The Muslim Communities of Nepal

The Muslim Communities of Nepal

David Seddon

ADROIT
Adroit Publishers
New Delhi

ISBN : 978-81-87393-51-1

First Published in 2017

Published by
ADROIT PUBLISHERS
4675/21, Ganpati Bhawan, Ansari Road,
Daryaganj, New Delhi-110 002
Phone : 011-23266030

Distributed by:

Akhil Book Distributors
4675/21, Ganpati Bhawan,
Ansari Road, Daryaganj
New Delhi, INDIA
Mob.: +91-9899717865

Typesetting—Gaurav Graphics, Delhi-110002
E-mail: gauravsingh1908@gmail.com
Printed at: Rajyoriya Prints, Delhi.

Contents

Preface

This book is based on a report that was itself based on research undertaken by myself during 2014 and 2015 in collaboration with the Nepal Madhesh Foundation (NEMAF) and the US-based International Institute for Democracy and Electoral Assistance (IDEA). The report combined a review and analysis of the secondary data available in published and unpublished sources undertaken over a period from 2014 to 2015 with the analysis of the findings of fieldwork undertaken by a NEMAF team during May-July 2015, in Kathmandu and in the districts of Banke and Dhanusha in the terai. The book now also contains additional material collected and/or analysed during 2015-2017.

My thanks to all of those at NEMAF involved in the research, notably its Director, Tula Shah, and also to Mohna Ansari, a leading human rights activist now with the Nepal Human Rights Commission, for encouraging this work at the outset and providing the link with IDEA. My thanks also are due to all those at IDEA Nepal for their support and to IDEA for funding the original research.

Although the Muslim community as a whole constitutes one of the larger groups in Nepal (accounting for some 4-5 per cent of the total population, and ranking ninth in the order of the largest groups), there has been relatively little effort to date to assess in a comprehensive fashion the distinctive economic, social and cultural traditions, beliefs and practices of this distinctive and disadvantaged community, or to identify the aspirations, needs and capabilities of its members, male and female, young and old.

Despite the contribution made by earlier research (see bibliography), there is still relatively little in the way of up-to-date information and analysis easily available in one place about the Muslim communities of Nepal who together a significant and distinctive minority. It is hoped that this book will remedy this situation.

July 2017 **David Seddon**

Foreword

This work by Dr. David Seddon, based on research undertaken over several years in collaboration with the Nepal Madhesh Foundation (NEMAF) and with support from the International Institute for Democratic Alternatives (IDEA), provides an overview of the issues facing the Muslim community - and the various Muslim communities of Nepal, together with an account of their historical development and contemporary economic, social, cultural and political characteristics.

I first met David when I was working with the Women's Commission, and encouraged him to take his interest in the Muslim minority further, putting him in contact with IDEA (with whom I had previously worked). This proved very successful and led to his initial collaboration with IDEA and with NEMAF during 2014 and 2015. Since then, I have moved on to work with Nepal's National Human Rights Commission (NHRC), and he has taken the initial report for IDEA considerably further; but we have maintained contact, and I have agreed to provide this short foreword to this book.

Although there are other studies of Muslims in Nepal, this is the first attempt to provide a coherent and comprehensive consideration of the Muslim Communities of Nepal. It also identifies areas for further consideration and research, which the author hopes will be undertaken in close collaboration with representatives of the Muslim communities, and the various institutions and NGOs that devote themselves to improving the spiritual, social and economic condition of men, women and children of Muslim faith.

As a long-term human rights activist, as a member of the Muslim Community, and as a woman, I welcome the publication of this book, and hope sincerely that it will be read by a wide range of Nepalis both Muslim and non-Muslim, including politicians, policy-makers, academics and intellectuals, and above all by activists concerned with the welfare of Muslims in Nepal and by all those committed to making a difference for, and in collaboration with, disadvantaged people across the country.

I also hope it will be read by non-Nepalis, both by people of influence in the international and foreign agencies and also by those in other institutions in Nepal indeed by all those concerned with helping to improve the economic, social and political conditions of Nepalis and particularly those from disadvantaged communities.

If only some readers are better informed or are moved to action by this study, then it will have achieved its objective. It might also lead on, in various ways, to further collaboration with the Muslim communities of Nepal and to a more concrete agenda or programme for future activities and interventions.

July 2017

Mohna Ansari

Introduction

The status of the Muslim minority communities in Nepal is undoubtedly one of economic and social disadvantage and political marginality, and we understand but cannot fully agree with the views of Mohammed Mozammil Haque, who argued in December 2009 that 'there is no need of any research work to be done to know the sectors of exclusion of Muslim communities in Nepal'. He suggested that 'a (rapid review) is enough to see that the presence of Muslims in all the structural and developmental is either zero or negligible' (Haque 2009). It is true as we shall see that a rapid review reveals the disadvantaged status and situation of the Muslim community as a whole, and the severe economic and social deprivation and political marginalisation of many local Muslim communities; but the precise determinants or causes and consequences of this situation and the implications for action by the Muslim communities themselves require, in our view, more investigation and analysis.

This book is an outcome of the action research programme mentioned above, involving a collaboration between IDEA, NEMAF and the author, and is intended not to be definitive, but to build the basis for a discussion and debate regarding the challenges facing Muslim communities in Nepal and the potential for economic, social and cultural development among the Muslim communities of Nepal. Our starting point is the observation that the Muslim community as a whole is both distinctive and generally disadvantaged, economically, socially and politically, and that, despite some specific involvement through official elected representatives and through lobbying by Muslim groups and associations, the various Muslim communities as a whole have been largely marginalised in the political process that has taken place over the last few years (2008-2017) following the replacement of the monarchy by a republic and the election of a first Constituent Assembly.

This does not mean that there has been no opportunity at all to make representations and to express the views of the Muslim community as a whole. Firstly, there have been politicians in various parties, including Muslim members of the two Constituent Assemblies, who have worked hard to make the voice of Muslims heard. Secondly, there is a network of associations and organisations that claim to represent the Muslim communities of Nepal and their interests in a variety of ways, some of which intervene in order to improve the status and conditions of Muslims, in different parts of the country as well as across Nepal as a whole (many of these are listed in Appendix 1).

Indeed, a clear statement was produced prior to the passing of the new Constitution in September 2015 which identified the 'special issues' relating to the Muslim community they hoped might be incorporated into the draft (see Appendix 2). This document effectively listed the perceived key issues deriving from the distinctiveness and general disadvantage of the Muslim community and provided a framework within which Muslims might be better represented and be able to improve their status and circumstances, in the medium and longer term future. This specific and comprehensive intervention was of considerable significance; so too was the fact that there were now more Muslim representatives than ever before in a position to put forward these demands.

It is important, however, to recognise various other initiatives, both within the Muslim community as a whole and among the different Muslim communities, by civil society groups and NGOs, in response to the ongoing political process and indeed to the wider social and economic changes taking place in recent years across Nepal. Many of these relate to education, which is widely identified, both by Muslim leaders and by many others, as a key issue for action, given the remarkably poor level of education of Muslims in general and of girls and women in particular. Others relate to other dimensions of distinctiveness and disadvantage, and to discrimination.

In this book we shall consider the history, as well as the present situation and status of Muslims in the wider context of Nepal, and the situation and status of the different Muslim communities within the Muslim community as a whole, in terms of a range of different social, economic and political characteristics. We shall also explore the responses of Muslim communities and, in so far as possible, Muslim individuals interviewed by NEMAF in the field as part of the IDEA supported project, to external forces, with particular reference to changing gender relations inside and outside the family, relations of social difference and differentiation (e.g. of caste, religious and other affiliation, association and decision making) within the local community and in wider social networks, economic relations and differences of wealth and income (class) in local communities and beyond, and education and skills acquisition as a key to social mobility and advancement. We shall also review the history of Muslim involvement in Nepali politics over recent decades and consider a number of key themes and issues.

We hope the book will, perhaps by its very deficiencies and 'gaps', encourage others to examine the situation on the ground particularly as regards the initiatives being undertaken by Muslim civil society, through NGOs and associations and organisations of various kinds across the country. We have not been able, in this particular project, to identify and examine as we would have liked to do, the full range of these NGOs and their activities, although we were able through the fieldwork to gain some idea of what exists and what is being done in at least two particular localities in the *terai*, in Janakpur and in Nepalgunj, through key informant interviews and focus group discussions.

1

The Muslim Community

A Disadvantaged Minority

In terms of 'religious affiliation', the vast majority of the population of Nepal is identified in the 2011 census as Hindu (21,551,492), with Buddhists the next most common group (2,396,099) and Muslims (or more strictly 'followers of Islam') the third most common (1,162,370)[1]. The Muslim community constitutes a significant social, cultural, religious and political minority in Nepali economy and society. Only 375,699 Christians were identified in the 2011 census, although the numbers are growing fast, largely through conversion.

In the *terai,* the proportion of Buddhists is significantly smaller than in Nepal as a whole, but the majority of Muslims live there, making them the second most common group in the *terai* in terms of religious affiliation after Hindus. In the 2011 census, the Hindu population of the *terai* amounted to 11,308,620 (a little over half of all the Hindus in Nepal), while the population of Muslims (1,105,533) constituted the vast majority of all Muslims in the country and about 10 per cent of the *terai* population. Muslims are predominantly rural overall in Nepal 986,844 in the rural areas and only 175,526 in the urban areas and even more strikingly so in the *terai,* although there are a few significant urban concentrations of Muslims in Birgunj (Parsa District), Nepalgunj (Banke District), Kathmandu, Biratnagar (Morang District) and Rajpur Farhadawa (Rautahat District), as we shall see in more detail below.

The distribution of Muslims within the *terai,* however, is very uneven. Gaige (1975: 209), for example, suggested that, in 1961, the proportion of Muslims in the far western *terai* was less than 1 per cent on average, except in Banke District, where, exceptionally, it was 22 per cent; in the central *terai,* the proportion ranged from 8 per cent to 18 per cent; in the central eastern *terai*, from 11 per cent to 17 per cent; and in the eastern *terai* from 6 per cent to 9 per cent. Banke was at this time the district with the largest proportion of the total population identified as Muslim in all of the *terai*. In a recent sample survey (NEMAF 2016) in five districts of the central eastern *terai* Saptari, Siraha, Dhanusha, Mahottari and Sarlahi 15 per cent were Muslims.

Muslims account for around 4-5 per cent of the total population of Nepal and 10 per cent of the population of the *terai*, according to the 2011 census. Some Muslim activists suggest that this is an underestimate, and that the national figure may be closer to 10 per cent, and the proportion of Muslims in the *terai* closer to 20 per cent[2]. Bandita Sijapati also suggests that 'many Muslims and even Hindus in Nepal claim that the total population of Muslims reported in the census is incorrect and that the precise figure of the Muslims is anywhere between 6 to 10 per cent of the population'. In his report, *Indian Ethnic Groups in the Nepal Tarai,* published by Centre for Nepal and Asian Studies (CNAS), Ansari (1980) showed that the population of Muslims living in Sunsari district in 1978 was more than 50,000 three times the number reported in the 1971 census (19,373 Muslims). The often cited reasons for the under-representation of Muslims include: fear of being discriminated against for being Muslim; the use of census data for possible conscription into the army and/or for the imposition of more taxes (see also Siddique 2001, Dahal 1978, Sijapati n.d.).

Formally, according to the Constitution, Muslims have equal rights as citizens before the law; in reality they are widely regarded, and to a large extent consider themselves, a distinct 'minority' subject both to a degree of social and political discrimination and also to a degree of self-definition and separation from other social groups in Nepalese society. In fact, as we shall see below, there are several different and distinct Muslim communities in Nepal, with different histories, different social and cultural practices, different economic roles, occupations and statuses, and living in different parts of the country. Nevertheless, Mozammil Haque has argued that the Muslims of Nepal and Muslims in Nepal should be recognized as a single distinct community, and not as divided into different groups (Haque 2009).

He does not accept that Muslims living in the *terai* are 'Madhesis', even if they are geographically associated with Madhes as a region and thus, arguably, for some, with 'Madhes' as a socio-political entity. Haque suggests that 'the identity of Muslims in Nepal should be Muslim, rather than Madhesi, because while many of them live in *terai* others reside in the hills'. This is an important and controversial suggestion, given the strong position adopted by some of the Madhesi political parties on the subject of Madhesi identity and the need for recognition of this through the delineation of a single Madhesi state or several Madhesi states, and the fact that the state also recognises specific quotas for Madhesis in public employment and the civil service (which do not include Muslims living in hill districts).

Haque sees the Muslims in Nepal, generally, as a disadvantaged and under-privileged minority. 'They are not generally involved in any commercial or industrial undertakings, and the majority of them are either unskilled labourers or small-scale subsistence farmers, with a sprinkling of merchants and lower-level civil servants'. So, 'most of them are living their lives below the poverty line; thus ignorance and backwardness are rampant among Nepalese Muslims, and this has led to their forfeiture of their human rights in the country'. This, though probably the case for the majority of those Muslims living in the *terai,* is not, however, the case for those in Kathmandu, where many are relatively well educated and have well-paying jobs in the public as well as there private sector and some have lucrative businesses (particularly in the gem trade).

Haque argues that, 'even in the faith that they profess, their knowledge of Islamic principles and culture is very meagre, and they do need proper guidance and direction in this respect (sic). Many of them are Muslims in name only, but hardly know anything about Islam. Muslims seek a basic and fundamental education regarding their religion so that they are able to become able to recite and understand Quran and Islam. They also need to know how to perform *salah/namaz* (prayer), *zakat* (alms), *roza* (fasting) and *hajj* (pilgrimage) in a (proper) manner. But the national educational system and curriculum lack these teachings... So the only solution of this problem is to establish such institutions privately to conduct the educational activities which would work for the production of well educated, skilled personnel and professionals having Islamic spirits of Islam'.

Again, he expresses very particular ideas which require further consideration. Not all Muslims would agree that the only way to improve the education of Muslims is through private and by implication Muslim 'faith' schools (*madrasas*) and Muslim colleges. Other options include: a better resourced state primary and secondary school system with 'room' for Muslims as well as those from all other groups, a parallel system of state and private Muslim 'faith' schools (*madrasas*); a focus on *madrasas* for primary education only. Haque argues that the very practice of Islam and the dynamics of the Islamic community (*'umma*) or local religious communities, has helped to establish a distinctive social and cultural awareness and the formation of socio-economic institutions of real significance, at the local, district and national level. Others might argue, as indeed do many Muslims, that this tends to result in a kind of self-centredness and social introversion which does not help with the integration of Muslims in the wider Nepali society.

He takes, for example, the role of the *Tablighi Jammat*, which is a worldwide Islamic network. 'The Tablighi Jammat in Nepal serves to educate Muslims regarding their religious obligations and duties, especially in relation to the *namaz* (Islamic prayer, five times a day), the *roza* (fast) and *zakat* (Islamic charity). Although those questioned stated categorically that Tablighi Jammat did not have a worldly objective, they agreed that this religious networking did help in spreading awareness about the distinctive religious identity of Muslim and their legal-constitutional rights' (Haque, drawing on an open public discussion with local shopkeepers and residents at Jama Masjid Chowk, Nepalgunj in December 2009).

Taken as a whole, the Muslims clearly constitute one of the most disadvantaged groups both in terms of economic and social welfare, and in terms of cultural and political rights. They generally score poorly on the multidimensional 'composite' exclusion index (MEI) which includes household consumption, stunting, access to drinking water, toilet, school enrolment, primary school completion, female literacy and access to influence. Fifteen years ago they were bottom of the list of the main social groups in Nepal (see Table 1).

The situation barely improved over the next decade. The poverty incidence among Muslims was 41 per cent in 2003/04 as compared with a national average of 31 per cent; only indigenous people in the hills and *dalits* showed a higher incidence (with 44 per cent and 45 per cent respectively), according to the NLSS II (CBS 2004). The decline in poverty incidence from 44 per cent to 41 per cent between 1995/96 and 2003/04 was only 6 per cent; this was the smallest decline experienced by any group in Nepal. Average per capita income in 2003-04 was Rs. 10,200 as compared with the national average of Rs 15,000. Life expectancy was 61 compared with a national average of 64 (see Table 2).

Table 1: A Comparison of Population, Literacy and Poverty Different Groups, 2001

Population groups	Population Percentage	Literacy percentage	Poverty index
All Nepal	100	53.70	0.325
Brahmin Hill	12.91	74.90	0.441
Newar	5.49	71.22	0.447
Thakuri	1.48	63.39	n.a.
Chhetri	15.98	60.11	0.348
Gurung	2.49	59.79	0.299
Rai	2.83	58.19	0.299
Limbu	1.62	58.12	0.299
Tharu	6.58	47.12	0.313
Tamang	5.63	45.04	n.a.
Yadav	3.70	40.83	0.313
Muslims	**4.27**	**34.72**	**0.239**

Source: UNDP 1998; Census, 2001

Table 2: Poverty Incidence and Trends by Social Group 1995/6 to 2003/4

Social group	1995/6	2003/4	Change in %
All Nepal	42	31	- 26
Newar	19	14	- 28
Brahmin/Chhetri	34	18	- 46
Terai middle caste	29	21	- 26
Terai janajati/indigenous people	53	35	- 34
Muslims	44	41	- 6
Hill janajati/indigenous people	49	44	- 10
Dalits	58	45	- 21

Source: NLSS II (CBS 2004)

In 2005, a study of 'gender and social exclusion' undertaken by a team specifically recruited for the purpose by DfID and the World Bank provided a detailed assessment of socially excluded and/or disadvantaged groups, which included Muslims in that category (GSEA 2005). This study was later published as *Caste, Ethnic and Regional Identity in*

Nepal: further analysis of the 2006 Nepal Demographic and Health Survey (Bennett et al 2008). The 'social barriers to exclusion' identified in this study consisted of gender, caste, ethnicity and/or race, language, religion, age and geo-political barriers; barriers that were economic in nature, such as unequal control of and access to land and other assets, and constraints on income generating opportunities and employment, were, however, not mentioned, except as 'outcomes' or results of social exclusion. Muslims were identified on the basis of religion, but it was noted that while 'technically not 'untouchable', Muslims are considered impure by the Hindu caste system'; hence 'following the Central Bureau of Statistics (CBS), Muslims have been retained as a separate group for poverty analysis along with gender, caste and ethnicity' (Bennett et al. 2008: 3).

It is noted in this study that Muslims had the second lowest per capita income on average among the major groups, after hill *dalits,* and they were 'significantly over-represented among the lowest income quintiles, with only 5 per cent in the top quintile' in fact their representation in the top income quintile was the lowest of all groups, including hill and *terai dalits.* Together with hill and terai *dalits,* Muslims were concentrated heavily in the lowest consumption quintiles with one in four households in the lowest quintile (pp. 20-21). On the other hand, they fared better as regards the proportion under the poverty line, with just over 41 per cent as compared with 43 per cent for hill *janajatis*, 46 per cent for *terai dalits* and 48 per cent for hill *dalits*. It was noted that 41 per cent of Muslims were landless the highest of all groups (37 per cent of *terai dalits* were landless and 32 per cent of *terai janajatis* (p. 25).

Hill *janajatis* had the highest proportion (31 per cent) of household members working overseas (ie not in India), but Muslims were second (22 per cent). Among those receiving remittances, this source of income accounted for about a third of annual household income; among Muslim households, who on average had among the lowest average per capita incomes, received a slightly higher proportion of household income from remittances than other groups. A shift out of agriculture, visible in most other groups, was taking place particularly among Muslims and *terai dalits,* with almost 53 per cent of *terai dalits* and 46 per cent of Muslims working outside agriculture. The share of Muslims in higher return occupations had declined (Bennett et al. 2008: 26-27).

As regards literacy and education, Muslims had progressed less than any other group in the decade 1991-2001, and female achievements were among the poorest; surprisingly, however, they had done better than *terai dalits* and *terai* middle castes in terms of the female/male ratio at secondary school and graduate levels. Muslims had the largest percentage of children under 15 of all groups. Current contraceptive use among *dalits* was 12 per cent lower than Brahmins and Chhetris, and 23 per cent lower than *terai janajatis*, but three times higher than Muslims. Muslim women had poor access to trained health practitioners and Muslim women and *terai* middle caste groups both of which practice female seclusion had the lowest awareness of HIV/AIDS prevention and the lowest immunisation rates (Bennett et al. 2008: 32).

The study considered women's participation in politics at all levels, including local politics, and their employment in the executive, civil service and judiciary, but made no specific reference to Muslim women. It also looked at responses to exclusion and involvement in social movements and NGOs, with particular reference to women; but again had little to say about either Muslims in general or Muslim women in particular. A specific chapter (chapter 8) was devoted to *dalits* but, although it was noted at the outset that while 'technically not 'untouchable', Muslims are considered impure by the Hindu caste system', there was no discussion in this chapter of Muslims and their 'caste' status.

A review of pretty much all special programmes for *dalits* and disadvantaged *janajatis,* whether supported by the government or by other agencies, also fails to refer to Muslims as indeed to all of the programmes. Chapter 9, on '*adivasi janajatis*' (indigenous nationalities), also fails to include Muslims, as do chapters 10 (on exclusion in the law), 11 (on improving access for women, *dalits* and *janajatis* in health), 12 (on bringing girls, *dalits* and *janajatis* into primary education), 13 (on group-based coalitions to promote empowerment and social inclusion), 14 (on affirmative action), and 15 (on priorities for action).

In 2006, according to the UNDP (2009), Bennett et al (2008) and the *Nepal Human Development Report* (2009), Muslims were ranked 19 out of 20 of all the recognised social groups, coming just above *madhesi dalits* in an overall ranking which included life expectancy at birth, adult literacy, mean years of schooling, per capita income, life expectancy index, income index, HDI and ratio to national HDI, In comparison with the national average, life expectancy at birth was 61 as compared with 64 and was lower than all except hill Chhetris and hill *dalits*. Strikingly, adult literacy (30 per cent) was worse than any other social group except for Madhesi *dalits (27* per cent), and the same was the case for mean years of schooling (1.60 and 1.21 respectively) and educational attainment (0.238 and 0.209 respectively). The Human Development Index (HDI) for Muslims was 0.4 in 2006, compared with an average for Nepal as a whole of 0.5 lower than that of the *dalits* of the hills and only just above the *dalits* of the *terai* (see Table 3).

Table 3: Human Development Index (HDI) by Social Group, 2006

Social Group	Human Development Index
All Nepal	0.509
Madhesi Brahmin Chhetri	0.625
Newar	0.616
Hill Brahmins	0.612
Other Undefined	0.599
Hill Chhetri	0.514
Hill Janjati	0.507
Terai Janjati	0.470
Hill Dalits	0.449
Muslims	**0.401**
Madhesi Dalits	0.383

Source: UNDP, 2009; Nepal Human Development Report 2009.

The human development index of Muslims remained low over the next few years. In fact, according to the 2011 census, the HDI index for Muslims, at 0.42 was still lower than that for hill *dalits* and for all *dalits*; again, only *madhesi dalits* registered lower, at 0.40 (see Table 4).

Table 4: HDI Values by Caste and Ethnicity, 2011

Caste/ethnic groups	Life Expectancy	Adult Literacy	Mean yrs of School	PPP in $$	HDI arith. Mean	HDI geom.mean
Newars	72.26	80.07	4.75	1522	0.627	0.565
Hill Brahmins	73.26	81.89	4.79	1247	0.626	0.557
Madhesi B/Cs	74.10	82.05	4.63	937	0.614	0.536
All B/Cs	73.99	76.32	4.41	1115	0.609	0.538
All hill/mountain groups	70.25	72.35	4.18	1056	0.574	0.511
all Madheshis excl. Yadavs	71.91	54.80	3.79	751	0.523	0.461
All hill Janajatis	70.51	71.21	4.15	1051	0.573	0.509
All Chhetris	70.32	72.04	4.13	1016	0.571	0.507

All Janajatis excl. Newars	69.86	66.93	3.99	844	0.546	0.482
Terai Janajatis	69.44	62.24	3.99	822	0.532	0.473
Madhesi other castes	72.35	53.93	3.83	732	0.522	0.460
Yadavs	73.42	51.78	3.91	671	0.519	0.455
All Madheshi	70.95	53.27	3.76	744	0.513	0.454
Hill Dalits	65.57	61.93	3.46	805	0.505	0.466
All Dalits	67.19	52.27	3.42	755	0.488	0.434
Muslims	**70.47**	**43.56**	**3.24**	**695**	**0.481**	**0.422**
Madheshi Dalits	70.45	34.58	3.35	616	0.455	0.400

The Nepal Living Standards Survey of 2011 by contrast, shows Muslims surprisingly high up in the ranking, with a poverty headcount rate of 20.2 as compared with *terai* Brahmins at 18.6, a national average of 25.2 and an average for *terai* and hill *dalits* of 38.2 and 43.6 respectively (see Table 5).

Table 5: Poverty Incidence (NLSS 2011)

Caste/ethnic group	poverty incidence % below poverty line	% of all poor	% of total population
All Nepal	25.16	100.0	100.0
Newar	10.25	2.5	6.2
Brahmin (hill)	10.34	5.2	12.7
Brahmin (Madhes)	18.61	0.4	0.5
Muslim	20.18	3.5	4.3
Chhetri (hill)	23.40	16.6	17.8
Janajati (Madhes)	24.93	7.3	7.1
Janajati (hill)	28.25	24.4	21.8
Middle caste (Madhes)	28.69	17.6	15.4
Dalits (Madhes)	38.16	6.9	4.6
Dalits (hills)	43.63	15.2	8.7

Source: NLSS, 2010/11

In 2013, a further analysis of the 2011 Nepal Demographic and Health Survey was undertaken (Pandey et al 2013). This reported that 'studies by Bennett and colleagues (2008), RTI (2008) and the Nepal Family Health Program II and New Era (2010) have revealed important differences among caste/ethnic groups, exposing gaps in health services utilisation and health outcomes that remain despite overall progress toward many of the MDGs' (2013: 1). It notes, furthermore, that 'trend analysis by Johnson and Bradley (2008) and RTI (2008) reveals evidence of severe and worsening economic inequities in access to and use of important health services, as reflected in such indicators as fertility rates, unmet need for contraception, use of ante natal care (ANC), delivery in a health facility and services received from a skilled birth attendant as well as in vitamin A consumption postpartum. These studies also found economic disparities in access to child heatlh services...' (2013: 4). Muslims, and Muslim women and children in particular, were still in a poor state, as regards health status and access to health services, as compared with most other groups.

It seems, from the available statistical data at least, that the situation of the Muslim community as regards overall poverty had improved markedly since the early 2000s, but that the Human Development Index (HDI) and particularly health status remained low. Poor educational attainment explains much of this. Many of those interviewed in the field during the summer of 2015 as part of the IDEA/NEMAF project were able to cite statistics (referring often admittedly from earlier periods, eg the 2001 census) which revealed the poverty and disadvantaged status of Muslims in Nepal. Lack of education and poor educational attainment was a predominant theme in these interviews. Mr. Asgar Ali, ex-Deputy Mayor of Janakpur and currently a local political leader of the RPP(Nepal), commented, for example, in an interview undertaken as part of this project in summer 2015, that

> 'According to the Human Development Report 2006, Muslim male literacy rate was 61.8 but female literacy rate only 26.5. Over 40 percent of children leave school (ie drop out) during their primary education; and the percentage of students obtaining their secondary certificate is 25.5 percent in male and 12 percent in female. The proportion of Muslims getting higher education is negligible. The census of 2001 showed that the number of graduate and postgraduate Muslims amounted to only 4,067. Very few Muslims are employed in the army, the police or governmental jobs. This situation adversely affects the self-confidence of Muslims.

According to the most recent *Nepal Human Development Report, 2014*, the Human Development Index values were poorest in the *terai* or Madhes for *dalits* (0.400), with Muslims next poorest (0.422) and

Madhesi 'other castes' the third poorest (0.460); *terai* or Madhesi *janajati* were less disadvantaged (0.473) and *terai* or Madhesi high castes the least disadvantaged (0.536) (NHDR 2014). The income index for Muslims is still lower than for the average Nepali; and as regards the average household wellbeing index, the NHDR suggests that 'the share of Muslims in the lower deciles has climbed sharply' in recent years (NHDR 2014: 49); meaning that a larger proportion of Muslims now fall in the lower deciles of the income distribution for this group. This suggests that inequality within the Muslim community, in terms of well-being, has grown, even while the average remains relatively low.

The assessment of 'productive ability' by the NHDR (drawing on information from successive National Living Standards Surveys) suggests that this has generally tended to decline in the period between 1995 and 2011 both among Muslim households and among Muslim individuals, with nearly 30 per cent of Muslim households in the lowest decile in 2011 compared with around 2 per cent in 1995, and nearly 20 per cent of individuals in the lowest decile in 2011 compared with about 7 per cent in 1995 (see NHDR 2014: 61). The implications of these statistics are not entirely clear, but they suggest low productivity and/or a low involvement or inclusion in the local economy, with an increasing proportion of Muslims in the lower deciles.

The NHDR comments that 'both Muslim households' and Muslim individuals' shares rose sharply in the lower deciles over the period from 1995 to 2011, 'by far the most significant departure from inclusiveness' (NHDR 2014: 76). This may be associated with an increasing rate of foreign labour migration among Muslim men and an exceptionally low involvement in local economic activity on the part of Muslim women (for a combination of social and cultural reasons), but it may also be due to increasing diversity in terms of economic and social activity within the Muslim community. The NHDR also notes that the gap between household ability and individual ability was increasing for Muslims, and that as regards individual ability there are signs of increasing inequality as some cluster in the higher deciles while others cluster in the lower deciles, while such a movement was less marked among households.

Unfortunately, the gender development index (GDI) and gender empowerment measure (GEM) used in the NHDR 2014 were not applied to ethnic groups and castes. This might have revealed the degree of gender inequality that exists in the Muslim communities of Nepal, particularly as regards access to education. At least, however, the NHDR states, in its recommendations, that 'clear and ongoing caste and ethnic inequalities are revealed in different educational achievements and earnings.

This strengthens the argument for deliberate strategies to increase inclusiveness by providing education and economic opportunities for disadvantaged ethnic and caste groups such as *dalits* and Muslims' (NHDR 2014: 66).

Overall, the status of Muslims generally remains one of a disadvantaged minority, with an exceptionally poor educational index, but one in which there is increasing diversification of well-being within the community, perhaps as a result of an increasing diversity and diversification of life paths (see Table 6).

Table 6: Status of Muslims in Nepal - 2014

Item	Muslim	Nepal
HDI	0.422	0.490
Life expectancy	70.47	68.8
Income index	0.324	0.409
Adult literacy	43.56	59.57

Source: NHDR 2014

A Growing Minority

According to the 1981 census, the Muslim population was 2.7 per cent of the total population. This increased to 3.5 percent in 1991 a larger percentage than that of the Rais (at 2.8 percent) and ninth in size of all caste/ethnic groups identified in the census. The total Muslim population in 1991 was officially recorded as 653,218; but many believed that the actual figure was much higher and that they constituted, even at that time, as much as 6 per cent of the population (CBS 1993, 1995).[1] In the 2001 census, when they were recorded as being just short of 1 million (971,056), Muslims accounted officially for slightly over 4 per cent of the total population of Nepal (4.3 per cent according to the census), suggesting a significant rate of population increase if the official figures are taken as given. Ten years later, in 2011, the total recorded number of Muslims was 1,164,255 (1.2 million), with the number of males recorded as 583,799 and that of females as 578,571, indicating a preponderance of males. Given the high rate of migration abroad for employment among the Muslim communities of the *terai*, where the vast majority of Muslims reside, which usually leads to an under-enumeration of men, this sex imbalance almost certainly indicates a higher rate of mortality among females and significant gender discrimination against girls and younger women in particular. We shall discuss this shortly.

The rate of population increase among Muslims is higher that the national average, and indeed higher than that of most other social groups. It was suggested by the statistician, Dr. Vikash Raj Satyal, writing in *Sambal,* the IIDS Newsletter (2003) that over 'the last five decades, the total population of Nepal has grown with an average inter-census annual growth rate of about 2.1 per cent, but ... the annual growth rate of the Muslim population was considerably higher'. With the current growth rate of 2.1 per cent, the total population of Nepal is projected to double in 33 years, whereas the Muslim population, with a current growth rate of 3.9 per cent, is projected to double in 18 years. It likely that Muslims today (2017) constitute at least 5 per cent of the total population of Nepal.

The Muslim population of Nepal is predominantly rural, with not far short of 1 million (988,515) living in the rural areas in 2011 (according to the national census), and a mere 175,740 living in urban areas. This situation is changing as migration from countryside to town takes place, but the transfer of population as a result of the rural exodus seems to be relatively small. There are more males (95,708) in the urban areas than there are females (80,032) by quite a margin, suggesting the preponderance of male migration to the towns, while the number and proportion of females is larger in the rural areas ie 499,469 females as compared with 489,046 males. The overall ratio of females to males in the total Muslim population (of 1,164,255) is below parity, with males amounting to 584,754 and females 579,501, indicating a demographic bias towards males and implying a social bias against females an issue to which we shall return later.

Distribution by Region

About 97 per cent of the Muslim community lives in the *terai,* while the other 3 per cent is found mainly in the city of Kathmandu and the western hills; very few (0.5 per cent) are in the mountain districts of Nepal. According to the 2011 census, fewer than 500 Muslims live in the mountain areas of Nepal, some 55,000 live in the hill areas, the majority of these in Kathmandu, and about 1.1 million in the *terai.* In the *terai,* the main concentration is in the central region (nearly 530,000), the eastern region (265,000) and the western region (200,000); the mid-west and far-west between them account for around 115,000. In 1991, however, the Muslims of the *terai* comprised only 3.28 per cent of the total population of Nepal. They constituted the third largest social group in the *terai,* after the Tharus (6.5 per cent) and Yadavs (4.0 per cent).

Nearly half of all Muslims (48 per cent) live in the central development region; after this the next highest percentage is in the eastern development region (23 per cent), followed by the western development region (19 per cent), the mid-western development region (10 per cent), with virtually none (0.5 per cent) in the far west (0.51 percent).

Table 7: Distribution of Muslim Population by Region, 2011

Region	Mts	Hills	Terai	Percentage
Far-West	139	431	5,389	0.5
Mid-West	169	3,518	109,147	10
Western	7	19,558	200,491	19
Central	93	30,104	527,645	23
Eastern	56	2,728	264,780	48
Total	464	56,339	1,107,452	100

Distribution by District

Muslims are found in most of the 75 districts of Nepal, although as we have seen there are very few indeed in the mountain areas and relatively few in the hills, apart from Kathmandu, and the vast majority of Muslims are to be found in the districts of the *terai.*

As regards the percentages of Muslims in the hill areas, the 2001 census recorded that in Kathmandu 1.1 per cent of the total population was Muslim; in Tanahun, 1 per cent; in Arghakhanchi and Gorkha, 0.9 per cent; in Kaski, 0.7 per cent; in Udaypur, 0.6 per cent; in Surkhet, 0.4 per cent; in Makwanpur, 0.3 per cent and in Lalitpur, 0.3 per cent. So, the concentration of Muslim hill population is largely in the central and western regions; with relatively few in the east.

Although there is considerable variation from district to district, there is a general concentration in the percentage of Muslims in total district population in the mid-western and central eastern *terai.* In the 1961 census, for example, the districts of the mid-western *terai* averaged 13 per cent Muslims, those of the central and eastern *terai,* 9 per cent. From Banke to Rautahat, the percentage of Muslims per district was, with only one exception, in double figures during the 1960s; from Sarlahi eastwards to Jhapa, it never exceeded single figures; and in Jhapa itself was as low as 3.5 per cent. This follows, roughly, the same pattern from west to east in the percentage of the Muslim population across the border in Uttar Pradesh and Bihar (cf Gaige 1975: 15).

This general tendency, however, obscures differences within different regions of the *terai. Gaige* (1975: 209), for example, suggests that in the far western *terai* the proportion of Muslims was less than 1 per cent in 1961, except in Banke, where it was 22 per cent; in the central *terai* it ranged from 8 per cent to 18 per cent; in the central eastern *terai*, from 11 per cent to 17 per cent; and in the eastern *terai* from 6 per cent to 9 per cent. Banke was at this time the district with the largest proportion of the total population identified as Muslim.

The vast majority of Muslims today live in 15 *terai* districts; over the last 30 years, the largest numbers have been found, generally, in the central eastern districts, of the *terai*, but some districts (eg Kapilvastu and Banke in the west central and western *terai* respectively) appear to have undergone a significant increase in population in recent years. It is not entirely clear why this is the case; but this trend has continued over the last decade, with those two districts moving into second and third place respectively as far as numbers of Muslims is concerned. Some of these changes in the proportion of Muslim population is due to immigration of other groups, including particularly, during the 1970s and 1980s, people from the hill areas. There is, it seems, relatively little internal migration of Muslims within Nepal, apart from a general move from rural to urban areas and from the *terai* to Kathmandu.

On the whole, however, the 'ranking' of districts has remained fairly steady over the years, albeit with some variations, as we shall see (see Tables 8 and 9).

Table 8: Terai Districts Ranked by Muslim Population

	District	1981		District	1991		District	2001
1	Rautahat	39,295	1	Rautahat	71,379	1	Rautahat	106,111
2	Bara	36,833	2	Kapilbastu	62, 512	2	Kapilbastu	87,573
3	Mahottari	36,106	3	Mahottari	53, 852	3	Parsa	76 567
4	Rupandehi	32,969	4	Bara	48, 648	4	Bara	75 051
5	Dhanusa	30,605	5	Banke	45, 787	5	Mahottari	74 364
6	Sunsari	28,535	6	Sunsari	45, 737	6	Banke	73 254
7	Sarlahi	26,468	7	Parsa	45, 662	7	Sunsari	69 187
8	Parsa	25,222	8	Rupandehi	42, 850	8	Rupandehi	61 563
9	Kapilbastu	23,080	9	Saptari	35, 020	9	Saptari	47 610
10	Banke	22,267	10	Sarlahi	32, 727	10	Sarlahi	47 364
11	Morang	17,175	11	Siraha	32, 116	11	Siraha	40 926
12	Siraha	16,621	12	Morang	26, 987	12	Morang	37 081
13	Jhapa	13,140	13	Jhapa	15, 557	13	Nawalparasi	21 722
14	Nawalparasi	6,381	14	Nawalparasi	14, 613	14	Jhapa	19 367
15	Bardiya	7,616	15	Bardiya	7,269	15	Kathmandu	11 982
16	Kathmandu	2,968	16	Kathmandu	5,409	16	Bardiya	10 671

Source: Population data from censuses of 1981, 1991 and 2001 (CBS).

In 1991, Muslims constituted the largest social group in four districts: Parsa, Rautahat, Kapilvastu and Banke (CBS 1995). Ten years later, in 2001, Muslims formed the largest single population group in five *terai* districts –one in the far west, Banke, one in the west, Kapilvastu, two in the central region, Rautahat, Parsa and Bara. They also formed the second largest group in five other districts in the central eastern and eastern *terai* Dhanusha, Mahottari, Sarlahi, Sunsari and Siraha. Seventeen districts had a population above 10,000 in 2001. On the other hand, there were virtually no Muslims in the three furthest western districts of Kanchanpur, Kailali[1] and Bardia, mainly because large tracts of dense forest to the south of these districts have tended to discourage immigration from the heavily populated northern areas of Uttar Pradesh to the south.

The next district to the east of Bardia Banke has the largest Muslim concentration (in terms of percentage of the total population) of any *terai* district; this was the case in the 1960s, when the figure was 22 per cent (according to Gaige 1975: 14), and remains the case today. This is, arguably, because there is no forest south of Banke to discourage immigration from areas of Muslim concentration to the south in Uttar Pradesh. It is also the case that Banke has one of the main cities of the western *terai*, Nepalgunj, which is an important commercial and administrative centre and a transport and communications hub for much of western and mid-western Nepal, and attracts significant immigration from surrounding areas.

Although the largest absolute number of Muslims lived in Rautahat throughout the period from 1981 to 2001, the district with the next largest number changed during the same period from Bara (in 1981) to Kapilvastu (in 1991 and 2001), the latter rising from 9th to 2nd; equally, other districts have changed relative positions over time as regarded their 'ranking' on the basis of total population. This is a function of many different variables, including of course both total Muslim population and total non-Muslim population. Interestingly Banke which was 10th, 5th and 6th respectively in 1981, 1991 and 2001 in the 'ranking' of districts by Muslim population was the district with the largest proportion of Muslims in the general population (just over one fifth) in 2001 (according to Haque that is), the largest concentration of Muslims within a district.

Fifteen years later, the overall proportion of Muslims in the population has tended to increase in most *terai* districts. In a recent sample survey

(NEMAF 2016) in five districts of the central eastern *terai,* Saptari, Siraha, Dhanusha, Mahottari and Sarlahi, for example, 15 per cent on average were Muslims, whereas, previously, even Mahottari, where the proportion of Muslims was the greatest of these five districts, had a smaller proportion than that, and the rest had less than 10 per cent.

Table 9: Percentage of Muslims by District (2001)

S. No.	District	Muslim Population	Percent of total pop.
1	Banke	76,188	20.49
2	Rautahat	106,131	19.68
3	Kapilvastu	93,094	19.57
4	Parsa	76,536	15.45
5	Mahottari	74,779	13.55
6	Bara	74,925	13.39
7	Sunsari	68,377	10.89
8	Rupandehi	62,850	8.93
9	Dhanusha	58,048	8.69
10	Saptari	47,114	8.28
11	Sarlahi	47,427	7.45
12	Sirha	41,033	7.29
13	Morang	40,321	4.95
14	Nawalparasi	22,022	3.92
15	Jhapa	18,295	2.98

Source: Mohammed Mozammil Haque, December 2009

Percentages, however, differ significantly from absolute numbers, as the total population size of districts in the *terai* has varied considerably, although most have seen increases in population in recent years. Also, the absolute size of the Muslim population has grown more rapidly in some districts than in others in recent years. Some of this is the result of natural increase, and a small proportion the result of migration between districts but much of it, we suggest, is the result of differential immigration from India. The dynamics behind this remain little studied.

In 2000, Mollica Dastider remarked that 'while the central *terai* districts record the highest concentration of Muslims, there has been a substantial increase in Muslim in the eastern region of the *terai* (ie the region bordering Darbhanga, Saharsa and Purnea districts of Bihar). The districts on the Nepali side and the population of Muslims there are as follows: Morang (26,987 in 1991), Sunsari (45,737), Saptari (35,020) and Siraha (32,116), according to Yadav 1992' (Dastider 2000: 766). Bista attributed this population increase to the latest arrival of Bihari Muslims and caste Hindus from across the border (Bista 1985). Dastider notes that 'there are also reports of alleged infiltration of Bihari Muslim refugees from Bangladesh, who entered the eastern *terai* region of Nepal in the post-1971 period (Sharma 1994). However, due to lack of adequate data on such infiltrations, it is difficult to confirm such reports' (Dastider 2000: 766).

Table 10: Muslim Population by District (2011) - Ranking Compared with 2001

S. No.	District	Muslim Population	% up ^/down v
1	Banke	93,298	18.98v
2	Rautahat	135,519	19.73^
3	Kapilvastu	103,856	18.15v
4	Parsa	87,212	14.51v
5	Mahottari	83,849	13.36v
6	Bara	89,834	13.06v
7	Sunsari	88,173	11.55^
8	Rupandehi	72,468	8.23v
9	Dhanusha	63,697	8.44v
10	Saptari	57,145	8.94^
11	Sarlahi	60,754	7.89^
12	Sirha	47,715	7.49^
13	Morang	45,750	4.74v
14	Nawalparasi	24,167	3.75v
15	Jhapa	25,997	3.20^

Source: Demographic Profile of Nepal, 2013/2014, MEGA Publication & Research Centre, Kathmandu NB the data in column 1 (Muslim Population) do not, for reasons which are not clear, coincide with the figures given by the national census (see below in Table 11).

Dastider does report that 'during a recent field study in the easternmost district of Jhapa, the author has observed that a large part of the Muslim population in the district are migrant Muslim workers from the adjoining districts of Kishanganj and Galgalia in Bihar. While most of them have their names in the voters list, very few of them are citizens' (Dastider 2000: 769).

There has been a significant increase over the last thirty years in the total Muslim population of Nepal and a marginal increase in their numbers as a proportion of the total population. There has been a significant increase since Dastider was writing in 2000. The main districts in which Muslims live and work, however, have remained much the same in the last ten years, with Banke, Rautahat, Kapilvastu, Parsa, Mahottari, Bara, Sunsari and Rupandehi providing both the largest absolute numbers and the largest proportions of Muslims in the total population (see Table 10).

The total population of Muslims by district across the whole of Nepal, according to the 2011 census was as follows:

Table 11: Total Muslim Population of Nepal by District (2011)

S.N.	District	Total Population of district	Muslim Population	Muslim %
1	Rautahat	686,722	135,283	19.70
2	Kapilvastu	571,936	103,838	18.15
3	Banke	491,313	93,263	18.98
4	Bara	687,708	89,685	13.04
5	Sunsari	763,487	88,072	11.53
6	Parsa	601,017	87,033	14.48
7	Mahottari	627,580	83,696	13.33
8	Rupandehi	880,196	72,428	08.23
9	Dhanusha	754,777	63,099	08.36
10	Sarlahi	769,729	60,679	07.79
11	Saptari	639,284	57,004	08.92
12	Siraha	637,328	47,566	07.46
13	Morang	965,370	45,755	04.74
14	Jhapa	812,650	25,974	03.20
15	Nawalparasi	643,508	24,160	03.75
16	Kathmandu	1,744,240	21,866	01.25

17	Bardiya	426,576	11,084	02.60
18	Chitwan	579,984	6,741	01.16
19	Kailali	775,709	4,930	00.64
20	Dang	552,583	4,781	00.86
21	Kaski	492,098	4,437	00.90
22	Tanahun	323,288	4,157	01.28
23	Lalitpur	468,132	3,080	00.66
24	Gorkha	271,061	3,056	01.13
25	Udayapur	317,532	2,168	00.68
26	Syangja	289,148	1,978	00.68
27	Surkhet	350,804	1,825	00.52\
28	Makawanpur	420,477	1,787	00.42
29	Arghakhanchi	197,632	1,773	00.90
30	Bhaktapur	304,651	1,503	00.49
31	Palpa	261,180	1,226	00.47
32	Dhading	336,067	1,037	00.31
33	Lamjung	167,724	952	00.57
34	Baglung	268,614	734	00.27
35	Parbat	146,590	624	00.43
36	Pyuthan	228,102	614	00.27
37	Kanchanpur	451,248	461	00.10
38	Dailekh	261,770	459	00.18
39	Gulmi	280,160	431	00.15
40	Nuwakot	277,471	351	00.13
41	Kavrepalanchok	381,937	318	00.08
42	Salyan	242,444	268	00.11
43	Accham	257,477	257	00.10
44	Ilam	290,254	229	00.08
45	Rolpa	224,506	216	00.10
46	Myagdi	113,641	180	00.16
47	Sindhuli	296,192	179	00.06
48	Dhankuta	163,412	161	00.10
49	Rukum	208,567	126	00.06
50	Doti	211,746	116	00.05
51	Jumla	108,921	111	00.10
52	Bajura	134,912	100	00.07

53	Panchthar	191,817	55	00.03
54	Dolakha	186,557	46	00.02
55	Khotang	206,312	43	00.02
56	Sankhuwasabha	158,742	41	00.03
57	Sindhupalchok	287,798	38	00.01
58	Dadeldhura	142,094	37	00.03
59	Ramechhap	202,646	33	00.02
60	Terhathum	101,577	31	00.03
61	Darchula	133,274	31	00.02
62	Kalikot	136,948	27	00.02
63	Okhaldhunga	147,984	26	00.02
64	Baitadi	250,898	21	00.01
65	Bhojpur	182,459	19	00.01
66	Dolpa	36,700	14	00.04
67	Solukhumbu	105,886	13	00.01
68	Humla	50,858	11	00.02
69	Jajarkot	171,304	10	00.006
70	Rasuwa	43,300	9	00.02
71	Bajhang	195,159	8	00.004
72	Mugu	55,286	6	00.01
73	Manang	6,538	4	00.06
74	Mustang	13,452	3	00.02
75	Taplejung	127,461	2	00.002

http://www.nmc.gov.np/site/cms/11

Distribution by Town and Village (VDC)

In 2011, the rural population accounted for 79 per cent of the total Muslim population, according to the Nepal Department of Health Survey, as compared with 21 per cent in the urban areas (Pandey et al 2013: 42). Not surprisingly, however, the urban areas tend to contain the largest Muslim population, with Birgunj (Parsa district) in the east and Nepalgunj (Banke district) in the west having the largest overall Muslim population, and Kathmandu and Biratnagar (in Morang district, also in the east) coming roughly third equal.

The total population of Muslims in Kathmandu Metropolitan area was 17,706 in the 2011 census; that of the larger Kathmandu area was 21,866, that is, 1.25 percent of the total population. The population of Muslims in Lalitpur and Bhaktapur districts was 3,080 and 1,503 respectively. The total population of Muslims in the Kathmandu Valley was 26,449, with the vast majority in Kathmandu itself. The 2011 census indicates the number of Muslims by VDC and metropolitan area[1].

Table 12: Muslim Population by VDC/Municipal Area (2011)

No.	Place	District	Number Muslims Over 10,000
39471	Birgunj Sub-Metropolitan City	Parsa	24,445
57652	Nepalgunj Municipality	Banke	18,900
30811	Kathmandu Metropolitan City	Kathmandu	17,706
6038	Biratnagar Sub-Metropolitan City	Morang	17,554
33947	Rajpur Farhadawa	Rautahat	13,237
			5,000 to 10,000
6336	Narsinghatappu	Sunsari	9,268
7340	Ramnagar Bhutaha	Sunsari	8,768
36953	Kalaiya Municipality	Bara	8,737
7073	Ghuskee	Sunsari	8,660
50749	Siddharthanagar Municipality	Rupandehi	7,642
51266	Tenuhawa	Rupandehi	7,598
22312	Parsa Dewadh	Mahottari	7,462
6684	Sripurjabdi	Sunsari	7,065
19063	Janakpur Municipality	Dhanusa	6,781
7390	Bhokraha	Sunsari	6,495
21907	Dhamaura	Mahottari	6,385
33450	Gaur Municipality	Rautahat	6,116
58028	Jaispur	Banke	5,321
			2,000 to 5,000
35025	Jatahara	Rautahat	4,954
7843	Jalpapur	Sunsari	4,874
34264	Karuniya	Rautahat	4,761
58121	Raniyapur	Banke	4,678
34445	Jowaha (Jokaha)	Rautahat	4,645
33802	Laxmipur (Do.)	Rautahat	4,606
34785	Akolawa	Rautahat	4,568
35090	Gamhariya Parsa	Rautahat	4,450

56931	Laxmanpur	Banke	4,332
34209	Jingadawa Belbichwa	Rautahat	4,325
23676	Sundarpur	Sarlahi	4,157
34317	Bairiya	Rautahat	4,074
34681	Pipra Bhagwanpur	Rautahat	3,927
53533	Abhirao	Kapilbastu	3,542
52036	Pipara	Kapilbastu	3,420
57236	Katkuiya	Banke	3,342
35131	Rajpur Tulsi	Rautahat	3,272
57565	Bankatti	Banke	3,106
57082	Piprahawa	Banke	2,900
36110	Bishunpur	Bara	2,868
20970	Bairgiya Laxminiya	Mahottari	2,545
33845	Lokaha	Rautahat	2,505
38313	Kauwa Ban	Kaṭaiyạ Parsa	2,480
34166	Fatuha Maheshpur	Rautahat	2,469
57792	Kalaphanta	Banke	2,395

The relatively larger size of urban population is explained by the importance of immigration from the surrounding rural areas combined with the more limited immigration from elsewhere in Nepal and India, as well as natural increase within the towns and cities concerned. Immigration generally has accounted for a more substantial proportion of the overall growth in the Muslim population than has natural increase, although it should be noted that natural fertility and family size tends to be relatively large within the various Muslim communities as compared with many other social groups (as we shall see below).

There is a general feeling among Muslims in Nepal, as well as among Muslim political activists, that their population is officially underestimated, whether intentionally or not. A focus group of 19 people interviewed in summer 2015 as part of the IDEA/NEMAF project in one of the largest VDCs in Banke District, Jaispur (Nepalgunj) and also, independently, a key informant, Mohammed Akram Ansari commented that, although the official government data suggest a population of 5,321 in Jaispur, a survey by an INGO in 2060 (2003) suggested a significantly higher figure, of around 8,800. 'The total population today, a decade later, must be at least 20,000 thousand', it was suggested. In the whole of

Nepal, this informant reckoned 'Muslims must account for around 10 per cent of the population'.

Table 13: Muslim Population of Banke District, 2011

Area Name	Data Value
Bageswari	244
Baijapur	20
Bankatawa	184
Bankatti	3,106
Basudevpur	1,415
Belahari	1,392
Belbhar	518
Betahani	1,946
Bhabaniyapur	1,566
Binauna	16
Chisapani	69
Ganapur	1,046
Gangapur	1,187
Hirminiya	3,359
Holiya	1,320
Indrapur	2,095
Jaispur	5,321
Kachanapur	70
Kalaphanta	2,395
Kamdi	2,218
Katkuiya	3,342
Khajurakhurda	792
Khaskarkando	674
Khaskusma	513
Kohalpur	715
Laxmanpur	4,332

Mahadevpuri	16
Manikapur	1,142
Matehiya	2,482
Narainapur	2,039
Nepalgunj Municipality	18,900
Paraspur	1,788
Phattepur	1,988
Piprahawa	2,900
Puraina	2,424
Puraini	1,835
Rajhena	1,073
Raniyapur	4,678
Saigaun	2,588
Samserganj	336
Sonpur	4,036
Titihiriya	40
Udayapur	425
Udharapur	4,652

The fieldwork undertaken as part of this project in summer 2015 found that the number of Muslims recorded in Banke district was very close to the 2011 census, with the total for Nepalgunj itself identical (at 18,900), and some discrepancies. These data are nearly five years out of date, however, so that the Muslim population (and the population as a whole) will have increased significantly since then, and may well now exceed 100,000.

This gives a total of 93,199 (official census figure 93,263). It reveals the very uneven distribution by VDC, with Nepalgunj municipality, not surprisingly, having the largest Muslim population at 18,900, but also with five VDCs exceeding 4,000, and one, Jaispur, where interviews were undertaken for the IDEA/NEMAF project in summer 2015, exceeding 5,000. These are effectively urban VDCs. Six, on the other hand, had a population of less than 100.

There can be no doubt that the Muslim population of the urban areas of Nepal, Nepalgunj included, has grown significantly in recent years, in part because of natural fertility but largely because of rural to urban migration. There has been no detailed study of 'Muslims in town', as far as I know, but it would be interesting to know how this growth has taken place and what changes it has brought about in urban Muslim economy and society. A glimpse can be caught, however, from a few descriptions, mainly by journalists, like Peter Gill who recently captured the distinctive atmosphere of Nepalgunj in an essay for *The Record*:

> 'The city's large Madhesi and Muslim population make the town unusual in a country where both these groups are minorities (according to the government census, Muslims and native speakers of Madhesi languages make up one-quarter and one-half of the city's population, respectively, compared to one-twentieth and one-fifth nationally)'....

Much of the real estate on New Road and Surkhet Road is owned by people from the hills, or Pahadis, whereas the old bazaar is predominantly occupied by people from the plains, including Muslims and Hindu Madhesis....

> 'The old bazaar is roughly a square kilometer, divided into four quadrants by the north-south and east-west roads that intersect at Tribhuvan Chowk. In the bazaar's northwest quadrant is Bagheshwori, the city's oldest Hindu temple, and the Junge Mahadev, said to be the world's only mustachioed Shiva. In the northeast quadrant lies the Jummah Masjid, and the cramped Muslim quarter known as Eklaini, where gullies wind around saints' tombs and betel wholesalers cut the nut in front of their homes. To the east, the bazaar abuts a stagnant pond called Rani Talau, built by one of the city's early tax collectors as a monument to his beloved wife. To the south of the bazaar lies Hospital Road, which is lined with government offices, and the zonal hospital, and eventually leads to the Indian border and the town of Rupaidiha in Uttar Pradesh'...

Gill writes about the way in which the different religious communities live side by side, distinctive yet proximate:

> I was struck by the way many people lived out their religious identities. It was usually easy to tell Hindu from Muslim if not by one's words of greeting (*namaste* versus *salaam-alaikum*), then by facial hair or dress. Although many Muslim women in Nepalgunj

> do not cover their heads, many do wear a hijab or the face-covering niqab. Groups of young men, students of the Barelwi organization known as *Dawat-e-Islami,* meander around in distinctive white robes and green turbans…

Buildings get claimed by one religion or another. Muslim houses fly flags with the Shahada, the declaration of faith, while flags of Hanuman the monkey god and symbol of strength favoured by Hindutva groups in India flutter above Hindu homes. In the northwestern part of the bazaar, the streets are lined with scores of gold and silversmith workshops, each with four or five men and boys sitting on cushions on the floor, tinkering away with blow torches, hammers, and tweezers. Each shop is nearly identical, save for framed images of the Koran, the Kabaa in Mecca, or posters of Hanuman, Laxmi, Ganesh, or Bishwokarma.

Even the women in Nepalgunj reflect this multiplicity of different communities, as Srijana, a gender specialist with an INGO, explained to Peter Gill:

> "Women' is not a homogenous group," she reminded me. "Nepali women come from all different backgrounds, and even in Nepalgunj, when you talk about women, there are Madhesi women, there are some Tharu women, there are Brahmin-Chhetri women, there is the urban-rural difference. There are Muslim women, and among them there are upper class and lower class. All women's experiences will be very different."

As an example of this, another woman activist and politician, Mohammadi Siddiqui, told Gill that she had the good fortune to receive an education, and then married an underground democrat, a Congress member, during the Panchayat era.

> 'Though she lived in *pardah* in her husband's house, he had encouraged her to read and do clandestine work for the party, hiding and filing secret documents. He died soon after the 1990 democracy movement, leaving her with three young children, but Mohammadi felt inspired to continue his unfinished work. He had been due to run for ward president on the Congress ticket, and she left *pardah* to run for the seat herself. Her mother-in-law, who was uneducated herself, supported her, helping take care of the children while she campaigned. Mohammadi won the election and continued to serve in the party, eventually becoming a member of the first Constituent Assembly in 2008'.

In 2004, Mohammedi established Fatima Foundation, an NGO that works to promote dialogue between Muslim and other religious communities, and empower women through education and job skill training.

> She explained that she founded Fatima Foundation as a Muslim women's NGO because she felt other women's organizations were too Hindu and Pahadi-centric. Muslim women face a different set of challenges, she said, and she sought to dispute the notion that Islam teaches female subservience. She spoke of the economic disparities among Muslim women. "In wealthy households, girls get to go to schools. There are a few wealthy Muslim women from Banke who have become doctors, or have master's degrees. But in the villages, there is still child marriage and domestic violence. Parents can't provide for their daughters, so they marry them off at a young age."

Natural Fertility and Population Growth

In 2001, the total recorded population of Muslims in Nepal was about 976,000; ten years later, in 2011, it had reached 1.2 million a significant increase (and now approximately the same size of population as the Tharus of the *terai).* Some continue to argue that this is an underestimate; and while population growth in Nepal as a whole has also increased over the last ten years, the rate of growth of the Muslim population has been faster than the national average, and faster than most other groups. Reasons for this include a relatively low use of contraception and a relatively high fertility rate in the Muslim communities of the *terai,* giving rise to larger than average families and households.

The analysis by Pandey et al indicates that 'while awareness of family planning is almost universal among Nepali women and men, there is still substantial variation in the use of family planning methods and in unmet need among different caste/ethnic groups'. It adds that, according to the 2011 National Health Survey, 'at 25 per cent, met need for family planning is markedly lower among Muslim women than among other groups' (Pandey et al 2013: 14). The national contraceptive prevalence rate increased between 1996 and 2006 to 44 per cent, but the rate among Muslims remained very low at 17 per cent (among *terai* Brahmin/ Chhetris by contrast it was 68 per cent). The data derive from an Analysis of 2006 Nepal Health and Demographic Survey (Bennett et al

2008), as do those cited below. The Core Group's report on its family planning project states that 'one in every ten Muslim women has a strong belief that the Quran prohibits the use of family planning, especially sterilisation' (Core Group 2009: 5). Women interviewed in Kapilvastu were reported to have said that 'birth and death are not under the control of Man, but of God, and we should not go against nature' (Khan 2011: 33).

On the other hand, Muslim women, like other women in Nepal, where the practice of abortion is linked with issues of morality and stigrna, are often obliged to resort to the termination of pregnancies using illegal or traditional 'remedies' which are often unsafe and threaten their health and life. Abortion has been legal in Nepal since 2002 and safe abortion services are available in government health facilities and in authorised private hospitals and clinics, as well as in facilities provided by some NGOs. Still, only two fifths of women aged 15 to 49 are aware that abortion is legal, and only three fifths know about places where abortion services are available (MoHP et al 2012). Higher percentages of Brahmin/Chhetri women and Newar women (in the 60s) had such knowledge, compared with *dalits* and *janajati* women (in the 50s). Wealth and poverty were better predictors than caste and ethnicity or religion in this respect, with knowledge ranging from 40 per cent among the poorest women to 71 per cent among the wealthiest. 62 per cent of Muslim women said that they knew about opportunities for abortion, slightly above the national average of 59 per cent (Pandey et al 2013: 18); but there is no data on the actual incidence of abortion, which is likely to be low.

The recent 'further analysis' of the 2011 Department of Health Survey data (by Pandey et al 2013) suggests that 'the unmet need for contraception among *dalit* and Muslim women continues to be much higher than in other groups. Closer attention needs to be paid to understanding the reasons that *dalit* and Muslim women continue to have higher levels of unmet need. While the intersection between gender, poverty and social exclusion (particularly for poor *dalit* women) might be creating barriers for *dalit* women, a better comprehension of the mechanisms to work through the existing cultural barriers that Muslim women face is a dimension that needs to be addressed' (Pandey 2013: 33).

One factor is that contraception is not encouraged and indeed is often actively discouraged by the *imams* and religious leaders, who have very considerable influence on family behaviour; another is the value attached by custom and practice and particularly by men to large families. The Core Group project on family planning (working in four *terai* districts Sunsari, Siraha, Dhanusha and Banke between 2006 and 2009) recognised this and explicitly tried to involve the Muslim clerics (*maulanas* and *imams*): 'initially, the NGOs working with the project faced challenges involving the Muslim community and women. Working with the support of Muslim *imams* and other religious leaders, the project was able to create continued support for the use of family planning practices within the Muslim community' (Core Group 2009: 10). Upadhyay found that among hill Muslims in Tanahun, 'Muslims do not practice family planning, permanent or temporary' (2014: 77), so this is not just a phenomenon confined to the Muslims of the *terai*.

The majority of births in Muslim communities continue to take place at home, with a mere 18 per cent of deliveries in a health facility. The percentage of pregnant women attending at least four ANC visits was lower among Muslims than any other social group apart from *terai/ madhesi dalits* (Pandey et al 2013: 41). Institutional deliveries were lowest for *dalit* women in the *terai* (9 per cent) but were also very low for Muslim women in general. In the *terai* at least, most deliveries of children by Muslim women are not only at home, they are without a skilled birth attendant. The percentage of deliveries attended by a skilled birth attendant (SBA) was lower (at 33 per cent) than most other social groups, but higher than *dalits* and *janajatis*.

The re-analysis of the 2011 Department of Health Survey data (by Pandey et al) in 2013 revealed that 'despite the dramatic increases recently, still only a little over one third of births have been attended by an SBA. The more privileged Newar and Brahmin women are twice as likely as women in the hill Chhetri, Muslim and *terai madhesi* 'other' categories to have an SBA on delivery'. For *dalits* and *janajatis*, the difference is even greater. Only 31 per cent of pregnant Muslim women received antenatal care from skilled birth attendant, compared with the national average of 44 per cent, and 76 for hill Brahmin women, only 33 per cent were delivered by a skilled birth attendant; 32 per cent were delivered in a health facility, but only 13 per cent of deliveries were with a midwife or assistant nurse midwife attending, compared with a national average of 19 per cent. The lowest was for *terai* dalit women (5 per cent) and the highest for *terai* Brahmin/Chhetris (70).

The mass media are an important channel for learning about health services and outcomes; studies have shown that exposure to mass media is related to childbearing behaviour, including preference for smaller families, weaker son preference and favourable attitudes towards contraceptive use (Barber & Axinn 2004). Exposure to mass media has also been shown to increase use of maternal health services (Navaneetham and Dharmalingam 2002). In the 2011 NHS, as in the 2006 NDHS (Bennett et al 2008), the level of mass media exposure varied among social groups in Nepal. Among women aged 15-49, exposure was much lower than the national average of 67 per cent among Muslim, *dalit* and *terai/madhesi* 'other' groups (Pandey et al 2013: 25). Not surprisingly, as a result of all this, infant mortality remains high, as does maternal mortality; under-5 child mortality in 2006 was 80 per 1,000 live births as compared with a national average of 68. The percentage of Muslim women breast feeding within an hour of the child's birth was lower than most other groups (apart from *terai dalits*) at 34 per cent (compared with the overall average of 45 per cent), as was exclusive breast feeding up to five months (48 per cent as compared with 70 per cent).

The Nepal Department of Health Survey of 2011 found that, while weight for age stunting (stunting) was relatively low among Muslims, compared with other groups, particularly *terai/madhesi* groups, as was weight for height stunting (wasting), low weight for age (underweight) was relatively high (exceeded only by *dalits*) and anaemia, particularly among girls, was higher than for any other group apart from *terai/madhesi dalits*. Furthermore, above average proportions of Muslim women were undernourished (37 per cent), which was higher than any other group apart from *terai dalits* (45 per cent), and almost double that national average (18 per cent); more than half (55 per cent) were anaemic, compared with a national average of 35 per cent (Pandey et al 2013: 22).

Furthermore, the percentage of Muslim children who received all basic vaccinations was 77 per cent, the second lowest after *dalits* (the highest rate was 92 per cent among hill Brahmin/Chhetris). The recent re-analysis of the 2011 Nepal Department of Health survey census data by Pandey et al suggest that, as far as vaccination coverage is concerned, 'the extent and equity in immunization coverage over the years has been highly encouraging in Nepal. Coverage has increased among nearly all social groups. The only exception to this improvement is among Muslim children, whose 'coverage' with basic vaccine actually decreased substantially between 2006 and 2011 and whose 'coverage' with measles vaccination was one of the lowest'. Thus, 'while it is important to ensure continuity of such coverage, it is equally important to better understand the causes of the recent decrease in coverage in one specific group, the Muslims, and to develop interventions that address the causes' (Pandey et al 2013: 35).

But all of this does not prevent indeed some would argue that, together with a desire particularly among men for large families it encourages high fertility rates and larger than usual families and households. On the other hand, there is some suggestion that, despite all of these disadvantages, Muslim life expectancy, at 70.5 years, seems to be better than the national average (68.8 years).

Household Size, Age and Gender

A sample survey undertaken in 2009 (Rana 2009) produced some revealing statistics relating to 240 households and 1,623 individuals in six districts (Table 14).

Table 14: Demographic Structure in Sample Survey (2009)

Age	Hill (% population)			Terai (% population)			Total (% population)		
	M	F	T	M	F	T	M	F	T
0-5	6.85	3.71	5.57	6.95	6.61	6.79	6.92	5.82	6.40
5-15	28.15	33.88	30.76	33.56	32.13	32.88	31.80	32.64	32.20
15-40	44.40	44.21	44.23	40.34	43.66	41.93	41.66	43.78	42.67
40-60	16.96	16.11	16.53	14.43	13.04	13.76	15.25	13.98	14.65
60 above	3.61	2.06	2.88	4.69	4.53	4.61	4.34	3.75	4.06
Grand total	100	100	100	100	100	100	100	100	100

The average household size was 6.5 in the hill districts and 6.9 per cent in the *terai* districts; 6.2 in the urban areas and 7.3 in the rural areas; that is, higher in the *terai* and in the rural areas. A study among Muslims in the hills in Tanahun District found that family size was, on average, 7.3, with a median of between 5 and 6; but a significant minority of households had between 8 and 15 members, and one had 23 members (Upadhyay 2014: 78).

The percentage of the population under the age of 15 in Rana's survey was nearly 40 per cent, with 6.4 per cent under 5 and 32 per cent aged between 5 and 15; 43 per cent of the population was between 15 and 40 years and about 15 per cent between 40 and 60. Thus about 55 per cent belonged to the economically active group (15 to 60 years) and 4.6 per cent above 60, giving a total figure for the 'dependent' population of around 43 per cent. In the hill areas, the dependent population was around 40 per cent, in the *terai,* 44 percent. This is a relatively high dependency ratio, and in the case of the Muslim community, where many women are obliged by custom and tradition (the *purdah* rules) to remain indoors, and not to work 'outside', even adult married women are, in effect, dependent as far as income generation is concerned.

In the 2009 study (see Table 14 above), the ratio of females to males in the *terai* areas was less than 100 in all age ranges, with the exception of 15 to 40 where there were more women than men; this was almost certainly a consequence of high rates of male out-migration, which means that a significant proportion of the men were away, usually abroad, for some time, and were therefore under-represented in the survey. This suggests that in all age ranges, if one discounts the effect of male outmigration, the sex ratio is in favour of men suggesting a clear demographic bias against females and implying a social bias against females.

This phenomenon is generally relatively common in the Nepal *terai,* according to a study by Seddon (1998) on 'missing girls' in Nepal. This is particularly the case in the Mithila-speaking region of the central eastern *terai* (Dhanusha, Mahottari, Sarlahi, Rautahat, Bara and Parsa), where the female-to-male ratio (FMR) is particularly low falling in a range between Parsa (883 women to every 1,000 males) and Rautahat (903). However, *all* the districts of the eastern *terai* have female/male ratios of less than parity, with Jhapa the highest (at 981), but the rest all below 965. In the western, mid-western and far western *terai,* only Chitwan, Dang and Kanchanpur have female/male ratios over 1,000, and those with the lowest ratios are Kapilvastu (932) and Banke (905). These data are not just for Muslims, but it may well be that in this region the gender concerns are similar in all groups. This would merit further study.

There is a statistical tendency, I suggest, for districts with low female/male ratios to be those with the largest numbers and proportion of Muslims; but it is also clear that in these districts the sex ratio for women is low in all social groups. Generally, when social groups are identified, the groups with female/male ratios of less than 1,000 are groups found in the *terai.* Seddon divides the social groups into six categories and finds that groups 4, 5 and 6 all of which have female/male ratios of 1,000 and over virtually all live in the hills and mountains, while groups 1, 2 and 3 all of which have female/male ratios below

1,000 are almost all in the *terai*. Group 1 all have female/male ratios below 925 and Group 2 are between 925 and 950. Muslim communities fall into Seddon's 'Group 2' with a female/male ratio of 942. All of those with FMRs below 950 (ie Groups 2 and 1) 'would appear to be particularly discriminatory towards females' (Seddon 1998: 34-35).

Even at the national level, the proportion of females in the total Muslim population is significantly below that of males, despite the absence abroad working in the Gulf and elsewhere of a large number of men, which would usually result in under-enumeration of adult males. In each age range in the 2011 census, for example, up to the age of 19, there are fewer females than males; this changes dramatically in the age ranges 20 to 44 when females outnumber males in each age range. A focus group held in Ek-laini Bazaar in Nepalgunj in the summer of 2015 as part of the IDEA/NEMAF project suggested that the ratio of females to males in Banke District was roughly 3 to 2. From ages 45 to 89, however, men again outnumber women, according to the census. This suggests a systematic demographic bias against females and behind these data a serious bias against females.

Health Status and Health Practices

The physical and demographic characteristics of the Muslim population result, in part, from poverty and lack of resources; but also in part from the maintenance of traditional patriarchal values with respect to the status and position of women. These manifest themselves also in the phenomenon of 'missing girls' (where the proportion of girls in the age range 5-19 is significantly lower than that of boys), low levels of literacy and education; in patterns of economic and social life, including entrepreneurial activity, employment and exposure to mass media; in limited involvement in domestic decision making as well as in 'public' life outside the home (which will be discussed separately below), and finally, in low levels of well-being and health generally.

Disability is a significant aspect of health status among Nepali people, with around 10 to 11 per cent of families on average reporting a disabled person in the family. In a recent survey by NEMAF in five districts in the central eastern *terai* (NEMAF 2016), 11 per cent of households reported a disabled person, with 12 per cent relating to females and 10 per cent to males. The average for Muslims was 11 per cent, for *janajati* 13 per cent and for *dalits* 15 per cent. Incidence tended to be higher among families identified as poor (13 per cent) and very poor (16 per cent).

The factors affecting Muslim women's health can be seen as both external and internal to the Muslim communities external relates to the provision of health services and their quality, and accessibility, internal to the constraints in terms of custom and practice which reduce women's real access to whatever health services are available. As regards the former, a small village study in Bardiya District undertaken in 2010 (Khan 2011) with a sample of 100 Muslim interviewees found that most explained the generally poor health status by the fact that they did not have good access to health care.

Two thirds of respondents (66 per cent) said that doctors were not available, while 17 per cent explained it by the fact that the health service institutions (health posts, sub health posts and hospitals) were far from their homes. Some said that employees in the health centres ask for money so they do not go there, or that they simply get the same medicines each time. Most (66 per cent) said that they were treated badly in health posts, sub health posts and in hospitals, but 31 per cent said that staff in the health centres behaved well towards them. Of those who said they badly treated, 73 per cent said that they were treated in this way because they are Muslim and cannot speak Nepali fluently, while 28 per cent said that being a Muslim one reason why they are treated poorly by health professionals.

On the other hand, a recent survey in 2016 undertaken by NEMAF in five districts of the central eastern *terai* reported that when asked if they received health services 'to your expectation', 84 per cent of Muslims said yes, and only 16 per cent said no; when asked if they faced 'any difficulty' in accessing health services, 62 per cent said no, and only 38 per cent said yes (2016: 28). Where problems were experienced, the largest proportion of those complaining (half) mentioned lack of medication available, while a relatively small proportion mentioned inadequate information, absence of health personnel, unhelpful behaviour and discrimination (15 per cent for each of these). *Dalits* and *janajati* both felt less discrimination (12 per cent and 7 per cent respectively); but, interestingly, half (50 per cent) of high caste Hindus complained of discrimination. It seems that feelings of discrimination are highly subjective.

Such factors as poor water supply and sanitation adversely affect health. Among the hill Muslims of Tanahun, studied by Upadhyay (2014: 79, 92), the majority (58 per cent) of households had no toilet and used the area surrounding the village, 36 per cent had a temporary or makeshift toilet and only four households (6 per cent) had a permanent toilet. Drinking water availability was also poor, with 22 per cent relying on a pond or water tank, which Upadhayay says was usually dry in any case and 27 per cent having to go to a spring, although 52 per cent did have access to tap water.

Several studies have shown that women's autonomy is linked with their use of health care and is often as important as other known determinants such as their education (Bloom et al 2001). In Nepal as a whole, one fourth of women (26 per cent) make their own decisions on health care, but a greater perentage do not participate in decisions at all. In nearly all caste, ethnic and religious groups, decisions on women's own health care are taken by the women theselved or jointly with their partners; two exceptions are *terai/madhesi* women and Muslim women, where the majority do not participate in decisions even about their own health care.

Among Muslims women, 19 per cent made decisions on their own, 27 per cent jointly with the husband and in 54.5 per cent of cases, decisions were taken by husbands alone (Pandey et al 2013: 24-25). Upadhyay suggests that among the hill Muslims of the village he studied in Tanahun, eight out of 64 women played no role in decision making, with 11 (17 per cent) playing a 'partial role' and 35 playing an 'advisory' role, and only 15 per cent actively involved (2014: 97).

Maternal and child nutrition also appears to be a critical issue among Muslim communities. Nearly 20 per cent of Muslim women were considered moderately or severely thin in 2008 as compared with a national average of 8 per cent of women, with only *dalit* women in the *terai* on average thinner (24 per cent moderately or severely thin), and stunting among children as a result of malnutrition was widespread. The re-analysis of the 2011 census data (by Pandey et al 2013) suggests that Muslim children under five who were stunted, wasted and/or underweight and who had anaemia were relatively common, with the proportion of those underweight higher than most groups, apart from all *dalits*. Anaemia was a particular problem, with figures higher than for any other group apart from *terai/madhesi dalits* (Pandey et al 2013: 23).

Focus programmes for specific communities, such as the *terai/madhesi dalits*, Muslims and *terai/madhesi* 'other', who have poor indicators for almost all services and outcomes, are considered essential. Specific programme initiatives to reduce anaemia among girls are called for along with activities to change gender-based discriminatory practices in families and communities (Pandey et al 2013: 36). Also, the health effects of marriage between blood relatives, notably between cousins, which is common among the Muslim population in Nepal, are the subject of considerable controversy. There is evidence from various studies that consanguineous marriages tend to have a deleterious effect on health.

A recent study in Nepal was designed to determine the prevalence, characteristics and health outcomes related to consanguineous marriage (Bhatta & Haque 2015). A cross-sectional survey was carried out using a cluster sampling technique to select a total of 400 women aged 15-49 years; they were interviewed from September 2011 to February 2012. It was found that the overall prevalence of consanguinity (marriage to close relatives) was 37 per cent. The median age at marriage and age at first childbirth was 15 and 18 years, respectively. Several factors including husband's educational status, 'dowry' practices and physical/emotional violence appear to be associated with consanguineous marriage. The association of being in a consanguineous marriage among women whose husband's education level were secondary or higher was 3.35 times greater than among those whose husbands were unable to read and write.

Woman who had a consanguineous marriage were less likely to have used contraceptive than those who had a non-consanguineous marriage. Women who had consanguineous marriage were more likely to have birth defects in their children than those who had a non-consanguineous marriage. The association of having a history of death after live birth among women who experienced emotional violence was 2.60 and physical violence 2.15 times greater than among those who did not experience violence.

Notes

1. The figures for Muslims as a social group are slightly different from the figures for Muslims by religious affiliation in the 2011 census.
2. 'Steady migration of Bangladeshi Muslims to the (eastern) *terai* contributed significantly to this increase' (*India Today*, June 12, 2000).
3. This belief derives from a report in the official daily *Gorkhapatra* (5 Baisakh 2038 BS) which, at the time of the visit of the Saudi foreign minister in February 1981, gave the total figure of the Muslim population as 1.4 million
4. According to Gaige 1975: 33, practically all the Muslims (in Kailali) are businessmen and constituted 22 per cent of all itinerant traders (1975: 35). In Kapilvastu, Muslims accounted for over a quarter of all itinerant traders (1975: 35) and about a quarter of all owners of small-scale industry (1975: 40).
5. I am indebted to Dr. Magnus Hatlebakk for this information

2

Muslim Communities

The discussion and the figures provided above relate to 'Muslims in Nepal' as a whole. But 'Muslims in Nepal' do not, in reality, constitute a homogenous category, despite the arguments developed by Haque and those who rightly wish to draw attention to the Muslim community as a distinctive and disadvantaged minority in Nepal. The Muslim community is divided along religious-sectarian & doctrinal, geographical or regional, linguistic, cultural, caste and classlines. The different Muslim communities also have different histories, known with different degrees of detail and depth. This, in itself, has an impact on the Muslim community as a whole. Megan Sijapati comments that 'at the outset of my fieldwork, Muslims in Nepal complained to me that they were endlessly divided and that their own religious and political prejudices were their greated impediments to social, economic and political development' (2011: 25).

The Coming of Islam

Islam spread rapidly to the east from its heartland in the Middle East from its very beginning in the early 7th century CE. Islamic influence first came to be felt in the Indian subcontinent during the early 7th century with the advent of Arab traders. According to historians Elliot and Dowson in *The History of India as told by its own Historians*, the first ship bearing Muslim travellers was seen on the west coast of India as early as 630 CE. The first Indian mosque is thought to have been built in 629 CE, purportedly at the behest of an unknown Chera dynasty[1] ruler, during the lifetime of Muhammad (c. 571–632), in Kodungallur in Kerala by Malik Bin Deenar. H. G. Rawlinson, in his book *Ancient and Medieval History of India*, claims the first Arab Muslims settled on the Indian coast in the last part of the 7th century. This fact is corroborated, by Sturrock in his *South Kanara and Madras Districts Manuals, and* also by Haridas Bhattacharya in *Cultural Heritage of India Vol. IV.*

In Bengal, Arab merchants helped found the port of Chittagong, and Sufi missionaries settled in the region as early as the 8th century CE. The earliest indication of contact between the Islamic world and Nepal is a mention of Nepal as a source of musk exports to Arabia in the *'Hudood-Al-Alam'*, published in 783 CE.

It was the Muslim conquest of the Indian subcontinent over the next millennium that really established Islam in the region. But before that, at least one Muslim traveller came to Nepal. Born in 973 CE, in modern day Khiva in Uzbekistan (then called Kwarizm), the great Muslim traveller and geographer, Al Birani, was forced south into exile in Afghanistan after Mahmud, king of Ghazna (997-1030 CE), invaded Kwarizm in 1017 CE. During his time in exile, much of it spent in India, he gathered the materials for his great book, *The Indica* (Edward Sachau, *Alberuni's India*. Kegan Paul, Trench, Truner & Co Ltd, 1910, p. 201). He started the work of writing after 1030 CE when Masud, son of Mahmud, came to the throne. In his book, he describes the geography, as well as the peoples and their cultures, of northern India, and indicates the route from Ajoda (Ayodhya, Oudh), via Banarasi, then eastwards via Sharwar, Pataliputra, Mungiri, Janpa, and Dugumpur to Gangasayara, 'where the Ganges flows into the sea'.

He also reports that 'marching from Kanoj towards the east, you come to Bari, Dagum, the empire of Shilatahat, and the town Bihat. Farther on the country ... is called Tilwat[2], and the inhabitants, Taru' - whom he describes as 'people of very black colour and flat-nosed like the Turks'[3]. He remarks that 'opposite Tilwat, the country to the left is the realm of Naipal. A man who had travelled in those countries gave me this report: when in Tanwat he left the easterly direction and turned to the left (ie northwards). He marched to Naipal, a distance of 20 *farsakhs,* most of which was ascending country. From Naipal he came to Bhoteshar[4] in thirty days, a distance of nearly 80 *farsakhs,* in which, he notes wryly, 'there is more ascending than descending country'.

'Bhoteshar is the first frontier of Tibet. There the language changes as well as the costumes and the anthropological character of the people. Thence the distance to the top of the highest peak is 20 *farsakhs.* From the height of this mountain, India appears as a black expanse below the mist, the mountains lying below this peak like small hills, and Tibet and

China appear as red. The descent towards Tibet and China is less than one *farsakh*'.

According to the Tibetan Muslim community's traditions, Islam first arrived in Tibet almost a thousand years ago, entering a region that has always, mistakenly, been viewed as characterized by a monolithic Buddhist culture. From the 12th century onwards, it is believed by some, Muslim merchants from Kashmir and Ladakh went to Tibet to trade, and in the 16th century the Fifth Dalai Lama asked some of them to stay, granting them religious freedom and rights. These 'Kashmiri' and 'Ladakhi' Muslims married into the local community and gained converts. Author Thomas Arnold, in his book, *The Preaching of Islam,* says that, gradually, marriages and social interactions led to an increase in the Tibetan Muslim population until a sizable community developed around Lhasa, Tibet's capital.

This eventually led to over 100 Muslim families to move to the Kathmandu valley (Dastider, chapter 4). It is not entirely clear what happened to these early Tibetan immigrants, or how they relate to the later wave of immigrants from Tibet - or, indeed, to the so-called 'Kashmiri' Muslims. Upadhyay even suggests that 'it is believed that when the Muslim ruler Bakhtiyar Khilji invaded Tibet in the 13th century, some of his soldiers entered secretly into Nepal' (Upadhyay 2014: 29); but he gives no source for this statement.

The first documented direct contact between Muslims in India and Nepal after the visit of Al Birani was in the early 14th century CE, when Gayasuddin Tuglaq, the emperor of Delhi, went to war with Hari Singh Dev, the King of Mithila (one of the kingdoms mentioned in the *Ramayana*) at Simraungarh. The King of Mithila was defeated and his capital destroyed; he then fled with his family into the hills of what is now Nepal, where he was well received. Not long afterwards, in 1349 CE, in the time of King Raj Malla, according to historical accounts, Sultan Shams-ud-Din Ilyas actually invaded the Kathmandu Valley through Banepa. This apparently resulted in the looting and destruction of the royal Hindu temple of Pashupatinath, the Buddhist stupa at Swyambunath and other sacred sites in the Kathmandu Valley. However, he and his forces remained only a short time in Kathmandu, due to the cold climate according to some sources and because he was unable to maintain his lines of provision for the army according to others.

By this time, the Hindu Malla kings of Nepal ruled over a settled urban society in the Kathmandu Valley, which already had a thriving economy, based on agriculture, horticulture and trade, with a complex division of labour into different occupational castes, including craftsmen of various kinds and farmers. The Newar of the Kathmandu Valley were already a sophisticated people, speaking a language akin to that spoken further south in Mithila, with which there were clearly strong cultural as well as economic and political links. Later, the Malla kingdom was divided between three sons, into the smaller kingdoms of Kathmandu, Lalitpur and Bhaktapur.

Although the royal family was of a Thakuri (Chathariya) Hindu caste, many of the people were Buddhists and Lalitpur had more than a hundred Buddhist monasteries (*baha*), inhabited by the descendants of Buddhist monks (*shakya*) who abandoned their vows and started to marry as early as the 13th century. Toffin remarks that 'Hinduism and Buddhism have cohabited within this small valley for nearly two millennia. The result is a syncretist religion…'; he also notes that 'these kingdoms were largely tolerant of other faiths. The Christian missionaries, for instance, Jesuits as well as Capuchins, were more than tolerated' (Toffin 2013: 53-54)

Hill Muslims ('Charaute' or 'Miya')

Another, arguably distinct category of Muslims apparently settled early in Nepal, coming from different parts of northern India during the 16th and 17th centuries, having allegedly been invited by the rulers of the Chaubise petty states in the western hills particularly, as previously mentioned, the rising petty state of Gorkha who wanted Muslim artisans and artillerymen from India to train their armed forces in Mughal techniques of making firearms (including cannon) (int. Siraj Faruqui and Athar Faruqui; Bista 1996). They also, apparently, came to Nepal to sell Turkish and Arab horses.

It is said by some that the 'Churaute' Muslims, who were said to be traditionally scent manufacturers, musicians and suppliers of bangles (*chura*) etc., were closely related to this wave of Nepalese Muslims (Gaborieau, 1972, 84-85). Some of these immigrants, it is said, remained in the hills as makers of agricultural implements, utensils and ornaments. The descendants of these migrants are widely known as 'Charaute' or 'Miya' (bangle-sellers), but a majority in fact survives as farmers, labourers and other occupations that they have in common with the surrounding non-Muslim hill folk.

According to Dor Bahadur Bista (1980: 150), 30 years ago, the hill Muslims numbered only a few thousand and constituted 0.01 per cent of the total population of Nepal. Today, their numbers are still relatively small. In the 2001 census only 4,893 individuals (0.02 per cent of the total population) were recorded as being 'hill Muslims'; in the 2011 census, however, although only 2,884 were recorded in the hill areas of the far west, the west and the east, some 20,000 were registered as Muslims in the western hills and 30,104 were recorded for the central hills as a whole which of course included the Kathmandu Valley and thus the Kathmandu Muslims.

The hill Muslims are scattered thinly through some 48 of the 55 hill districts of Nepal, but the main area of concentration is, apparently, in the western and central hill districts of Gorkha, Tanahun, Kaski, Syangja, Palpa, Pyuthan, Arga Khanchi and Dailekh. The hill Muslims have been greatly influenced by the local hill milieu. Although they follow Islamic customs such as prayer (*salam*), circumcision, and ritual burial of the dead, other Islamic practices like *nihth (*bride price) and *zakat* (charity collected during religious festivals) are not always observed. They generally speak Nepali and in their dress, food habits and some of their customs are apparently indistinguishable from their Bahun and Chhetri neighbours.

Upadhyay spent some time in a Muslim hill village (in Kihun VDC in the District of Tanahun, in western Nepal) and provides an account of their circumstances, living as they do as a significant minority among other groups Magars, Brahmins and Dalits (2014). The Muslims constitute the fourth largest group in the VDC 466 people in 64 households and tend to live in their own village, known as 'Miya Gaon' or Hukka, in ward number 5. Interestingly, given the usual 'history' of such people, only one old man actually gained an income as a bangle-seller.

Upadhayay suggests that, according to respondents in the village, one group of Muslims 'came from Lhasa and settled in Basantapur village in Tanahun District and later migrated to Sundhara, Gajarkot VDC in Tanahun and finally settled in Miya Gaon, Hukka'. Others came from Rampur in Palpa District. These groups were mainly, he says, 'Tibetan' and 'Kashmiri' Muslims. The migratory history of this village goes back about 250 years, according to Upadhyay; but he also suggests that 'in the historical phase' (ie before then), Muslim groups were invited by Shah and Sen kings to supply butyl or cosmetic materials for the palace, as well as to make weapons and provide military training, and Muslim medicine. These, it seems, were Bihari, Bengali and Awadhi Muslims (2014: 73).

In general, these immigrants, although Muslim rather than Hindu, were over time broadly accommodated in Nepal, wherever they settled, within the Hindu caste based structure and, as a result, acquired a well defined if relatively low social status in the overall caste hierarchy. This aspect became very evident in the 19th century when the Muluki-Ain codified the social status of different social groups, including Muslims.

The 'Kashmiri' Muslims of Kathmandu

Fadzakir explains that the term 'Kashmiri Muslims' may be used in several different senses: those who are 'Kashmiri by descent, those who are Kashmiri by geographical origin and those who are 'Kashmiri' by religious affiliation' (2001: 28).

According to the *Vamshavalis*, the first Muslims to settle in Nepal, as opposed to just visiting or invading, arrived in Kathmandu from Kashmir in the late 15th and early 16th century during the reign of King Rama Malla (1484-1520 CE). Some of them, who were educated and literate, helped create a Munshi Khana, a government department which used to manage official documents and letters. This department, we are told, was also instrumental in making contacts with the Delhi Sultanate (Siddika 1993, 103). They built a mosque, the Kashmiri Takia (Kashmiri Jame Masjid), on the king's way (Raj Path), only a few hundred metres from the king's palace. There are two tombs within the compound of the mosque, one of which is that of Haji Mishkin Shah, considered the first Muslim to have arrived in Kathmandu, and the second is of his nephew, Khwaja Gyasuddin Shah.

There was at least one other wave of Muslim immigration before the rise of the petty kingdom of Gorkha and the integration of the kingdoms of the Kathmandu Valley into this 'Gorkhali' kingdom. In his book on *Kathmandu*, Thomas Bell cites one leader of the so called 'Kashmiri Muslim' community as saying that 'we have some family papers from 367 years ago. The king (then) was Prateep Malla. We came from Saudi Arabia to Baghdad and from Iraq to Samarkand and Bokhara, then Afghanistan to Kashmir and Kashmir to India, Nepal and Tibet. Pratap asked us to stay here and do business'. According to Bell, 'he adopted the voice of Prateep Malla: 'I will give facilities, customs duty free, for the Kashmiri Muslims'. He still had cousins in Lhasa, who came to visit from time to time'.

'He picked up the phone and spoke in Urdu. A while later, someone came in with a sheaf of papers', which he handed to Bell. 'It was a university thesis, written thirty years ago by a member of the community, about the community. 'Read this and give it back', he said. 'There were four families of Kashmiris: first came Syed, then Joo, then Sheik, then Khan, the old man explained. He was from Syed. Now the four families fill 200 households in the city, a total of around 1,000 people. Later other Muslims came, but they are not the same' (Bell 2014: 126).

Fadzakir suggests that not all of those who refer to themselves as 'Kashmiri' Muslims are actually descendants of the earliest arrivals from Kashmir, but also of healers, cooks and Persian language specialists (not all of whom by any means were from Kashmir), invited by the Malla and Shah kings to serve in their court. Until the early 19th century, virtually the only mosque in Kathmandu was the 'Kashmiri' mosque, and it is their association with the management of that mosque that identifies this heterogeneous group of Muslims in Kathmandu as 'Kashmiri'. The descendants of the original Kashmiris, Fadzakir remarks, carefully record their genealogies, so as to avoid any disputes over authority and/or inheritance. According to one Kashmiri historian, he reports, there are about 70 Kashmiri households in Kathmandu. These are given special burial privileges on the Kashmiri side of the cemetery at Swayambhu.

The term 'Kashmiri' is also used to apply generally those who worship at the Kashmiri mosque. Fadzakir explains that these are generally likely to be recent immigrants to Kathmandu from the *terai*. These, who refer to themselves as a Barelwis, practice saint veneration, and the fact that the Kashmiri mosque is the main locus of saint veneration in Kathmandu has meant that the mosque has become the primary 'marker' of their religious and cultural identity. But this group is not allowed burial rites at the Kashmiri cemetery nor are they eligible for membership of the mosque management committee. Finally, according to Fadzakir, the term is also used to refer to the more recent arrivals in Kathmandu from Kashmir, who are general traders in handicraft and woollen products which they sell in Thamel. These 'Kashmiris' have little in common with the two other groups; most are opposed to saint veneration and do not pray at the Kashmiri mosque.

The history of the successive waves of Muslim immigrants is actually poorly known or documented and can be both confused and confusing. Upadhyay (2016), for example, suggests that those Muslims who came to Kathmandu at the time of King Ratna Malla (1484-1520 CE) were different from the group that came later, at the time of King Prapa (Prateep) Malla (1641-1674). The latter, to whom he refers (misleadingly) as 'Hindustani' Muslims, he says, 'put up their own mosque in the southern part of the property belonging to the Kashmiri Takia'. He suggests (2014: 29-30) that this 'Hindustani' mosque, now known as the Nepali Jame Masjid, 'is originally said to have been a Shi'a mosque, which was converted at a later date, by Maulana Sargaraz Shah, who arrived with the followers of the Begum Hazrrat Mahal, former wife of the Nawab of Awadh, when she fled from India after the suppression of the so-called 'Great Mutiny' in India in 1857' hence the reference to 'Hindustani' Muslims.

This is very confusing and it seems clear that the early Muslims, who came in the 15th-16th and in the 17th centuries respectively, are different from those who came in the mid-19th century, who are commonly referred to as 'Hindustani Muslims'.

The 'Hindustani' Muslims

Clearly distinct from the earlier two waves of immigrants (in the 16th and 17th centuries) is a much later wave, often known as the 'Hidustani' Muslims, associated with those who, like the Begum Hazrat Mahal of Lucknow, the former concubine and wife of the Nawab of Oudh (Ayodha), fled from India after the 'Great Mutiny' of 1857 during which she had supported the rebels against the British and after spending some time in the western *terai,* settled as a refugee, together with many of her entourage in Kathmandu. Her husband, the Nawab, was the last of a dynasty of Shi'a rulers of Qaraqoyunlu origin from Nishapur, Iran which had been established in Awadh in 1724, by Nawab Sa'adat Khan.

The Begum had been born at Faizabad, Awadh and became a courtesan by profession. She had been taken into the royal harem as a *khawasin* after being sold by her parents. She was then sold to Royal agents, and later promoted to a *pari,* and was known as Mahak Pari. She became a *begum* after being accepted as a royal concubine of the King of Oudh, and the title 'Hazrat Mahal' was bestowed on her after the birth of their son, Birjis Qadra. She became the first wife of the last Tajdaar-e-Awadh, the Nawab Wajid Ali Shah, who rebelled against the British.

After her husband had been exiled to Calcutta, she took charge of the affairs in the state of Awadh despite her divorce from the Nawab and seized control of Lucknow. When the forces under the command of the British recaptured Lucknow and most of Awadh (Oudh), she was forced to retreat. Hazrat Mahal worked in association with Nana Saheb, but later joined the Maulavi of Faizabad in the attack on Shahjahanpur. She also arranged for her son, Prince Birjis Qadra, to become *Wali* (ruler) of Awadh; he was forced, however, to abandon his position after a short reign. She sought asylum in Nepal, and was initially refused asylum by the Rana Prime Minister Jang Bahadur, who had supported the British; she then, according to the librarian at the Mahendra Library in Nepalgunj, as reported by Peter Gill (in *The Record*, February 2017)

> 'with a retinue of her guards ...escaped across the border into Nepal, and spent some time hiding out in the jungles of the western Terai. Meanwhile, in Kathmandu, Jung Bahadur (Rana, the Nepali Prime Minister) became incensed upon hearing the British offer to return only the area now known as Naya Muluk as compensation for his military support apparently, he had expected much more territory. In a gesture calculated to irk the British, he sent word to the Begum and her retinue in the jungle that they would be welcome to take up residence in Kathmandu. She accepted. When she arrived, the Rana promptly confiscated her remaining treasure, and she lived out the rest of her days in the Nepali capital. When she died in 1879, her body was interred in a tomb, which today can be found in a dusty, forgotten corner of the Nepali Jama Masjid compound on Durbar Marg, by the stairs to the sky bridge to Ratna Park'.

In fact, she arrived in Kathmandu with her son and various courtiers and followers. She is said to have commissioned the building of a palace, a mosque and an *imambara*, where she is buried. She died in Kathmandu in 1879 and was buried in the grounds of Kathmandu's Jama Masjid, where her tomb (*mazar*) is looked after by the Jama Masjid Central Committee. On 15 August 1962, she was honoured at the Old Victoria Park in Hazratganj, Lucknow for her role in what is now referred to India as 'the First War of Independence'. Along with the renaming of the park, a marble memorial was constructed, which includes a marble tablet with four round brass plaques bearing the Coat of Arms of the Awadh royal family. On 10 May 1984, the Government of India issued a commemorative stamp in her honour.

Her son lived in Kathmandu for eighteen years, paying for his stay with jewels kept out of the possession of the British before moving to

Kolkata, where he died in 1893. He, like his parents, was a Shi'a Muslim. He was a poet and *shayar.* He organized many *tarahi mahfil e mushairah* in Kathmandu, which were recorded during the same period by the writer Khwaja Naeemudddin Badakhshi. His *majlis e mushalirah* were discovered in Kathmandu in 1995, by Professors Abdul Rauf and Adil Sarwar Nepal, and published in *Nepal mein Urdu Shairi,* a collection of the *sha'ari* (poems) of Birjis Qadr and his followers produced in Kathmandu over a period of several decades (and published initially by Tribhuvan University).

In between the early 'waves' of Muslim immigrants in the 15th, 16th and 17th centuries and that of the mid-19th century, it is entirely possible that there were others. The rise of the petty state of Gorkha, under the Shah kings, during the 17th century and the eventual unification of the Gorlkhali state under Prithivi Narayan Shah, for example, were both associated with increased links with India and the import of guns and other material of war; as we have already seen, it is said that some at least of the so-called Charaute 'hill Muslims' of Nepal are the descendants of Muslims brought in as armourers and military advisers during this period.

Daniel Wright, in his introduction to his *History of Nepal,* written in the latter part of the 19th century, refers specifically to the 'Kashmiri Muslims' and recounts how 'a few Musalmans, consisting of Kashmiri and Iraki merchants live in Kathmandu. The former have been established there for generations. Altogether they do not number more than about one thousand' Wright, 1877). The implication here is that the so-called 'Kashmiri' Muslims came earlier than those from Iraq, and that they constituted district communities, but Wright does not elaborate. Perhaps significantly, there is still a mosque referred to as the Raqi mosque in Kathmandu between Indrachowk and Asan Tol.

The descendants of all these early Muslim immigrants tended to remain in the Valley, and in particular in Kathmandu. Today, they are said to be, for the most part, well-educated and to speak a mixture of Nepali and Urdu at home. Many of the longer standing families of Muslims of Kathmandu are also fluent in Newari the language of the Kathmandu Valley; Sijapati even refers to 'Newari Muslims' and insists that such do exist, having met those 'who identify themselves as such and who speak Newari' (personal comm.). Fadzakir mentions Sheikh Idris, who had lived all his life in Chhetrapati, who explained that when he moved there, there were hardly any Muslims and most of the local families were Newar: 'even now', he said, 'my good friends and neighbours are Newars. We Muslims also follow some Newar culture. We eat the *dhao bhaji* (curd with beaten rice) and we can also speak Newari'.

Having said that, his relative Sheikh Khalil refers to himself as being 'treated like an outcast I even had to wash my own cups after drinking tea in the shop' (Fadzakir 2001: 27). Sijapati adds that there are also those who identify themselves as Iraqi Muslims, and draws attention to the old Raqi/Iraqi mosque (*masjid*) near Asan Tol (pers. comm.). While many of these Muslims are businessmen, some have apparently joined government service or entered politics.

Tibetan Muslims in Kathmandu

There is also a distinctive community of 'Tibetan Muslims' consisting of those who came relatively recently to the Kathmandu Valley. In 1952, China took over Tibet and declared it Chinese. Many Tibetans, including some Muslims, fled south at that time into Nepal. In their language and dress these Muslims were virtually indistinguishable from their Tibetan Buddhist counterparts. Some, like the parents of the present day owner of the Utse restaurant and hotel (who is not a Muslim) managed eventually to set up businesses, notably (like their counterparts in Pokhara) into the production and sale of rugs. Today, many of them are engaged in the trade of Chinese consumer durables and selling curios. It is said that, on the whole, the Tibetan Muslims tend to be more affluent than the other Muslim communities.

Although this migration was insignificant in terms of numbers Fadzakir (2001) suggests that 'there are about 30 Tibetan Muslim households in Kathmandu' it offered a new dimension to Muslim plurality and cultural and linguistic diversity. It is not certain precisely how many Tibetan Muslims there are now in Nepal, but one source suggests about 300-400 individuals (Clare Hennig, 11-17 July, 2014, *Nepali Times Buzz*). It is not also clear to what extent they have adapted to speak local languages as well as their original Tibetan, although Fadzakir suggests that 'it is common to see Tibetan Muslims at a wedding wearing the Tibetan national costume, chatting amongst themselves in Tibetan, and then switching effortlessly to Urdu or Nepali when conversing with non-Tibetan Muslims' (Fadzakir 21001: 30).

Hennig reports that 'like many others, Rehman and Tako's families first fled to Kashmir and Darjeeling because of their ancestral links to

India, later moving on to Nepal for economic opportunities. The shared history of migration and the efforts to preserve their heritage have forged strong bonds within Nepal's Tibetan Muslim community. And the mutual experience of Ramadan each year keeps it strong. The combination of the Islamic faith with Tibetan culture is being passed down to the younger generation as a joint effort between the family and the community. Tako's 17 year-old daughter and 14 year-old son attend a secular school in Kathmandu. But they read the Quran at home and worship at Jame Masjid on Fridays. On the streets, they speak Nepali but at home, it is Tibetan.

Fadzakir suggests that 'they are perhaps the most clearly defined ethnic category within the Muslim community, both in terms of appearance and language'; he also states that 'Tibetan Muslims are also unique among the Muslim groups in that marriages are commonly arranged with other Tibetan Muslims. Out of 32 Tibetan marriages surveyed, only four were with non-Tibetan Muslims, and out of these four only one was with a Muslim from Kathmandu. The rest were with foreigners'. In her piece, Clare Hennig talked to Abdul Rehman, a 63 year-old jewellery boutique owner in Thamel. He explained that: "The migration was purely on the basis of religion during the Cultural Revolution," Rehman said. "The elders thought, 'Ok for us we would stay but what about the future of the children?' So therefore they migrated." Abdul Rehman's nephew, Enayat Tako said that both Muslim and Tibetan are equally important elements of his identity. "We want to save our culture, that's why we mostly marry within our community," he said.

Amina Banu, the Tibetan Muslim founder of Banu's Total Fitness gym, described how the community comes together each night for *iftar*, the breaking of the fast, and how the holy month provides the time to grow closer to God and to one another: "Iftar is always celebrated in my sister's house; everybody comes together and we pray...we cook and it is like a festival. We stay together overnight."

Hennig suggests that 'despite cultural and language differences, Tibetan Muslims have integrated well with the other Islamic communities in Nepal. Kashmiri, Indian and Tibetan Muslims all pray together at the same mosques, and celebrate Ramadan together. "A Muslim is a Muslim, we don't differentiate," said Rehman. On the other hand, there are still some Tibetan Muslims who hold Indian passports, despite having lived in Nepal for several decades (according to Fadzakir 2001: 26); as a result of this, they still do not feel entirely secure in Nepal. Furthermore, he also states that 'they follow the Deobandi sect and align themselves with the Nepali mosque' not the Kashmiri mosque. He adds, tellingly, that 'ideologically, a Nepali Muslim is one who subscribes to the Deobandi sect and observes its prohibition of saint veneration and the role of mediators in Islam. Used in this way, the terms 'Nepali' and Kashmiri' (and by extension the Nepali Jame and Kashmiri mosques) represent ideological opposites, and are the local idioms for the Deobandi and Barelwi sects in Islam' (Fadzakir 2001: 31). For further discussion of religious communities, see Chapter 4 below.

Muslims of Kathmandu Today

The 2011 national census shows that the majority of Muslims in the Kathmandu Valley are in mainly in Kathmandu itself (where they numbered 21,866, or 1.25 per cent of the total national population), with very small numbers in Lalitpur (3,080 or 0.66 per cent of the total population) and Bhaktapur (1,503 or 0.49 per cent). The population has grown significantly since the 1991 census when Muslims in the Kathmandu Valley accounted for only 0.93 per cent of the total population of Nepal, at just over 6,000 people. Of these, Kathmandu itself accounted for 5,377, Lalitpur for 593 and Bhaktapur for 110. These Kathmandu Muslims constitute a number of identifiable communities that are themselves heterogeneous in many ways, although the existing rather limited literature on Muslims in Nepal tends, as indicated above, to group them in a rather standardised fashion.

The Muslims of Kathmandu are, for the most part, located within a 1.5 km radius of Ghantaghar, where the two main mosques in the city are located. The area with the highest number of Muslims is Bagh bazaar, the area directly adjacent to the Nepali Jame mosque. Fadzakir (2001) provides a 'Muslim map' of Kathmandu to show where the main places of importance and the Muslim households he surveyed for his study are located. The former include: Ghantaghar in central Kathmandu, where the 'Nepali Jame' and 'Kashmiri' mosques stand on the same side of the road; the Madrasah Islamiya School at the Nepali Jame mosque; the Islamic Library, between the two main mosques, and adjacent to the office of the Islamiya Yuva Sangh, the Muslim Youth organisation, established in 1985.

They also include: the Jame market, with Muslim restaurants and the tomb of Hazrat Begum Mahal (who sought refuge in Nepal after the 1857 'mutiny' in India); Sundhara to the south of Nayasadak where there are Muslim butchers; Thamel, where there are also Muslim butchers and restaurants (in 'Muslim tol') and the 'Thamel mosque'; and Indrachowk, where the Kashmiri bead market and the 'Raqi mosque' are located. Out to the west is the Swyambhu Muslim cemetery. These are all described in some detail, and their significance for the Muslim community of Kathmandu explained (2001: 12-18).

In west central Kathmandu, Fadzakir surveyed households in Thamel, Chhetrapti, Asan, Indrachowk, New Road and Putalisadak; in east central Kathmandu, in Kantipath, Kamal Pokhari, Kamaladi, Dilli Bazaar, Matidevi, and Ghattekulo. Far out to the east, he surveyed households in Chabahil. To the north he surveyed households in Maharajgunj, Samakhusi, and Lazimpat and Naya Bazaar. To the west, he surveyed households in Swyambhu; and to the southwest, he surveyed households in Kalimati and Soltimode. This gives some idea of the physical and geographical distribution of the Muslim 'community' of Kathmandu.

My own limited field research so far in Kathmandu suggests that the history, the economy and society, and the culture of the Muslims of Kathmandu suggests a far more complex, varied, divided and yet interactive 'community' than the standard classification (which tends to be repeated by almost all of those who have written on the Muslims of Nepal, and which I have largely followed above) would suggest. But this remains to be explored. Fadzakir provides a useful introduction, but his research was undertaken nearly 15 years ago, and much had changed in that time.

Inter-regional migration within Nepal is generally very low, although there has been a general tendency to move from the rural to the urban and peri-urban areas, and also, for the few relatively well educated Muslims of the terai and the hill areas, to migrate to Kathmandu. Those relatively few Muslim government officials and civil servants have also often moved around the country as part of their contract. The Muslim population of Kathmandu seems to have remained largely stable at a few thousand over the centuries, although it has undoubtedly grown over time as a result of the combination of natural increase and immigration. Although this population is also internally differentiated, by virtue of the different 'waves' of immigration, it has historically constituted a distinctive hill community as a whole, by contrast with the much larger communities of Muslims scattered across the *terai.*

In recent years, however, increasing numbers of Muslims from the *terai* have been coming to Kathmandu, for work or for study, or for other reasons, and the distinctiveness of 'the traditional Kathmandu Muslims' may well be compromised as this process accelerates. Even now, many Muslims with their family origins in the *terai*, live and work in the Kathmandu Valley as Fadzakir indicates in his discussion of the Muslim factory workers he surveyed, many of whom were from the *terai* or from India. Given the lack of detailed information on internal migration, it is hard to say what proportion of the population of the Kathmandu Valley Muslims is now originally from the *terai;* but it could be as much as half. We shall return to a consideration of the Muslims of the *terai* shortly.

In addition to recent Muslim immigrants to Kathmandu from the *terai,* there have also been recent Muslim immigrants from further afield, including from Kashmir. In Kathmandu, the next 'wave' of Muslim immigrants, after the influx of Tibetan Muslims in the 1950s and 1960s, was that of the Kashmiris who first arrived in the 1970s to set up curio shops in Kathmandu's tourist quarters. Many traders and merchants apparently arrived at that time with their stocks of handicraft, rugs and furs. There was a further 'spurt' in arrivals from Srinagar after the political turmoil in Jammu and Kashmir escalated in 1990 (according to Upadhyay 2014: 31). These more recent arrivals the 'new' Kashmiri Muslim community Upadhyay suggests, 'have little or no interaction with the older Muslim residents', and 'it is reported (although this seems unlikely) most do not even know that there is an 'old' Kashmiri Muslim community in Indra Chowk and other areas of the Kathmandu Valley'. This is broadly confirmed by Fadzakir (2001).

In October 2016, however, I spent some time talking to young Muslims who were managing gem and pashmina shops in Thamel and found that many had come quite recently from Jaipur and Agra, and even from Fatehpur Sikri, while others were actually from Kashmir. Most had come only in the last few years and appeared to be doing well in comparison with the local Nepalis selling similar goods. Most were familiar with many of the other young Muslims who worked in similar shops in Thamel and were clearly part of a larger 'young Muslim community' in the city; they variously attend the main two mosques and evidently mingle with others at the mosque and also socially, although their families appeared in most cases to be back in India and/or Kashmir. They all seemed to interact freely with other younger local Nepali Muslims and did not recognise the distinctions some fellow-Muslims made between 'different' Muslim groups in Kathmandu; they were also unaware of the 'deep' history of Muslims in Nepal.

The most clearly identifiable group of Muslim immigrants in Kathmandu in recent years has been that of the Rohingya Muslim refugees from Myanmar/Burma. The first of these came to Nepal in 2012 via India, arrived at the Jama Masjid in Kathmandu and were advised to register with the UNHCR; they were offered shelter and accommodation for the women and children but they preferred to stay together and selected cheap hotels in Bag Bazaar. Some families now live together in rented accommodation in Kapan, to the north of the city. In July 2015, the Nepal Muslim Women's Welfare Society distributed clothes for Eid to the children of Rohingya Muslims who fled to Nepal from Burma because of the genocide taking place in Myanmar. Little, however, was done for the small Rohingya community over the next few months and in December 2015, after a month long sit-in, Rohingya refugees launched a fast-onto-death outside the UN High Commissioner for Refugees (UNHCR) office in Nepal to support their demand that the UN agency either create the environment which would allow them to return safely home or help them resettle in a third country.

The UN agency recently cut down the allowance to urban refugees citing larger refugee operations in other parts of the globe. The unofficial blockade imposed by India in September 2015 made their lives worse: as the price of daily essentials shot up, their allowance was no longer sufficient to even pay their rent. "The UN agency can ask Nepal government to give us jobs," said one man. With a mere Rs 4,000 allowance and no job, the refugees have been finding it hard to sustain themselves. Nepal has not signed the 1951 Refugee Convention and the 1967 Option Protocol relating to the status of refugees. In the absence of the legal framework, asylum seekers in Nepal do not get refugee status; they are treated as illegal immigrants. Nepal refused to adopt the refugee convention during the second Universal Periodic Review (UPR) in November 2015.

Muslims of the *Terai*

Although considerable attention has been paid to the Muslims of Kathmandu, in fact, the vast majority (97 per cent) of Nepali Muslims live in the *terai*, as we have already seen, although the extent to which they identify with the other communities of that region and with the growing political-cultural demands for the social, economic and political recognition of a distinctive Madhesi identity, is variable and highly debatable as we shall see.

The history of the Muslim communities of the *terai* is little known. Gaige (1975) suggests, as regards Muslim settlement in the *terai*, that 'plains Hindus and Muslims appear to have moved into Mahottari-Dhanusha and Bara and the districts contiguous to them earlier than into other parts of the *terai*. Villages in the southern part of both districts were mostly settled seven to ten generations ago, although one village in each of the two districts was reportedly established fifteen generations ago' (maybe as much as 500 years). 'Farther north... villages were settled four to five generations ago...' On the other hand, 'Jhapa district is experiencing in a three generation span the transition that Mahottari-Dhanusha and Bara districts underwent in two or three hundred years (sic), from a dense forest region hiding a few tribal villages to an uninterrupted, cultivated plain dotted with many villages'.

He also reports that 'in Kapilvastu and its two neighbouring mid-western *terai* districts, the villages were all settled within the last eight to ten generations'. He even suggests, controversially, that 'Kailali district, representative of the far-western *terai*, is about at the stage of settlement in which Kirkpatrick found Bara district in 1793... (1975: 61). Gaige identifies a systematic trend as regards chronological settlement, with the earlier settlement in the east, and later settlement in the west. But, given that villages have not always been fixed, and relied historically on shifting cultivation, the 'depth' (or lack of 'depth') in the generational 'history' of contemporary villages does not necessarily mean that there was not settlement, and villages, in any given part of the *terai* at an earlier period. There is no evidence, however, so far of Muslim settlement in the *terai* before the 17th century.

Upadhyay suggests, but without any empirical justification, that 'some of the *terai* Muslims were present here at the time of Nepal's unification in 1768, while others migrated from British India from the 19th century onwards as wage labourers' (2014: 30). We know that, after the Anglo-Nepal war of 1814, when the boundaries of southern Nepal and India were clearly marked, a large part of areas near present day Indian states of Uttar Pradesh and Bihar, which as a matter of fact, inhabited by a significant numbers of Muslims, became the territory of Nepal. In this way, a significant Muslim population was almost certainly effectively 'incorporated' into Nepal.

It seems likely that the history of Muslim immigration into the *terai* is a long one, going back atleast to the time of the Mughals; but to be frank, there is little concrete evidence of this history. It seems likely also that the influx of Muslim immigrants has always been less than that of other Indian groups, given the religious demography of Bihar and Uttar Pradesh, the other side of the border, where Muslims constitute only between 15 and 20 per cent of the population. There is considerable further work to be done, however, on the history of settlement in the *terai*, and indeed in other parts of Nepal. Generally, a broad brush history of Muslim communities in Nepal indicates successive waves of immigration, up to and including recent times, in the *terai,* leading to the development of different and often quite distinctive Muslim communities in a palimpsest of colonisation and settlement.

Most Muslims living in the *terai* have ancestors who crossed at various times in the past into Nepal from India (and perhaps more recently from Bangladesh), perhaps as Bista (1980) indicates initially in search of seasonal or even more permanent agricultural work, and then settled in the border areas of the *terai,* to constitute communities that have, perhaps in some cases, been living there for centuries at least from the mid-18th century onwards. There is also evidence to suggest that there has been more recent that is, 20th century immigration also, particularly at the time of Indian Independence and Partition, and since then, in the 1950s, when malaria eradication made the settlement of the *terai* more attractive to would be immigrants, and thereafter as the area opened up to immigration and settlement on a large scale. A small investigation by me in a village in the south of Dhanusha district in 2014 revealed that most of those now living there could trace their origins in the Nepalese *terai* back to a grandfather or earlier ancestors who migrated there from further south, now across the border in India, but within living memory.

Today, as a consequence of this long history of immigration, there are various communities, sects and caste groups among the Muslims of Nepal, all of which contributes to the social and cultural diversity of the Muslim community of the *terai* as a whole. Many of these differences are historical and relate to the precise circumstances of the immigration of various groups into Nepal over possibly many centuries. But there are also important cultural and particularly linguistic distinctions between the three major Muslim geographical communities in the *terai* for while the majority of Muslims in the mid west speak Awadhi, the majority of those in the central *terai* speak Bhojpuri, while those in the eastern *terai* mainly speak Maithili, having largely adopted the local language of the indigenous population of those particular areas.

Notes

1. The Chera dynasty existed in what is today Kerala and Tamil Nadu; its capital was at modern Karur (Ptolemy's Korura). The Chera state had extensive trade relations with countries of the outside world. Sulaiman and al-Mas'udi, the Arab travellers who visited the Malabar Coast during the period, have testified to the high degree of economic prosperity achieved by the state from its foreign trade.
2. Tirhut or Mithila
3. This may be the first written reference to the Tharus of the *terai* and suggests that they were present there as early as mediaeval times.
4. The Bhote Koshi (in Nepali) the river from Tibet is also known as Rong-shar Tsangpo meaning, in Tibetan, the river flowing through or from Tsang', (ie Tibet west of Lhasa).

3

Language and Religion

Linguistic Communities

The social, economic and political importance of linguistic and other social and cultural differences among Muslim communities in Nepal is not at all clear. The majority of Muslims tend to speak the language of the dominant local non-Muslim community, although in Kathmandu, and also in the *terai*, many of the older generation at least speak Urdu among themselves, even if they are also fluent in Nepali and often Newari; but the linguistic map of Muslims in Nepal remains to be drawn in any detail. Some words of Arabic, Persian and even Turkish/Turkic origin have found their way into Nepali, but it is not clear whether these were simply borrowed through the indirect influence of the Mughals who for centuries dominated north Indian culture, or were brought in by Muslims who settled in Nepal. Examples of 'borrowed' words include: *mazhab, sardar, kitap, umrao, kotwal, hazir/hazur, badam, halwa, adalat, dushman, awaz, jabaf, kalam,* etc.

In the *terai,* it is not always possible to distinguish local languages and dialects, although Nepali, Awadhi, Hindi and Urdu are all 'registered' as distinct languages. In part this is because the differences between all of these languages and dialects are not so great. Nepali is essentially a language derived from Hindi (and other components) and includes numerous Hindi words and linguistic constructions as well as using the Devanagri script. The differences between Maithili, Bhojpuri and Awadhi, also, do not seem, at least to the untutored ear, to be too great or the languages too dissimilar, even though they are defined as distinct languages.

Certainly, the distinction between Urdu and Hindi is not so marked as often suggested. As Gaige remarks, 'it is more difficult to define

Urdu than to define Hindi. The Urdu of educated and urbanised Muslims contains many more words of Arabic and Persian derivation than does Hindi. However, Muslims and Hindus at the village level use about the same vocabulary for speaking. The difference is primarily in the script; literate Muslim villagers employ the Arabic script and literate Hindus the Devanagri that is also commonly used for Nepali' (1975: 208).

Gaige indicates that there were four major indigenous (i.e. non-Nepali) linguistic groups in the *terai*: Tharu, Awadhi, Bhojpuri and Maithili (based on the census of 1952-54 and the census of 1961). In the far western *terai* most indigenous language speakers spoke Tharu; and few of them were Muslims. In Banke, some 77 per cent of the population spoke Awadhi, and in the mid-western *terai* figures ranged between 87 per cent and 96 per cent Awadhi. In the central eastern *terai*, figures for Bhojpuri ranged from 93 per cent to 99 per cent and for the eastern *terai* figures for Maithili ranged between 85 per cent and 95 per cent. These data do not refer to Urdu and imply that the vast majority of the local population Muslims included in these three *terai* areas spoke Awadhi, Bhojpuri and Maithili respectively.

Linguistic affiliation and usage in the *terai* have always been controversial, at least since the 1950s; and classification has depended on more than purely linguistic factors. Thus, according to the 1952-54 census, around 30 per cent of the *terai* population spoke a local language as their 'mother tongue' while only 5 per cent spoke Nepali (4 per cent) or another hill language (1 per cent). Most (63 per cent) were assigned to no language classification, and only 3 per cent were specifically identified as speaking Hindi as their mother tongue. The census identified only 68,932 people who spoke Hindi as a second language clearly a gross underestimation.

Even in 1961, it was recorded that only 6 per cent spoke Nepali as a mother tongue, with another 2 per cent speaking a hill language first. Gaige estimated by contrast that the real figure for those speaking Nepali as a first or second language was closer to 25 to 30 per cent of the total. In the 1961 census, the majority of those previously 'unclassified' were re-classified as speaking a specific *terai* language or what was termed Awadhi defined in the 1961 census of India as one of six dialects in the 'Eastern Hindi' category. The number identified specifically as speaking Hindi as a first language was actually reduced from 80,181 in the previous census to a mere 2,867 in the 1961 census.

Gaige calculated that 'it can be concluded that in 1961 at least 46 per cent of the *terai* population spoke Hindi as a second language. If one adds to the 46 per cent the 17 per cent who speak Hindi or dialects of Hindi as mother tongues, at least 63 per cent of the *terai* population spoke Hindi as either a first or second language in 1961. It is doubtful if this percentage has declined since 1961...' On the other hand, the number of those speaking Nepali, particularly as a second language, also increased; as a result, as Gaige remarks, 'debate about the use of Nepali among the *terai* people became as much a part of the language controversy as the question about Hindi' (1975: 119).

Migration from the hills into the *terai* increased dramatically in the next few decades, through the 1960s and 1970s and into the 1980s, and this coincided with a major thrust by successive governments, as well as most political parties which continued to exist even though they were banned to make Nepali the national language. This proved very controversial. Even so, the spread of Nepali as both a first and second language has been one of the most dramatic features of linguistic development in Nepal over the last fifty to sixty years.

The linguistic importance of Maithili, not only in the eastern Nepalese *terai* but across a large area of northern India in the region of the ancient Mithila, cannot be underestimated. There is a substantial and ancient literature in Maithili, which is currently being explored and documented by intellectuals from the region. It is not clear whether the Muslims of this region have contributed, and if so in what way, to the development of the Maithili language and literature, nor is the extent to which Muslims in the central eastern *terai* speak other languages than Maithili. This will be subject to further research in future.

In the 1991 census, it was recorded that Maithili was the main mother tongue among the people of the *terai*, with 12 per cent of the total population of Nepal; Bhojpuri came second, with 7 per cent, 'Tharu' (although there is no single 'Tharu' language, but rather a set of different dialects) accounted for 5 per cent, with Awadhi only 2 per cent, Urdu 1 per cent and Hindi 1 per cent, even though Hindi is effectively a lingua franca across the region and is spoken as a second language by most people. Jha (1993) observes that these figures appear to a gross underestimate, with only 29 per cent of the total population of Nepal apparently speaking a non-Nepali *terai* mother tongue, despite the fact that something like half the population of Nepal resided in the *terai* at that time.

In the 2001 census, the situation appeared to be much the same, largely because of the number of people registered as being native Nepali speakers, even in the *terai.*

Table 15: Number and percentage of Population by Mother Tongue (Census 2001)

Mother Tongue Total 22,736,934	Number 100.00	Percentage 100.00	Cumulative
Nepali	11,053,255	48.61	48.61
Maithili	2,797 582	12.30	60.92
Bhojpuri	1,712,536	7.53	68.45
'Tharu'	1,331,546	5.86	74.31
Tamang	1,179,145	5.19	79.49
Newar	825,458	3.63	83.12
Magar	770,116	3.39	86.51
Awadhi	560,744	2.47	88.98
Bantawa	371,056	1.63	90.61
Gurung	338,925	1.49	92.10
Limbu	333,633	1.47	93.57
Bajjika	237,947	1.05	94.61
Urdu	174,840	0.77	95.38

Ten years later, according to the 2011 census, the order was different.

Table 16: Percentage Population by Mother Tongue (2011)

Language	Percentage of Speakers
Nepali	44.6
Maithili	11.7
Bhojpuri	6.0
Tharu	5.8
Tamang	5.1
Newari	3.2
Bajjika (sic)	3.0
Magar	3.0
Doteli	3.0
Urdu	2.6

Source: CBS 2011 Census

The proportion of those speaking Nepali as their mother tongue appears to have declined somewhat over the first decade of the 21st century. The same is the case for Maithili and Bhojpuri. On the other hand, the percentage of Urdu speakers appears to have increased very considerably. It is not clear what explains this, although it is possible it reflects an increase in the number of Muslims some of whom speak Urdu. The general increase in the number of those claiming to speak *janajati* languages as their mother tongue may explain the decline in the top three languages, but the reasons for the growth of declared Urdu speakers are not evident. Might this be an indication of 'an Islamic revival in Nepal' of the kind Sijapati identifies, in her book of the same name? Do Nepali Muslims who leave the *terai* and move to Kathmandu drop their *terai* languages and take up Urdu or do some of them already speak Urdu?

Migration certainly alters the distribution of languages spoken in any given region if it is significant enough. For example, the *terai* is now populated not just by indigenous peoples speaking indigenous languages, but also by immigrants, who have been coming into Nepal for decades if not longer and who sometimes bring their languages with them. Many of those migrating into the terai over the last decades have come from the hills and presumably have, to some extent at least, retained their hill languages, increasing the proportion of those speaking *janajati* hill languages and decreasing the relative proportion of those speaking indigenous *terai* mother tongues.

Immigration into the *terai* has also been cross border from India. The boundaries between India and Nepal have always been very permeable even today, people need not to get any permit or official document to visit either country, an arrangement that has encouraged people from both sides to move freely across the borders, with significant numbers entering Nepal and settling there but the influence of Indian culture has become ever greater, bringing with it a wider understanding and usage of Hindi, and it is possible that unofficial cross-border movement is now greater than ever. This requires further study. It takes place for a variety of reasons, including income generating opportunities and economic transactions, cultural and religious reasons (ie pilgrimages and festivals), employment opportunities, social visits and marriage, and for political and security related reasons. Most cross-border movement is transitory, but movement may eventually become permanent (as is often the case when marriages taken place or people move to find employment).

Most of the Muslim immigrants into Nepal came – as did most other, predominantly Hindu immigrants: in search of employment or land, as economic migrants; but some came also as political refugees. As a result, although the bulk of the population is today involved in agricultural work or cattle herding, there are important distinctions, not only of language, but also of class and caste between and within different Muslim 'communities', depending on their particular history. Some Muslim communities have a history in their present locality that goes back many generations, possibly centuries, but others are more recent arrivals.

Probably the major historical event of recent times that led to a significant increase in immigration into the *terai* of Muslims from India was Indian independence and partition in 1947-48. The malaria eradication programme (sponsored by USAID and the WHO and undertaken by the government of Nepal in the late 1950s) undoubtedly encouraged immigration from the hills; but it may well also have attracted migrants from India from the late 1950s onwards, and particularly during the 1960s and 1970s. Migration from the hills and across the border brought hundreds of thousands of squatters to settle in the *terai;* and at the same time, at least until the 1970s, there was a significant flow of labour migrants from Bengal, Bihar and Uttar Pradesh into the terai, to assist with the local harvest. Many of these may well have decided to settle, given the relative difference in wages between their place of origin and the *terai.*

Muslims in the *terai* have not been unaffected by these movements and trends, and it is likely that even if the majority still speak local *terai* dialects, the spread of Nepali (and hill languages) and Hindi cannot have left them unchanged. But we just do not know at the present time what the linguistic map of the *terai* would look like if first, second and third languages were to be considered, or indeed the precise history and pattern of immigration that is responsible for this heterogeneity.

At home, it is said, some Muslims speak Urdu, but those living in the *terai* mainly speak the local languages of the *terai* Awadhi, Bhojpuri and Maithili, depending on whether they are of the western or central eastern or eastern *terai,* while those living in the hills tend to speak the dominant local languages of their neighbours, or Nepali. It is increasingly recognised that there is a distinctive Mithila region in the central eastern terai. Maithili is spoken widely as a mother tongue in Dhanusha District, where the project undertook fieldwork during the summer of 2015, as well as in Rautahat, Sarlahi, Mahottari, Siraha, Saptari, Sunsari and Morang. A recent report by NEMAF (2016) refers specifically to five districts of 'the Mithila Belt', in which 80 per cent of the local inhabitants speak Maithili. In Banke, where the project also undertook fieldwork in the Nepalgunj area the main language is Awadhi, which is also spoken in Rupandehi, Kapilvastu, Bardiya, Kailali and Kanchanpur. The Muslim communities are not therefore so easily distinguished by their 'mother tongue', although, as is said, some speak Urdu at home and in the mosque.

Whether there are still 'Bihari' Muslims or Muslims in the eastern *terai* who immigrated from Bangladesh and who speak differently from those around them, remains to be discovered. A recent study of labour migration from Nepal and Bangladesh refers only to migrants from these two countries to India and seems not to consider migration between Nepal and Bangladesh or vice versa (Asia Foundation 2013).

As to the hill Muslims, I had assumed that, given that they are generally small local communities living 'cheek by jowl' as it were with many other local groups, including groups that speak local ethnic languages and local dialects, as they do in the *terai,* or else that they would generally speak Nepali and perhaps a smattering of these other local languages. But Upadhyay is not entirely clear on this matter. He says that 'the Western Hills Churoute Muslims', as he calls them, speak 'a mixed language of Urdu and Nepali' 'Churoute or Miya Bhasa', or at least they do in Miya Gaon, Hukka, where he worked. He then goes on, however, to state that 'Muslims are greatly influenced by the languages spoken in these parts like the Magar ethnic group language. They hardly speak Urdu and speak fluent Nepali' (2014: 129). Elsewhere again, however, he says that 'Miya language' is part of their identity (2014: 74). The picture is somewhat confused.

In Kathmandu, obviously most Muslims speak Nepali on an every day basis, but some of the Muslim communities retain, as we have indicated above, another language which they use among themselves and at home, whether that be Tibetan or, more commonly, Urdu. Sijapati has referred to Newari Muslims and, although she does not say so, I presume that some at least of these speak Newa among themselves, rather than Nepali.

Religious Communities

The Muslims of Nepal are almost entirely Sunni, although it is often stated that there is a 'small minority of Shi'a' some say in the west, some say in the east and others (eg Sijapati 2011: 17) in the southwest. Megan Sijapati suggests 'that an anti-Shi'a sentiment is prevalent and growing (as it is in much of the Sunni world), fuelled in part by Wahabbi anti-Shi'a discourses' (pers comm). I have, so far, however, not been able to identify *any* communities of Shi'a Muslims in Nepal, although many of the so-called 'Hindustani' Muslims who fled from India with the wife of the Nawab of Oudh to seek refuge after the 'Great Mutiny' in 1857 were in fact Shi'a, including her son. It is not clear, however, what happened to their descendants; and the mosque they founded has since been converted to one where the so-called 'Wahabis' tend to congregate.

Among the Sunnis, there are four main schools of thought (*maktab-i fikr)* Hanafi, Maliki, Shafi' and Hanbali. In Nepal, the vast majority of Muslims, as far as I can determine, are of the Hanafi persuasion. The main religious groupings identified in Nepal are the Deobandis and the Barelwis, although other terms are used to identify and define what are considered important distinctions and even divisions between the different Muslim groups. For example, some commentators and some Muslims also refer to 'Wahabis' as a distinct group or sect. These are considered to be 'more extreme' and to pray in slightly different ways. In India, the Deobandi movement has certainly been influenced by Wahabism from its early days; in Pakistan, nearly 65 per cent of the total seminaries (*madrasas*) are run by Deobandis, 25 per cent by Barelis, and 6 per cent by Ahl-e Hadith.

Although the Deobandi *fikr* has undoubtedly been influenced by Wahabism from its early days, the Wahabi *fikr* is more usually associated in Nepal with the Ahl-e-Hadis/Hadith. Ahl-el-Hadis/Hadith literally means 'the people of the *hadith*'. This is a reformist some would say fundamentalist movement, and (as previously indicated) is often referred to by other groups as 'Wahabi'. Sijapati suggests that the followers of this 'sect' are 'growing in number and in influence' (2011: 17) although no statistics are available on this. She also suggests that 'Deobandi and Jama'at-i Islami oriented Muslims from the *terai* areas are spokespersons and leaders for a renewal and reform of Islam'.

As regards the situation in Kathmandu, Sijapati comments that 'throughout my time in the Kathmandu Valley I heard stories, comments and histories that suggested significant tension between those of the Barelwi and Sufi orientation and those of the Deoband, Ahl-e Hadis, Jama'at i Islami and Salafi orientations' (2011: 26). These were as much doctrinal and/or theological differences i.e. sectarian as they were political or community based. The practice of saint veneration, for example, that takes place at the Kashmiri Takiya's *dargahs* conflicts doctrinally with the more orthodox prohibition of tomb veneration upheld by the latter groups. Hence, the Nepali Jame Masjid is the preferred ritual space in Kathmandu for those of Deobandi, Ahl-e Hadis, Jama'at i Islami and Salafi orientation, as well as the small number of Tablighi Jama'at followers, and not the largest mosque in the capital, the 'Kashmiri Masjid' (Sijapati 2011: 26-7).

Sijapati contrasts the outlook and position of the 'Kashmiri Muslims' (which clearly includes Barelwis and Sufis) with those of 'the revivalists' and quotes 'a number of Kashmiri Muslims' as saying that they were not interested in mixing religion and politics in the way the revivalists were: 'we want to be free, not involved in political parties'. The revivalists were often those that Sijapati refers to as 'Hindustani Muslims' including those from outside (i.e. the *terai)* who have recently relocated to the Valley and who 'mix politics and religion'.

When, in 2010, she discussed the *Islami Sangh's* sectarian affiliation(s) with its President, Nasrul Hasan Falahi, he said that of all the sects, 'we are most like Salafis, but not so extreme in dealing with non-Muslims'. He went on, however, to describe their *maslak* as 'the right one' looking only to the Quran and Sunna as authoritative. He confirmed that the Islami Sangh is heavily influenced by Mawdudi's ideas and the work of the Indian Jama'at-i Islami. Some Islami Sangh members explained to Sijapati that non-Islami Sangh Muslims refer to them as 'Wahabis' or 'Deobandis', but that this was not accurate they were admittedly *somewhat like* Deobandis but were *not* Deobandis.

They were primarily concerned, she argues, to build a tradition that is distinct from and opposed to 'folk' or 'vernacular' Islam, which involves practices of shrine veneration, or the veneration of 'saints' (*pirs)*, local healing traditions, and other forms of practice deemed *bid'at* (literally 'innovations', but best perhaps 'accretions'). They disapprove of shrine veneration and the veneration of 'saints' because they see it as a practice based on a lack of knowledge and an intermingling of local non-Islamic and Islamic beliefs and practices; even to revere the 'saint' (*pir*) as a spiritually elevated Muslim is *bid'at* and *shirk* (Sijapati 2011: 109). This position as regards 'the Islam of the book' and 'the Islam of folk tradition' has been discussed by Gellner with respect to the Middle East and North Africa, and to Morocco in particular, and is compared by him to the difference between the Protestant and the Catholic traditions in

Christianity, particularly as regards the veneration of saints (Gellner 1969, 1981).

In the Kathmandu Valley, it seems that a loose affiliation exists among those of the Ahl e Hadis, Deobandi, Wahabi and other Salafi type orientations who see themselves in distinction to the Barelwis and Sufis. Sijapati suggests that 'there is a palpable tension between them' (2011: 109) and adds that 'this is seen in the strain between the two mosques that represent these opposing orientations, the Kashmiri Masjid and Nepali Jame Masjid. The former holds *'urs* celebrations and houses *mazars* that attract other Muslims, and even Hindus, for veneration. In contrast, the Nepal Jame Masjid, which is newer and yet claims religious authority in the Valley, condemns these practices, quietly, hoping in some way to disabuse fellow Muslims of the belief in saints, which they see as 'accretions'.

This is an important topic, and the interested reader is referred to the later discussion of relationships of cooperation and conflict between the various Muslim communities, as well as between Muslim communities and other, non-Muslim communities in Nepal over the years and at the present time, and also to Megan Sijapati's fascinating account of what she calls 'the Islamic revival in Nepal', which explores these kinds of relationships between the different religious and political communities among the Muslims of the Kathmandu Valley for the most part. In the *terai*, however, where a detailed investigation of these distinctions and divisions has not yet been undertaken, it seems that there is a similar ambivalence expressed by several of the key informants interviewed as part of this project during the summer of 2015 regarding the unity of the Muslim community as a whole on the one hand and the differences between different Muslim communities on the other.

In Dhanusha District, for example, where fieldwork was undertaken in June 2015 by a NEMAF team, a key informant, Maulana Mohammed Rahamatullah, indicated that there were four subgroups of Muslims: 1) Barelis, 2) Ahal e Hadis, 3) Deobandis and 4) Jamaat-e Islami. The group with the largest number in Mahottari and Dhanusha were, he reported, the Barelis. He suggested that 'their economic status was generally 'higher and middle class both; but most were middle class'.

For some within the local Muslim community, it would seem, these divisions are of social and cultural as well as religious significance; for others, they are not of great importance. According to Ibrahim Rain, a well-educated farmer and local politician living in Janakpur, and interviewed as part of the IDEA-NEMAF project during fieldwork in the *terai* in summer 2015, the major distinction in Islam is between Sunni and Shi'a. He said that Shi'a are 'very few or rare in Nepal' and, if they are to be found 'it may be in the west of Nepal'.

According to him 'Shi'a consider the land as symbol of purity so they do *namaj* (prayers) at stones'; he also added that 'Shi'a are not the main part of Islam, as they are against Nabi[1], but that Muslims from any part of the world follow and respect the Quran and the Hadith because the Quran and the Hadith are respected by all Muslims'. Megan Sijapati has commented on this, saying that 'Ibrahim R's comments on Shi'a Muslims should not be taken at face value. This represents an anti-Shi'a view held commonly by certain Sunnis, but (one that) is not accurate. Shi'a are not 'against the Prophet' and do not worship stones' (pers comm). This may be factually true, but it is also the case that Ibrahim R's remarks do represent a certain anti-Shi'a sentiment that Sijapati herself suggests is prevalent and becoming more common in Nepal as it is in the Sunni world as a whole.

Ibrahim R, however, insisted that there was 'no big difference' between Deobandis, Barelwis, Wahabis, or others 'all follow their culture according to their beliefs. All follow the belief that no one is above Allah, and he can do whatever he wishes'. It was education, he suggested, that really made a difference and led to divisions within the Muslim community as a whole. In reality, however, as we have seen (and will see further in later chapters) the differences and indeed the divisions between the different Muslim groupings or sects in Nepal in both Kathmandu and in the *terai* are significant, and, at one level, inhibit the project of those whose priority is to emphasise the distinctiveness of the Muslim community as a whole and its systematically disadvantaged status and condition.

Sijapati suggests that the differences between different *masalik* or *firk* (sects) 'appear less stark (in the Kathmandu Valley) than they do in the *terai* due to the much smaller and more heterogeneous character of the Valley's Muslim population'. I am not convinced by this argument, for the Muslim population of the *terai* is also highly heterogeneous from this perspective (of different traditions and/or sects). It is, I suggest, significant that she adopts the perspective of the *Islami Sangh* members from the *terai* who argued that 'among *terai* Muslims there is an increasing emphasis on difference, which some *Islami Sangh* members attribute to the higher concentration of *madrasas* and *masjids* there as compared to the Kathmandu Valley' (2011: 110). She also cites one member of the *Islami Sangh* who asserted that 'the areas of conflict over sectarian differences, which revolve around what he called small things such as the practice of *rafa yadain* (the lifting of the hands in *namaz*, before and after *ruku*), the volume at which one says '*amin*' following the imam's recitation of the Surah al Fatiha, and the veneration of *pirs*' shrines have come to be increasingly emphasised in the *terai* over the past twenty years'.

Fadzakir, in his study of the Muslims of Kathmandu, considers the differences between the main religious groupings, notably between the Deobandi and Barelwi movements, as he calls them (Fadzakir 2001). He notes that the Deobandi movement was founded in India by Muslim religious leaders at the time of the so called Great Mutiny of 1857, essentially as a reformist movement; but also that the Deobandis are sometimes referred to pejoratively by their opponents as 'Wahabis', although in fact, ironically, the term 'Wahabi' came into use in India somewhat earlier (in the late 1840s and early 1850s) when the British (wrongly in fact) identified the war being fought by a group of rebels in the North-West frontier area, led by Sayyid Ahmed Barelwi, to reclaim Muslim land, as involving the importation of 'Wahabi' *jihadi* beliefs and practices, and condemned it as such (Fadzakir 2001: 32).

'Reformism' in Islam, which usually means a return to basic spiritual values and a stripping away of what are defined as 'accretions' or 'un-Islamic traditions and customs', has often been equated with 'fundamentalism', and even with 'extremism', by those uncomfortable with its search for 'purity'. The fact that the founders of the Deobandi movement, like the Deobandis of Nepal today, are hostile to such practices as the veneration of saints, has led to their being seen as 'fundamentalist' and defined as 'Wahabi' by other, arguably more 'tolerant' groups and sects like the Barelwis of Nepal. As Fadzakir remarks, 'in Kathmandu, the term 'Deobandi' is used as the opposite of the term 'Barelwi'... and often rests solely on the rejection of saint veneration' (Fadzakir 2001: 34). He adds, interestingly, that 'these terms, although used quite liberally in academic and media circles, are not commonly used among the Muslims themselves'.

One of the major critics of the Deobandis in India was Ahmed Reiza Khan Barelwi, a religious scholar from a well-established family in Bareilly. His followers were also called the Ahl-e Sunnat wa Jama'at (people of the *sunnat* and the community). A distinguishing feature of the Barelwis was their belief in the role of the Prophet Mohammed as a mediator between the faithful and their God, and in his continued presence and power of intercession; and also in the spiritual power (*baraka)* of other prophets and saints, even after their deaths, and their continued ability to intercede 'from the grave or the tomb'. Fadzakir suggests, however, that the use of the term 'Barelwi' itself 'is not commonly used' by the Muslims of Kathmandu. In an interview with a Muslim woman from the *terai,* she associates herself rather with the 'Kashmiri Muslims' of Kathmandu because she, like them, 'venerates the sacred shrine (*dargah sharif*)' (Fadzakir 2001: 36).

His interviews with Muslim workers in Kathmandu, most of whom were actually from the *terai,* are equally revealing of the loose and effectively interchangeable use of the various terms in play. In Kathmandu, they said, 'all are Sunnis... Deobandis do not allow the worship of tombs (ie veneration of saints)... here only 10 per cent are Deobandis and the rest are Sunnis... there is no difference (between Deobandis and Sunnis).. we all go to the same mosque.. the Kashmiri mosque..'. When asked 'why do you not go to the Nepali mosque?' they replied: 'it is always full. Whenever it is empty we go there. Also sometimes the Kashmiri mosque gives food, which is good'. When asked 'have you heard of the term Barelwi? They replied, with a smile: 'of course, we are all Barelwi... Sunni and Barelwi are the same' (Fadzakir 2001: 34).

Fadzakir concludes from this that the concepts are vague and only loosely applied, but notes that the workers from the *terai* did not see themselves as Deobandis. For Kathmandu Muslims, he suggests, a more common way of describing those who reject veneration of saints or 'tomb worship' is to refer to them as 'Nepali Muslims', a reference to the mosque at which the Deobandis worship which is widely referred to as the 'Nepali Jama' (mosque). Those 'Kashmiri Muslims' of Kathmandu who consider themselves the descendants of the original early immigrants and settlers would recognise this commonality, while at the same time rejecting any notion that this woman or any other Muslims from the *terai* could really be 'Kashmiris'.

The situation in the *terai* is somewhat different, although here too, there is a looseness of definition and a degree of ambiguity as to what different groups of Muslims have in common and what distinguishes or differentiates them. Peter Gill reported in *The Record* from Nepalgunj in February 2017 on some local views regarding the differences between the various 'sects' or tendencies:

'In Nepalgunj, the main revivalist school is Deobandi, which was founded as an anti-colonial religious movement in the wake of the 1857 revolt, spreading from a seminary known as the Darul Uloom Deoband in Uttar Pradesh. Deobandi mosques and *madrasas* in Nepalgunj, like their Barelwi counterparts, maintain connections with those in India, but compared to Salafi and Ahl-e-Hadis groups, which are more prevalent in eastern Nepal and receive support from the Gulf, they have fewer connections with the Middle East.

I first became aware of the separate schools in Nepalgunj at a religious teaching event that Chaand *dai* invited me, Bijaya, and his partner Madan to one evening. (I was somewhat surprised that Bijaya accepted the invitation, given his ardent atheism. He had become convinced of the absence of god as young boy, he once told me, after stealing *laddus* from a temple and observing that nothing happened.) At one point during the function, which was held to mark the tenth day after the holiday Muharram, I found myself seated next to one of the *maulanas* (Islamic teachers). His name was Wajahul Kamar Khan, and he was from a Banke VDC on the far side of the Rapti River, and ran a *madrasa* in Nepalgunj.

Wajahul Khan told me that not all of Nepalgunj's Muslims were honouring the holiday. Deobandis, he explained, worship the same god but do not observe many of the holidays celebrated by Barelwis, and hold different views on the nature of God, the Prophet, and the honouring of great teachers. Regarding the latter, he explained that Barelwis sometimes pray to God by visiting saints' tombs, whereas Deobandis believe that doing so is a form of idolatry. I had seen one such tomb, located in the courtyard of the *musafir khana*, or guest house, attached to the Jummah Masjid in Eklaini.

The evening I visited I saw a group of women place a tapestry on top of the tomb and sprinkle it with flowers before bowing to it. The *maulana* spoke respectfully about Deobandis, even if he did not subscribe to their teachings himself. A man sitting next to us was less diplomatic, chiming in: "They say that the Prophet, peace be upon him, was just another human being, only a *dai*. But he lived 1400 years ago, so how can he be your

> *dai?* If anything, he is your great, great, great, great, great grandfather. And if he was your *dai*, what does that make his wife? Your *bhauju?!"* The last point seemed to particularly incense him.
>
> As we were returning home later that night, Madan told me he had learned as much about Islam as I had from the evening. "You think that the conflict is between Muslims and Hindus, but no, they have conflicts among themselves!" Another evening, as we were having dinner in a restaurant in the bazaar, a friend, Ameer, told me he was Deobandi. I was surprised; he seemed in most regards a modern Muslim man. He was clean shaven, usually wore jeans and a T-shirt, and worked at an INGO. Most of his friends were Hindu. He seemed a far cry from the puritanical ideals of Deobandism I had heard about. He said his family became Deobandi about 15 years ago, when his older brother married a Deobandi woman who introduced them to it. Later, I met his father, the son of a Barelwi imam, who told me he was attracted to the Deobandi movement because Barelwi traditions had become old-fashioned. The world is changing, he said, and some of those traditions have no place in modernity.
>
> I also met a young Deobandi engineer who told me something similar. He said Deobandism is necessary because Muslims have begun to stray with drinking, gambling, taking interest on loans. He described Deobandi beliefs as more "scientific" than Barelwis', which he said were clouded by superstition. It occurred to me that the Deobandi followers I knew were more forward thinking, in some ways, than they are often given credit for. The lure of Islamic revivalism seemed in some ways similar to that of "development," driven at once by a fear and an aspiration for one's identity'.

In the *terai*, it would seem that the Barelwis and Sufis are more common than Deobandis, for there is certainly a significant practice of the veneration of saints and shrines, and other less orthodox beliefs and practices, including the use of local faith healers in case of sickness. But there has been no systematic assessment of the numbers of Muslims in the *terai* affiliated to or associated with any one particular group or sect or set of religious beliefs and practices, and so even this assertion cannot be strongly substantiated. Furthermore, it seems clear, from the previous discussion, that the views of Muslims in Nepal in the Kathmandu Valley, in the hills and in the terai - regarding the precise differences between the various Islamic socio-religious groupings are complex and sometimes even contradictory. Here again, there is ample scope for further research.

Muslim Religious Culture

In many respects, if language and 'theology' (the profession of one or another version or *fikr* of Islam) are not always clearly defining features of Muslims in Nepal, other cultural characteristics of Nepali Muslims set them apart as a whole from Hindus and Buddhists, particularly the former, who predominate in the *terai.* Muslims actually do things differently and look different. Even if they may differ between themselves as to whether they venerate saints or not, or how precisely they pray, there are many features of Nepali Muslim religious culture, if we may call it that, which distinguishes them from non-Muslims. As Gaborieau remarked, 'they pray facing west instead of the east, they bury their dead instead of burning them, they grow beards instead of shaving them, they kill animals by slicing through the neck instead of cutting off the head, they circumcise their males instead of leaving (it) alone (Gaborieau 1972). The men, at least, also wear distinctive clothes (and skull caps), and generally grow their beards in a fashion uncommon among non-Muslims.

Upadhyay has relatively little to say about the distinguishing features of Muslims in the hill village of Miya Gaon in Tanahun District, where he worked, apart from the fact that 'they are Muslims' and are 'highly drenched in traditional Muslim norms and values', adding that there are local *madrasas* and three mosques in the village (2014: 74) and that 'all Muslims perform their religious rites jointly in the mosques and other places' (2014: 139). He also remarks that family members visit 'the courtyards' (he probably means 'tombs or graveyards') at night to remember, honour and receive blessing from God for their dead. Elsewhere, he indicates how important the mosques are in defining the Muslim community and reflecting its distinctiveness (2014: 94-95). He does not, however, explain why there are three mosques for 64 households, suggesting differences and distinctions even within the local Muslim community.

He also refers to a specific conflict between local Muslim groups that used to exist, over differences in the way in which the evaluation of the moon's position based on the lunar calendar took place when determining the time to celebrate the Eid (Eid ka Chand). This seems to have been quite serious, as he refers to the fact that 'the conflict was prone to take a bloody form' before being averted by the intervention of 'senior fellows and some senior politicians of the Muslim community' (2014: 83). How systematic were such divisions, and whether they were based on any kind of theological or other religious difference is not discussed.

He lists all of the distinctive holy days and holidays observed locally including Al-Hijra, celebrated as the New Year, Muharram as the first month with Ras as San as the first day of the year, celebrated in the local mosque. He mentions Ashura, which involves fasting on the 10th day of the first month, and Akhari Chahar Sambah, the last Wednesday of the second month. They celebrate Miladunnabi, the birthday of the Prophet Mohammed, and remember the eleventh Sherif (Abdul Kadir Jilani); they celebrate the Night Visit of the Prophet Mohammed to Heaven (Isra and Miraj), and the Shab e Barat, the yearly record night, on the 15th of the eighth month. They celebrate the Night of Power or Night of Command (Layalat al Qadr) when the Qur'an came to earth, and of course the Eid ul Fitr at the end of Ramdan and the Eid ul Adha (2014: 94-95).

On the other hand, he suggests (2014: 64) that 'there is also the intricate co-operative feeling among the Muslims and Hindus; and they participate in each other's local fairs and festivals' there is good participation from the Islamic community in the sociocultural activities of the village, especially in the festivals of the Hindus. In this regard, there is harmony (called *miteri saino* in Nepali)'. But it seems clear that in terms of the local caste hierarchy, although the Muslims themselves do not adopt or practice caste differences, they are, as a whole discriminated against, as Muslims, by the local high caste (mainly Brahmin) Hindus, who constitute, after the Magars, the second largest group in the VDC.

For example, the Muslims are not allowed to slaughter cows at their festivals and fairs and are apparently 'not allowed to propagate Islam openly' (2014: 96). Observation of festivals and many of the Islamic traditions of Miya Gaon have changed, Upadhyay remarks, due to the influence of the dominance of their Hindu neighbours. He also indicates, apparently with regard to Miya Gaon, that, if they go to ordinary schools, their Hindu teachers 'pass insulting remarks or proverbs or examples against Muslims in the class. Muslim students sit separately on back benches (as they are regarded as untouchables) and also deprived from using educational materials and equipment in many cases. Muslim student's participation in sports and extracurricular activities is very low. Muslim students feel discriminated against, depressed, frustrated and terminate school' (2014: 140-141).

There are various cultural characteristics that appear to be generally associated with Muslims in Nepal in the *terai* at least. Interviews undertaken during the course of the IDEA/NEMAF project in summer 2015 produced numerous rather generalised statements about the characteristics of 'Muslim culture', although it was also recognised that in reality they varied from place to place, from community to community, from town to rural area, and according to social class. The project was unable to explore these variations between different Muslim communities in any detail. That remains a piece of research yet to be done. As we have seen in the previous section, these variations and differences may be of considerable significance and to mark the difference between Barelwis, Sufis, Ahl-e Hadis, Deobadis, Wahabis, Salafis etc.

Some generalisations follow, drawn partly from the remarks made by key informants and focus groups during the fieldwork that was undertaken for this project in the *terai* during the summer of 2015 and in part from existing written sources. This is just a brief summary and lacks detail; it does, however, provide a starting point for a more detailed description of the characteristics of Muslim religious culture in Nepal.

Dress

Older Nepali Muslim males generally wear *lungi*, pajama, *qamiz* etc. and often wear skull caps. Upadhyay remarks that in his hill village of Miya Gaon, Hukka, in Tanhun District, men and women appear to dress in the same ways as other local people, but Muslim men 'usually wear a kind of lower garment called *lungi*' (2014: 69). Even younger men may be bearded and older men are usually bearded, but sometimes shave around the mouth. Muslim females wear pajamas and *qamiz*; and also wear *saris*. Many Muslim girls and women prefer to wear extra piece of cloth called *dupatta orna* over their upper part of the body. Muslim women in the Nepalgunj area put on what they refer to as *burkas* when going out, though Muslim women of other areas are not very keen on wearing the burka. In his hill village of Miya Gaon, Hukka in Tanahun District, Upadhyay comments that 'in the field observation, not a single Muslim women was found wearing the veil or *burka*' (2014: 105).

Food Habits

Muslims do not eat pork (or tortoise) these are forbidden (*haram).* Fish and locusts are also not eaten. Mutton, buffalo and chicken are, however, very popular among Muslim communities, although Nepali Muslims do not apparently like to eat the skin of bigger animals like goat, sheep, and buffaloes. Most Muslims kill their own animals or buy their meat from Muslim meat shops only. This is because animals must be slaughtered according to Islamic law, that is, by drawing the knife across the throat and cutting the windpipe, the carotid arteries and gullet, repeating at the same time the words "BISMILLAH ALLAHUAKBAR", that means, "in the name of God, God is great". An animal slaughtered by following these rules becomes clean and lawful (*halal*) food for Muslims. Muslims tend to prepare and mainly eat food at home plain and fried rice, *pulau, biryani, kawab, kofta, korma, semai* etc. and also presumably, in the hills at least *daal bhat,* or whatever local food is commonly consumed.

Birth

At the time of birth, the father or a guardian recites the words of the *adhaan* the call to prayer in the infant's ear, for its welfare. This is the only ceremonial element of childbirth.

The Seventh Day

Washing of the baby and also the mother is performed on the sixth day. Between the seventh and the 21st day cutting of hair of the new born baby is observed. During this period, the name is given to the new born and a feast is organized for the friends and relatives. The name giving ceremony is termed *akika (or aqiqah).* The *aqiqah* is a celebration of the new birth, ideally on the 7th day after the baby is born. One goat for a baby girl and two goats for a baby boy should be slaughtered on the 7th day; if that is not possible, then on the 14th days, if not even then, on the 21st; but the *aqiqah* is a must: 'If you don't do this for your child, your child will not intercede for his parents on the day of resurrection'.

Washing

Again, the washing of the mother (and the baby) is performed on the twentieth day, and after this she is considered to be pure.

Circumcision

Muslim boys are circumcised usually between the ages of four and eight. On this day also, a feast is prepared for family members, relatives and closest ones. According to Sunni clerics, the circumcision of the male child should take place in his seventh year. This operation is generally performed by a barber. In Arabic circumcision is called *khitnah* or *khatnah* (literally 'cutting'). *Khatna* is not compulsory in Islam; it is *sunnat* (proper, appropriate). But if someone follows *sunnat, they* will be rewarded; a milder sin will be recorded under their name if someone does not follow *sunnat.*

Marriage

According to the 2011 Nepal Department of Health survey, the vast majority (66 per cent) of Muslim women are married - a higher proportion that in any other social group, except *dalits*; some 34 per cent were recorded as 'never married', lower than most other social groups apart from dalits (especially *terai/madhesi dalits*) and on a par with all *terai/madhesi* groups.

The celebration of marriage in Islam is called *nikaah*. Nepali Muslims follow the Islamic traditions as regards the marriage ceremonies and practices. The bridegroom comes to the bride's house, where the marriage is solemnized in presence of witnesses, relatives and friends. During the ceremony, the bride remains all the time inside the father's house. The bride is taken to the groom's house on the completion of the ceremony. The bride is decorated with ornaments, her hands decorated with *henna*; she wears a veil over her head, which is an extra decorative cloth. After the wedding, dinner is served. Bride and grooms accept the relationships by uttering the word '*kabul*'.

Marriage Payments

Marriages are based on negotiations and arrangements, although the proposal usually comes from the bridegroom's side. In Islam, a *mahr* (also transliterated *mehr*, *meher*, *mehrieh* or *mahriyeh*) is a mandatory payment, in the form of money or possessions paid or promised to pay by the groom, or by groom's father, to the bride at the time of marriage; this then legally becomes her property. While the *mahr* is often money, it can also be anything agreed upon by the bride such as jewellery, home goods, furniture, a dwelling or some land. *Mahr* is typically specified in the marriage contract signed during an Islamic marriage. 'Dower' is the English translation that comes closest to Islamic meaning of *mahr*, as "dower" refers to the payment from the husband or his family to the wife, especially to support her in the event of his death.

However, *mahr* is distinct from dower in two ways: 1) *mahr* is legally required for all Islamic marriages, while dower is optional, and 2) *mahr* is required to be specified at the time of marriage (when a certain amount is promised, if not paid immediately), while dower is not paid until the death of the husband. *Mahr* also can be classified as a form of "bride wealth", described by anthropologists as payments made from the kin of the groom to the kin of the bride; however, *mahr* is paid directly to the bride and not her parents. In fact, as her legal property, *mahr* establishes the bride's financial independence from her parents and in many cases from her husband, who has no legal claims to his wife's *mahr*.

In the *terai*, it is Hindu practice for the family of the bride to provide a 'dowry' which is a transfer of funds and/or a set of gifts given to the family of the groom. This is often be a considerable burden on the family and both reflects and contributes to the widespread notion that to give birth to girls is regarded as bad luck, in so far as they will later constitute a financial burden when the time comes for their marriage. It is not entirely clear what is the practice of Muslims in the *terai as* regards 'bride price' and 'dowry', given the frequent confusion of terms in the literature. It is significant, however, that Muslims, like Hindus tend to experience the giving of gifts at marriage as a burden, and that the burden appears to be largely something that on the family of the bride, in so far as it commonly needs to be paid by the family of the bride to be, rather than by the family of the groom to be, and in so far as the amount paid as dowry appears to be increasing at a rapid rate.

Interestingly, it was reported in the press on 7 November 2016 that the Muslim community of Rautahat was protesting against 'the dowry system' and against child marriage. Religious and civil leaders from the Muslim community apparently organised a massive gathering in Rajapur and pledged to end 'the dowry system' practised by local Muslims. 'On the one hand, the dowry system puts extreme financial pressure on the bride's family and on the other it causes discord in her in-law's home, so it must be abolished', said Haji Jikurullah, adding, significantly, that 'Islam never approves of the dowry system'. The main guest of the programme was Hajarat Maulana Ijaharul Haq, who also spoke on the issue, as did the Principal of Mahamudiya Madrasa. They both underlined that this was not directed against any religion but against 'the dowry system' and child marriage. It was proposed that an eleven member committee be formed at the district level to monitor the prevalence of 'the dowry system' among the Muslim community in Rautahat. It will be interesting to see whether this committee reports on local practices.

Marriage Rules

Muslims can marry with almost any other Muslim of opposite sex, except those prohibited by incest laws. Parallel and cross cousin marriage is acceptable; indeed, here as in many parts of the Muslim world, parallel cousin marriage is considered desirable, as it tends to keep property 'in the family' and to maintain 'family solidarity' as the bride is not coming from 'outside'. The negative health implications of this have been discussed previously. Widow marriage has no stigma in Muslim society and it is significant that the 2011 Department of Health survey indicates no divorced, separated or widowed women among the Muslim population (the only other groups with zero divorced, separated or widowed women recorded were *terai/madhesi* Brahmins and Chhetris and Newars). Muslim priests can also marry, unlike Buddhist monks and Christian priests.

Most Muslim men in the *terai* have only one wife, but there is provision in Islam for marrying up to four wives, if they can be looked after in an adequate fashion. In such cases, all the wives in theory have equal status in the eyes of their husband and his family. Children of all wives also, in theory, have equal status. There are certainly some patriarchs in the Muslim community, in the terai and elsewhere, who have more than one wife. Cross-border marriages are not uncommon in the *terai*, and these bring with them problems of citizenship where the groom is of Indian nationality; this will be a problem, particularly after the promulgation of the new Constitution.

In areas where there is a large Muslim community, as in most parts of the *terai,* finding a marriage partner is usually not a difficult matter; but in the hills, where in any one locality there may be limited pool of suitable husbands and wives, families seek relationships over a wider territory and may even engage in 'searches' far afield. Sometimes they seek *terai* brides or grooms, but in doing so, their matrimonial relationships are affected by language differences as well as physical distance (the bride lives after marriage at her husband's home and so potentially far away from her own natal family, which is not regarded as ideal). The Muslims of Miya Gaon for example, in Tanahun District, maintain strong links with the Muslims of Rampur, which lies some 70 kms east of Tansen, in Palpa District, for what Upadhyay calls ' sociocultural, economic, marital and relationships of many other sorts' (2014: 112). Rampur is relatively large, with a total Muslim population of about 700 people and 70 households, compared with Miya Gaon's 466 and 64. There is a tradition that some of the Muslims of Miya Gaon at least came originally from the Rampur area.

Divorce

Divorce is applicable in Muslim society when the marriage does not function properly. Shamima Siddika (1993) writes that, before getting divorce, which a desperate step, some attempts are made as follows:

1. The two parties involved should try to settle their disputes and resolve their problems
2. If they fail, two arbitrators, one from the husband's relations and other from the wife's, should be commissioned try to make peace between them and settle their differences.
3. If this attempt also fails, the divorce (*talak)* proceeds.

Divorce should be agreed upon by both parties. Both man and women can exercise this right. After the divorce takes place there is a waiting period, normally of three to twelve months because divorce is taken to be the last resort in Islam. So, the procedure attempts to encourage reconciliation wherever possible. For three months husband remains responsible for the welfare of wife and also her maintenance. If they are reconciled during this waiting period they may resume the marriage. If further problems arise, divorce (*talak)* is pronounced for the second time and the same procedure is followed. Only if the matter reaches a third divorce, it becomes irrevocable. It is rare for a divorced woman not to marry again.

Death and Burial

Muslims always bury their dead, whereas the Hindus burn their dead. When a Muslim dies, the whole body is washed a few times with soap or some other detergents and cleansed of all visible impurities. After the cleansing process, the body is anointed with camphor and perfumes. A man washes a man and a woman washes a woman and a man or woman may wash the young children. After the washing is done, the dead body is wrapped in one or more white cotton sheets covering all the parts of the body. After this, the dead body is placed in a coffin and carried to the grave yard by male relatives. The body is then, put in a position with the face toward the direction of Mecca. All the participants perform ablution (*wuju)* and read the funeral prayer (*janazah)*[2]. The Imam stands beside the body facing the Qiblah in Mecca with the followers behind him in lines. After completing the prayer, the body is lowered for burial with the face resting in the direction of Mecca in grave.

The period for condolences to the family of the deceased is of three days. At the end of this period, relatives pray to God for the deceased. On the tenth and twentieth day, relatives are invited for prayer. Also, on the 40th day they pray for the deceased. For these forty days, one needy person is given full meal in the name of the deceased person. On the last day, he is provided with the clothes of the deceased person and some money; *chhamai* and *barsi* are observed at six months and a year after the death respectively. Some families observe mourning for one year. If a man dies, his widow does not leave her house for four months and ten days.[3]

Festivals and Religious Practices

The place of worship for Muslims is called 'mosque' in English and *masjid* in Arabic. A Muslim, when he enters the *masjid*, stops at the barrier and takes off his shoes, carries them in his left hand, sole to sole, puts his right foot first as he passes into the square devoted to prayer. The chief of the *masjid* is the Imam or the leaders of prayers, but there are generally *maulawis* or learned men, attached to the *masjid* for the instruction of the students.

The Muslim calendar is lunar and its months are determined by various positions of the moon. In every year, there are twelve months and each month is either thirty or twenty nine days depending on the position of the moon.

The names of the Islamic months

1. Moharram
2. Safar
3. Rabi-ul-awayl
4. Rabi-os-saani
5. Jamaadi-awayl

6. Jamaadi-s-saani
7. Razzab
8. Shabaan/Shabe-barat
9. Ramadan (month of fasting)
10. Sauwaal (Eid al Fetr on 1st day)
11. Jilqaida
12. Jilhijja (Hajj and Bakra-Eid on the 10th)

The month of Ramadan is the ninth month of the Islamic lunar calendar, which, according to Islamic belief, is the month when The Quran, the Islamic holy book, was revealed by the Archangel Jibril to Prophet Mohammed. Fasting (*roza*) in Ramadan is one of the five pillars of Islam that all Muslims are expected to follow. The other four pillars are *shahadat* (creed), *salat* (prayer five times a day), *zakat* (alms or charitable giving), and *hajj* (holy pilgrimage to Mecca/Makkah).

The three major religious festivals recognised by Islam are the Eid al Fitr, the Eid al Azha and the birthday of the Prophet. Only the first two of these are now recognised officially by the government as national holidays; but in Nepal, Muslims celebrate a number of other festivals.

Eid-al-Fitr

The Eid-al-Fitr is one of the biggest festivals of Muslims in Nepal and across the Muslim world. The government of Nepal has also declared holiday in this festival. The festival puts an end to the month long fast of Ramadan, when Muslims across the world observe *roza* (fasting), that is, abstaining from food, water and all other physical needs from sunrise to sunset. The practice of *roza* is compulsory for all Muslims except for children, the sick, the pregnant and the elderly, and travellers.

Eid al-Ajha/Adha

Eid al-Azha or Bakra-Eid falls on the 10th day of the twelfth month. This feast is known for sacrifice and is observed for three days. The festival also follows the completion of the course of Hajj, which is an extremely devotional course. According to tradition, a goat or sheep suffices for one household and a cow or steer suffices for seven different households. In Nepal, many people sacrifice goats in the *terai* and buffalo in the hills. On this occasion, people assemble in the mosque for their special prayers. They prayer is led by *imams*.

Mohurram

This is the first month of the Islamic calendar and marks one of the greatest festivals of Muslims celebrated on the death anniversary of Hassan and Hussein, grandsons of Prophet Mohammad (SM). The Hijrah (al Hijara) also falls on the eve of the first day of Mohurram. The prophet Mohamed had two grandsons, named Hassan and Hussein. The *khalipha* of Damascus poisoned Hassan. Hussein fought with the *khalipha* for long time. At last Hussain was surrounded by the soldiers of the *khalipha* on the plains of Karbala. Hussein fought there for ten days and was ultimately killed. He remained without food and water for these ten days.

The Muslims observe ten days in the month of Mohurram. The observance begins in the first day of the month and ends at the tenth day. Muslims give expressions to their sorrow of death of Hussein and fast on the tenth day. Some Muslims, mainly Shi'a, it is said, make *tazia* with split bamboos; in India, *tazia* is regarded as the replica of tomb over Hussein's grave. In the *terai*, Muslims also play a special game with sticks at this time.[4]

Upadhayay reports, in his study of a hill Muslim village in Tanahun District, on the religious festivals and holy days recognised and celebrated by the people of Miya Gaon, Hukka in Kihun VDC. These include: Muharram and Al Hijara, with the first day of the first month celebrated in the mosque as Ras as Sana (the 'head of the year'), Ashura (on the tenth days of the first month), Akhari Chahar Sambah (the last Wednesday of the second month, when the Prophet Mohammed recovered from illness), Miladunnabi (the birthday of the Prophet Mohammed, in the third month), the memorial day for Abdul Kadir Jilani, the eleventh Sarif, Isra and Miraj (Prophet Mohammed's 'night visit' to Heaven from Mecca), Shab e Barat (the night of the 'yearly record' on the fifteenth day of the eight month, when God records the births, deaths and lives of certain men), Laylat al Qadr (the 'night of command' or 'night of consultation' when the Prophet Mohammed received the Quran), the Eid ul Fitra (at the end of Ramadan) and the Eid ul Adha (when goats and buffalo are sacrificed).

Notes

1. Nabi-A-Karim Mohammad Mustafa (S.A.A.W), the last messenger of Allah.
2. *Janazah* is the Arabic term used to mean Muslim burial.
3. Shamima Siddika; op. cit., p. 196.
4. Ibid., p. 216.

4

The Relevance of Caste

Legal Classification – the Muluki 'Ain

Although, clearly, the Muslim communities of Nepal are not Hindus, they have, nevertheless, been very much affected by their status as a minority in an overwhelmingly Hindu country and arguably even more importantly through being a minority in a Hindu state, whose laws have been, and remain binding. The 'Muluki Ain' of 1853-1854 was the first codified legal text, which defined the status of various communities and ethnic groups. In this text, Hindus and others, pure and impure, natives and foreigners, *parbatiya* and Madhesi, and various other caste-based social groups in Nepal were graded and classified based on their origin and customs. The 'Muluki Ain' itself claims that it was basically a compilation of the *thithibandeg* (the established 'social order' issued by various kings of the past). Perhaps for that reason, the conventional sources such as *Dharamshastra* and *Lokdharma* found a very clear expression in the 'Muluki Ain'.

The existing literature on the 'Muluki Ain' shows that the objective of this codification was to conceptualize the idea of a unified nation in a strict political religious sense. However, the nature of this Hindu nation was very different from that of European nation states, as Megan Sijapati emphasises in chapter three on 'a Hindu kingdom and Muslim alterity' of her study of *Islamic Revival in Nepal,* particularly in her discussion of 'the history of an *asal* Hindustan (a true land of Hindus) (2011: 33-40) and 'new conceptions of the nation' (pp 40-42).

This argument is further elaborated by Andreas Höfer's study of the 'Muluki Ain' (Höfer 1979). He claims that on the one hand there was a clear European influence on it, but at the same time it was an outcome of some very specific Nepali political practices. In this sense, the 'Muluki Ain' was a social and cultural text, which simply recorded the beliefs and customs of a ruling class/caste in relation to other social groups. Prithivi Narayan Shah's famous dictum, that Nepal, not India, was the real Hindustan (home land of Hindus), could be taken as an important point in this regard.

We know little in detail of how the early Muslims 'fitted' in practice into the surrounding economy and society of Nepal although Gaige suggests that even before unification, there were 'a few middle-caste Muslims in the mid-western *terai*' who were large landowners' but certainly from the mid-19th century onwards there was a formal or official classification into which Muslims, like all other social groups, were integrated, for better or worse the Muluki Ain of 1854. More recent immigrants tended to assimilate, to a degree at least, taking on some of the caste characteristics of local Hindu communities. At the time of the 'unification' of Nepal under the rulers of Gorkha during the late 19th century, they were generally considered as 'outcasts'.

Throughout the period of Rana rule, which lasted nearly a century, from 1846 until 1950, Muslims were considered as *mlekshya (mleccha)* or foreigners; and hadan impure and inferior status in the rigid fourfold caste hierarchy of Brahmin, Kshetriya (Chhetri), Baishya and Sudra, below that of the Sudra. The 'Muluki Ain' offers an interesting classification of Muslims. Although Muslims are seen as members of a single caste group, they are classified in two different ways in order to underline the distinctiveness of each social group in relation to Hindu castes. First, Muslims are defined in terms of 'touchability' and 'untouchability'. In this sense, Muslims in general (that is all Muslims) were regarded as an impure but touchable caste; however, the categorization of 'native' Muslims (*ajlaf* or *Nepal ka Musalman*) and 'foreign' Muslims (*ashraf* or *pardesi Musalman*) marks a second kind of classification (Höfer 1979: 131).

In much of the earlier ethnographic literature on Muslims in South Asia (not only Nepal), it has been argued that this *ashraf-ajlaf* dichotomy provided a primary 'caste-like' differentiation amongst the region's Muslims.

Ashrafs were considered to be descendants of distinguished foreign ancestors and hence of a superior caste group as opposed to the *ajlaf castes*, descendants of local converts (i.e., people who converted to Islam from Hinduism). *Ashrafs* are traditionally divided into four subgroups:

the *Sayyads*, who are considered to be descendants of Fatima, the Prophet Muhammad's daughter, and Ali, the fourth caliph of Islam, and hence are of the highest social status; the *Sheikhs*, who claim to be of Arabic origin; the *Mughals*, who are descendants of central Asian invaders; and the *Pathans,* who claim to descent from Afghan conquerors. In Nepal, they are considered to constitute approximately 45 per cent per cent of Nepal's Muslim population.[1] Kashmiri Muslims would be included in this category of 'distinguished foreigners' (indeed, they claim to be such).

The *ajlafs,* by contrast, are locals (including the progeny of Hindus who converted to Islam). Included in the category of *ajlaf* are occupational groups like *ansari* (weavers), *sabji farosh* (vegetable vendors), *dhobi* (washermen), *naddaf* (cotton teasers carders), *doffali* (tassel and bangle sellers), *mocchi* (cobblers), *darzi* (tailors), *hajam* (barbers), etc., who are placed at the bottom of the social hierarchy.[2] It is generally believed that *ajlafs* are accorded a lower status because these castes converted to Islam in the hope of improving their status and not 'through the sword'.[3] Furthermore, it is also argued that, being local converts, they have retained their original caste practices and status, and that the change of religion did very little to dissolve existing caste relations. This would include the hill Muslims and Charaute groups.

Either way, despite the prevalence of caste practices in Nepal, caste relations among Muslims are not as rigid as among the Hindus and most inter-caste restrictions are confined to matrimonial matters and less applicable to commensality and other forms of social interaction.[4] It is important to contextualize this 'process of codification' simply to avoid two possible misconceptions. Since the various identified communities were not enumerated in any detailed fashion at the time of the 'Muluki Ain', the only possible mode by which legal norms could be codified was to acknowledge the fuzzy and unclear boundaries of social groups. This is precisely what the 'Muluki Ain' does in relation to Muslims. There is no doubt that the 'Muluki Ain' exercised some sort of power in mapping the customary existence of various groups including Muslims, and the nature of this power cannot be understood in terms of modern census-based stratification. That could be a possible reason behind the complex terminology of the 'Muluki Ain', which is full of Persian and Sanskrit terms.

The argument that the 'Muluki Ain' is simply a part of the larger project of the Hinduisation of Nepal does not help us in understanding the complex structure of this text. Secondly, the process of codification should not be seen in isolation from the direct and indirect impacts of British colonialism in India especially at a time when the mighty Mughal Empire was declining. The presence of East India Company, a powerful modern political player in the subcontinent, not only posed a serious challenge to the ruling class of Nepal in relation to its geopolitical existence but also forced them to search for a religious-political legitimacy.

The legal status of non-Hindus generally and Muslims in particular in the overall caste structure is discussed in detail by Andreas Höfer (1979) and Marc Gaborieau (1972). But Muslims were not just assigned a caste status of their own; they had and continue to have their own castes and sub-castes.

Caste and Sub-Caste

Mark Gaborieau's study of the *Muslims of Nepal*, especially in relation to the 'Muluki Ain', explains that although the codification of religious status of different groups provided them a clear placing in the conventional caste ranking, the practices of these castes and sub-castes continued to be governed by their everyday cultural milieu (Gaborieau, 1972).

It is not always entirely clear precisely what relationship exists between caste and sub-caste as regards the Muslim communities; or between religion and ethnicity. Muslim groups are not normally identified as *janajati*, but Sijapati refers to conversations she had with a Muslim whom she refers to as 'a Newar Muslim', commenting that 'it is significant that he is a Newar Muslim and not a recent migrant to the valley from the Terai, as many of the other members (of the Millat-e Islamiya) are' (Sijapati 2011: 138). Indeed, she refers to 'Newar Muslims' on a number of occasions (Sijapati 2011: 25, 27, 78-79) and emphasises (in pers. comm.) that Newar Muslims 'do exist', commenting that she had met 'Muslims who are Newar and identify themselves as Newar Muslims', and that 'these belong to some of the older (ie long-standing) families in the Kathmandu Valley'. Many Newar today claim to be *janajati,* and even *adhivasi* (indigenous inhabitants of Nepal), but this is an ethnic claim, whereas to claim to be Muslim is to select a specifically religious minority identity.

The Muslim communities of the *terai, as* well as those of Kathmandu, are not only affected by the dynamics of linguistic change taking place around them, they are also although by definition *not* Hindus organized along the principles of caste; as Gaige remarks, 'there are high-caste as well as low-caste people among the Muslims' (1975: 74 fn). But caste among the Muslim communities differs in many respects from the caste system found among the *madhesi* Hindus. Jha suggests that 'the caste system has also shown its presence in Muslim religious communities: eg Sheikh, Shaiyad, Dhuniya, Pathan and Julaha. However, this system is not as rigid among the Muslim community as that of the Hindu. Most of the people of the Muslim community (in the *terai*) serve as masons, tailors and butchers' (Jha 1993: 7).

Sijapati suggests that 'many Muslims feel as the General Secretary of the *Islami Sangh* does, that, in theory, the institution of caste does not exist among Muslims. He admits that a caste system exists in Muslim society, but explains that Muslim castes operate 'on a horizontal plane rather than a vertical one, as among Hindus'. It is not entirely clear what he means by this, and it could be regarded as wishful thinking, as caste is inevitably a matter of hierarchy and thus 'vertical'. However, it is certainly the case, as Sijapati indicates, that 'shifts in social status are taking place across caste boundaries in unprecedented ways that are not exclusive to Muslims or to programs of religious revivalism. .. while many Nepali Muslims who have settled in the Valley from the *terai* are not of high caste backgrounds their professional, political and religious accomplishments and not just through their participation in Islamic movements have catapulted them into positions of higher social status both within their Muslim communities and in Nepali society at large' (2011:8).

It is certainly the case that, although Muslim groups are largely endogamous, and there are undoubtedly elements of hierarchy, there is no religious and ideological principle in Islam providing foundation for the concept of caste. For example, there is no basis for ideas of ritual pollution by touch or restriction on inter dining; even if these restrictions actually apply within Muslim communities and between Muslims and others. But in reality, in Nepal, each grouping does maintain a separate and distinct identity, especially with regards intermarriage. It would be interesting to discover the rate of intermarriage in the Kathmandu Valley and in the hills between Muslims and other groups, and also between different Muslim 'castes'.

In the *terai*, however, Muslims are certainly divided into castes. Below is a brief list of the larger 'caste' groupings in a rough order of social hierarchy (derived from the literature and partly confirmed by my own fieldwork in Dhanusha district in the central eastern *terai* during 2014).

Table 17: Main Castes and Sub-Castes Among Muslims in the Terai

Sayyid	- none throughout the terai region
Shaikh	- none throughout the terai region
Pathan	- mainly landowners and cultivators, throughout the terai
Thakurai	- mainly landowners and cultivators, Parsa and Bara districts
Jat	- landowners and cultivators, mid-western terai
Gaddi	- traditionally cattle herders, most now cultivators, mid-western terai
Ansari	- traditionally weavers, today mainly cultivators& businessmen, throughout the terai
Teli	- traditionally oil manufacturers, some now cultivators and petty traders, central terai
Halwai	- traditionally sweet makers, most now cultivators and petty traders, throughout the terai
Dharkar	- weavers and manufacturers of cane chairs, throughout the terai
Rangrez	- traditionally cloth dyers and calico printers, throughout the terai
Dhuniya	- traditionally cotton carders, most now cultivators, central terai
Darzi	- tailors and thread manufacturers, central terai
Kasgar	- traditionally potters, central terai
Chikwa	- butchers, mid-western terai
Hajjam	- barbers, throughout the terai
Kabaria	- traditionally fruit and vegetable sellers, mid-western and central terai
Patihar	- selling threads, needles and ribbons, throughout the terai
Kawasi	- selling threads, needles as well as fruits and vegetables, throughout the terai
Churihar	- bangle makers and sellers, central terai
Dhobi	- traditionally washermen, throughout the terai
Natuwa	- labourers, throughout the terai
Halalkhor	- scavengers and labourers, throughout the terai
Nat	- traditionally tumblers and acrobats, throughout the terai
Faqir	- traditionally mendicants/beggars, throughout the terai

Table 18: Another List is to be Found on the Internet in Wikipaedia

Community	Traditional Occupation	Distribution
Sayyid	holy person (Laxmanpur, Banke)	Throughout the Terai
Shaikh	local leader	throughout the Terai region
Pathan	mainly landowners and cultivators	throughout the Terai
Thakurai	mainly landowners and cultivators	Parsa and Bara districts
Ansari	traditionally weavers, most are cultivators, business man	throughout the Terai
Chikwa	Butchers	Mid-west Terai
Faqir	traditionally mendicants	throughout the Terai
Jat	landowners and cultivators	Mid-west Terai

Kabaria	traditionally fruit and vegetable sellers	Mid-west and Central Terai
Gaddi now cultivators	traditionally cattle herders, most	Mid-west Terai
Hajjam	Barbers	throughout the Terai
Patihar	selling threads, needles and ribbons	throughout the Terai
Kawasi	selling threads, needles as well as fruits and vegetables	throughout the Terai
Churihar	bangle makers and sellers	Central Terai
Teli	traditionally oil manufacturers, some are cultivators, and are petty traders	Central Terai
Dhuniya	traditionally cotton carders, most are now cultivators	Central Terai
Darzi	tailors and thread manufacturers	Central Terai
Kasgar	traditionally potters	Central Terai
Halwai	traditionally sweet makers, most are petty traders and landowners	throughout the Terai
Rangrez	traditionally cloth dyers and calico printers	throughout the Terai
Dhobi	traditionally washermen	throughout the Terai
Dharkar	weavers and manufacturers of cane chairs	throughout the Terai
Natuwa	Labourers	throughout the Terai
Nat	traditionally tumblers and acrobats	throughout the Terai
Halalkhor	scavengers and labourers	throughout the Terai

Source: Wikipedia.org

Some of these occupational groups are clearly similar to those found among local Hindu communities and can be explained by assimilation into those local communities, but some appear to be distinctively associated with the Muslims.

One of the key informants from Nepalgunj, Ms Mahmuna Siddiqui (Vice President and Acting Chair of the Fatima Foundation Nepal, a Board of Member of Sankalp Kathmandu, working as a member in Amnesty International Nepal, and a member of the Trafficking Control Committee at the district level) made some interesting comments on the issue of caste. She pointed out that there is no mention of 'caste' in the Qur'an, but remarks that although the Prophet belonged to a Sayyad family he had spent most of his time with the Koresh tribe, who were involved in livestock trading.

She had an essentially 'class-based' analysis of the origin of castes. For example, she said that some of those involved in making cloth became known as 'Jolaha', and eventually these Jolaha became Ansari; some people started the business of making sweets, so they become known as 'Halwai'; some were involved in selling and buying meat, these then became 'Kureshi'; and some were involved in making and repairing shoes, sandals and slippers – these were then called 'Mochi' or 'Farooqui'. So, the Muslim 'caste' system, she said, is simply a matter of occupational differentiation, and not, she emphasised, the basis of discrimination. This, however, is precisely the argument made by Hindus as regards the caste system namely that it reflects a division of labour between occupational groups (*jajmani)* involving various forms of exchange and is not a hierarchy.

When asked about the fact that there is a tendency in Muslim communities for intra caste or intra family group marriage, so that Ansaris marry Ansaris and Khans marry Khans, while in Islam there is no reference to, or justification for, 'caste' divisions, she replied that this existed because of the lack of education and awareness. 'It is certainly true of Nepalgunj. The area is near the border with India and sometimes Nepalgunj seems like India, with its full-blown caste system and even the wearing of the *burka* by some Muslims there. But this type of rigid intra caste marriage system, where one is bound to marry within one's caste is common only in UP, she said, and not so common in Lucknow, Delhi, Gwalior, Bombay or Pune. Within Nepal, even in Butwal, Bhairahwa, Pokhara, Birgunj, Kathmandu etc., they do not practice this kind of intra-caste marriage'. 'There, if we ask them, what is your caste, if he is a man, he will reply 'Miya' (ie Muslim), and of a woman, they will say 'Bibi". 'This 'caste system' derives', she argues, 'simply from occupational differentiation, and does not imply serious divisions within the Muslim community as a whole'.

According to Islamic Law, marriage is performed between two families, without 'dowry', and in a very simple way; in theory there is no caste-ism and one marriage partner may be from an 'upper' caste, the other from 'lower' caste. According to Islam, all are same if they follow the basic principles of Islam. But in 'the real world' here in Nepal, people do things differently, she said. For example, 'Ansari caste people marry their daughter only with a man from another Ansari family; the same is the case with Khans, Siddiqis, etc. In Islam there are two *firka* (paths or groups) between which marriage should not take place: Shi'a and Sunni; a Shi'a cannot be married to a Sunni and vice versa'.

Another key informant from Nepalgunj, Mohamed Akram Ansari, a member of National Muslim Commission and active member of the UCPN-Maoist, stated that among Muslims in Nepal 'there is no casteism'; but also recognised that it does exist and 'it is affected by Indian culture'. This, he said 'creates misconfusion about Islam'. He also suggested that 'various caste groups, like Khan, Ansari, and Siddiqui, are generally the upper category of people who accepted Islam: they make strategy, they make policy of divide and rule for their own purpose (eg casteism, religious division and racial discrimination)'.

It is less clear that caste distinctions operate in the hill Muslim communities, where the local communities are arguably too small to allow for that kind of internal differentiation or to inhibit marriages between persons of different 'caste'. Upadhyay is insistent that in the hill village of Miya Gaon, Hukka that he studied in Tanahun District there were 'no caste distinctions among the Muslims'. He identifies the different groups in Kihun VDC within which Miya Gaon is situated, referring to them as 'caste/ethnic groups': Magar, Brahmin, Muslim, Dalits, Gharti, Chhetri, Other. The Muslim community was the third largest of the various groups in the VDC and is largely confined to Miya Gaon. The Muslim community in Miya Gaon is differentiated in various ways but not, Upadhyay insists, by caste: 'unlike the Hindus, there is no untouchability prevailing among Muslims. All can dine on one table; they are allowed to change their occupation. They can marry and have good relations with (those of) high class after improving their economic condition'. He adds that 'their worship place is common', even though there are three mosques in Miya Gaon (2014: 129). We shall examine the other forms of differentiation social, economic and other in this community below.

5

Occupation and Class

There is relatively little basis yet for a detailed analysis in terms of caste and class in the Muslim communities of Nepal, although there is no doubt that even if Muslims as a whole constitute a marginalised and disadvantaged minority in Nepal, the Muslim communities are themselves, as we have seen, differentiated not only by history, origin, language, etc.; they are also divided and differentiated by class.

The vast majority of Muslims in Nepal work in agriculture, in the rural areas of the hills or, to an overwhelming extent, in the *terai*. Details of the structure of landownership, the relations of production and of exchange, and of consumption needed to provide the basis for an understanding of the Muslim agrarian economy are, however, relatively sparse, although economic and social change has been considerable and the growing importance of non-agricultural employment and other economic activities (eg in the industrial, commercial and services sectors), including labour migration and the flow of remittances that has become such an important feature of the economy of both the hills and the *terai* in recent years, is evident from the available data. Given the importance of these aspects of the local economy and society for an understanding of the status of Muslims in the wider economy and society of the *terai* and of Nepal as a whole, it is important that further research be undertaken in this area, in particular.

Gaige suggests that 'a few Muslims' could be classed as being part of the 'upper- and business-caste plains people' (1975: 162), but this is hardly a sufficient basis for a class analysis of Muslim entrepreneurs and their relationship to other classes of Muslims or non-Muslims for that matter and much remains to be done in this regard. The overall economic profile of Muslims in terms of occupations and sectors, is distinctive. It is necessary, however, to distinguish between the structure of 'occupational' castes and subcastes (as discussed above) and the actual occupational structure to be found today among Muslim communities. One interpretation of the difference between these two is to see the former as a 'traditional' division of labour and occupational structure and the latter as the contemporary or 'modern' and thus arguably relatively recent version of the 'traditional' structure; but often there is no relationship between the 'occupational caste' and the actual occupation of an individual.

Dastider, for example, identifies a number of what are specifically referred to as 'Muslim occupational castes' eg *hajjam* (barber), *darzi* (tailor), *rajmistry* (mason) and *julaha* (weaver) and explains that, in fact, 'all of these work in the fields during the harvesting season, either on their own lands or as tenant farmers. Inadequate income opportunities in their hereditary profession have forced many occupational castes to fall upon tenant farming or even work as daily wage labourers in bigger farms, usually at four kilograms of rice per day' (Dastider 2000: 767). This implies that the shift from 'traditional' occupation to current occupation is relatively recent; this may be the case, but it is also entirely possible that the so-called 'occupational castes' of Nepali Muslims have not been 'real occupational groups' for quite some time, and are in fact social and cultural categories or 'identities' (rather like British surnames like Smith, Tailor, Farmer etc.) rather than socioeconomic class formations. This remains to be explored through detailed fieldwork among these different groups.

A key informant in the Janakpur area, Maulana Mohammed Rahamatullah, suggested that the majority of Muslims in Mahottari and Dhanusha Districts were Barelsis and that the majority were also either upper or middle class (mostly the latter). However, in spite of having relatively good income sources, he remarked that their ability to save was limited, in large part because of the large number of family members and life style. He pointed out that if male and female both work together, then both income and savings would increase, which would be helpful in case of emergency. At present, a single income source cannot fulfil the needs of all family members, but it is relatively rare for Muslim women to undertake paid work, so joint families are common to ensure economies of scale and sufficient sources of income.

Occupational Structure

In Kathmandu, Fadzakir (2001) surveyed households from a number of different local Muslim communities (as indicated previously) and found that, overall, the adult males (265 in all) tended to be predominantly either in business of some kind with a significant proportion of these being associated with artisan production (eg embroidery, handicraft, watch repair, dyeing, etc.) or working in the service sector (eg restaurants, hotels, 'tourism', salesmen or shopkeepers) or else employed as factory workers (the largest group at 62 - 20 per cent of the total). While the majority of the former were Nepali Muslims, most of the latter were immigrant workers, many of them from India or from the *terai.*

The workers in the survey were mainly employed in two clothing factories which employed almost exclusively men from Bihar, Uttar Pradesh and Darjeeling (all in India) and from Biratnagar (in Nepal). Fadzakir comments that these factory workers were only a small percentage of the total number of Muslim immigrant workers employed in the capital, and that there were at least 10 such clothing factories in Kathmandu. Another industry in which a considerable number of foreign Muslim immigrants are employed, apparently, is embroidery (28 of his respondents); but this, by contrast with the clothing industry, is a largely artisan system of production, located for the most part in small workshops, in Jyatha, Jhocche and Thamel, producing both for the wholesale and for the retail market.

There are also producers of handicraft (including hand woven carpets, wool and pashmina shawls, papier-maché ornaments and leather goods), who have retail outlets or shops; most of these claimed to be 'Kashmiri Muslims' and part of a larger population of first generation Muslims from Kashmir who have shops all over the city, although notably in Thamel and Durba Marg. These are the 'new' Kashmiri Muslims referred to earlier. Another group of shopkeepers are sellers of gems, beads and bangles; in Thamel, for example, many of the gem stone and jewellery shops are owned and run by Muslims. On the whole, these have done relatively well for themselves and can be seen as largely belonging to the petty bourgeois and even bourgeois class, with relatively well educated children and decent standards of living for the most part. It is not only the old 'Kashmiri' and/or 'Hindustani' communities that are involved in such business; many of the gem shops in Thamel are now managed or 'kept' at least by young men from Kashmir, Jaipur, Agra, Fatehpur Sikri and other places in northwest India.

The bead sellers are a rather distinctive group. The bead market at Indrachowk is known as *pote* (bead) bazaar. The shops have been there in this location for as much as three hundred years. Originally, these enterprises were owned by the early Kashmiri Muslims who used to trade in glass beads. This is why the *pote bazaar* is also known by older generation Muslims as the 'Kashmiri Bazaar'. Today, as a result of intermarriage and transfers of ownership, the prorietors of these businesses are no longer exclusively Kashmiri Muslims, although most are Muslims. Only one shop out of 34 identified by Fadzakir was owned by a Hindu. The bazaar, somewhat curiously, caters to a local, largely Hindu market. The beads, which now come mainly from Japan and 'Czechoslovakia' (according to Fadzakir) are usually made into sacred necklaces called *mangal sutra*, which are worn by Brahmin and Chhetri brides; Muslim women do not wear the beads or bangles produced and sold in this market.

Many Muslims in Kathmandu are also involved in some way with the mosques, either as teachers or as administrators and caretakers; but some are employed in the civil service or in other forms of private enterprise; some have sons working abroad, and a number have sons and daughters studying abroad; others have more mundane sources of income (eg book sellers, butchers, shopkeepers and other 'petty bourgeois' trades). Interestingly, none of those surveyed by Fadzakir in central Kathmandu claimed to be involved in agriculture, and although a few described themselves as landlords it seems that these were property owners getting an income from rent, rather than landowners. Only a few (6 out of 265) were working abroad.

Apart from this very interesting study, relatively little is known of the occupational and class structure and dynamics of the Kathmandu Muslim community, whether Nepali Muslims or immigrant Muslim workers, often from India. Further research is badly needed.

The predominant impression gained from a variety of sources is that most Muslims outside the Kathmandu Valley live in the rural areas and that most are involved in farming. Dastider states that 'like other Indian settlers, Muslims ... entered the *terai* as farmers, and a majority of them continue to remain linked with agriculture'. This is probably the case for hill Muslims as well as for those living in the *terai*, although it is important not to underestimate the process of rural emigration and the increasing importance of employment and entrepreneurial activity in the urban areas, and also the significance for Muslims, as for other Nepalis, of foreign migration to live and work abroad and send remittances back home.

Data from the UNDP 2009 (cited in Bennett et al 2013) suggest that, among Muslim men, agriculture was an important but minority activity, with only 38 per cent involved in this sector. Over a third (37.4 per cent) was employed as skilled or unskilled labourers and 18.5 per cent were in the service sector; nearly 5 per cent were clerical workers and 1.3 per cent was classified as 'professional/technical/managerial'. The majority of Muslim women, however, still worked in agriculture (76.7 per cent). Although this was the lowest proportion of virtually all groups in Nepal (85.8 per cent for Nepalese women as a whole). Some 13 per cent were employed as skilled or unskilled labourers, while just over 10 per cent worked in the service sector a higher percentage than in any other group apart from Newar women.

In the hills, Upadhyay provides an account of the division of labour in the local economy of the Muslim community of Miya Gaon, Hukka in Kihan VDC in Tanahun District (in 2012) and indicates that the greatest number of respondents 46 out of a hundred - declared themselves to be working in agriculture, as farmers or labourers; 38 were working abroad; six were teachers; five were in business; four were labourers, and one was in government service. Others (number unspecified) were landowners renting out their land to others or students.

Of the 64 households in the community, all had some land. 25 households had less than 3 acres of dry land and 23 had between 4 and 8 acres (75 per cent of all households); 10 had between 9 and 15 acres and six had between 16 and 23 acres. Upadhyay describes the six households with the larger land holdings as 'the elite of Miya Gaon, Hukka' (2014: 103). In addition, some households (38 out of 64-60 per cent) had irrigated paddy land, although 26 (40 per cent did not). Of those with some paddy, 25 households had between 1 and 2 acres, 9 had between 3 and 4 acres and four had between 5 and 10 acres. Unfortunately, these data on landownership does not allow us to determine which households had how much dry and irrigated land combined.

Nevertheless, on the basis of landownership do it would seem that the community was indeed divided into a small landowning elite, a majority of 'middle farmers' and a significant minority of small and micro-farmers. Some of the larger landowners rented out land to those with significantly less and some of the near landless worked for the larger landowners. It is not clear whether these arrangements involved relationships of the kind that some have termed 'semi-feudal' or simply pragmatic arrangements on a more or less temporary basis to resolve imbalances in access to cultivable land and to agricultural labour. Also, we are not able to determine how far foreign labour migration and remittances accentuated these landowning divisions or counteracted them. But earnings from employment abroad were a significant source of income to 38 individuals.

Overall household income appears to allow us to identify a significant proportion of households earning Rs 8,000 or more a month, with a small number in the middle earning Rs 4,000 to Rs 8,000 and a significant minority earning less than Rs 4,000 a month. So, it seems, a better off half and a less well-off half, with considerable inequality between the wealthiest and the poorest. None of the Muslim households, however, were well off in comparative terms, within the larger community of the VDC, with only half earning Rs 8,000 or more a month and the rest earning less (compared with the situation described by the 2009 survey of hill and *terai* Muslims Table 20 where Rs 8,000 a month is what hill *dalits* earned on average at that time).

This seems to be confirmed by the very low ownership of domestic assets or consumer durables (eg cupboard, radio, mobile phone or solar panel/device): 79 per cent of the inhabitants had none of these. A few people (35) owned a radio, 23 people owned a mobile phone and 18 owned a solar panel out of 466; one person owned a motorbike. Most households (58 per cent) had no permanent toilet and 36 per cent had only a temporary structure. Only four households had a proper permanent toilet. One third of houses were *pukka* (built of stone walls and tin roofs), and two third were *kaccha* (mud, wattle & daub and thatch.

In the *terai,* it seems, although many remain involved in farming, having entered Nepal originally for the most part as farmers, farm labourers and livestock keepers as well as traders and small business owners, the proportion of those employed in the non-agricultural sector has grown over time. It appears to have increased significantly between 1998-99 and 2008 (on the basis of New Era calculations from the NLFS, cited in Bennett et al 2013: 15). What these data do not reveal, however, is the rapid growth in the importance of labour migration, particularly foreign labour migration, among Muslim communities as part of the wider growth in labour migration among the various communities of the *terai* as a whole (see Seddon 2017).

Dastider remarks that 'in the few urban centres in the *terai,* Muslims are... conspicuous in small scale trade. In the towns of the middle and western *terai* (viz Birgunj, Kalaiya, Taulihawa, Krishnanagar, Nepalgunj and Mahendranagar) Muslims form a significant part of the small traders'

(2000: 767). Some of this is the result of recent immigration from the rural areas, but some has its roots in the more distant past. In Nepalgunj, probably the most important centre of urban Muslims in the *terai*, the main commercial centre, Ek-laini Bazaar, is dominated by Muslim shop owners who are the direct descendants of the original traders invited there by the Rana rulers around 1860-75 from the Awadh region (Nandpara) to establish a trading centre along the Indo-Nepali border. Further research into the history of immigration by Muslims into the Nepal *terai* is, as has already been remarked an urgent necessity.

Recent trends, however, probably account for most of the recent growth in commercial or at least non-agricultural activity in the urban areas of the *terai*. The proportion of Muslim men and women in the urban areas over 15 respectively employed in the non-agricultural sector grew from 74 per cent and 59 per cent respectively (with an overall figure of 70 per cent) in 1998-99 to 89 and 63 per cent respectively (with an overall proportion of 78 per cent) between 1998-99 and 2008 an 8 per cent increase (on the basis of New Era calculations from the NLSS, cited in Bennett et al 2013: 15).

In the rural areas, the figures for non-agricultural employment by Muslims were much lower 30.7 and 13.5 per cent for males and females respectively, with an overall proportion of 23.3 per cent for 1998-99, and 41 and 12.7 per cent respectively, and 26.6 per cent overall for 2008 a 3.3 per cent increase. In the period concerned, however, the overall percentage of men and women combined in the non-agricultural sector increased from 27 per cent to 33 per cent a 6 point increase. Clearly, the trend is away from agriculture, even if the majority of those in rural areas, particularly in the *terai* are still farmers or agricultural workers something that is now by no means certain, given the rapid growth in foreign labour migration.

Dastider refers to the lack of statistical data, but a study undertaken by sample survey among the Muslim communities of selected hill and terai districts (Rana 2009), revealed an interesting snapshot of the occupational structure of these communities (see Table 19).

Table 19: Occupations of Survey Communities (2009)

Occupation	Hill			Terai			Total		
	M	F	T	M	F	T	M	F	T
Agriculture	34	0	34	83	2	85	117	2	119
Trade	41	1	42	25	2	27	66	3	69
Tailoring	3	0	3	17	0	17	20	0	20
Artisan	0	0	0	13	0	13	13	0	13
Service	0	0	0	7	0	7	7	0	7
Labour	0	0	0	6	0	6	6	0	6
Student	0	0	0	0	2	2	0	2	2
Foreign employment	0	0	0	2	0	2	2	0	2
Contractor	1	0	1	0	0	0	1	0	1
Household	0	0	0	0	1	1	0	1	1
Total	79	1	80	153	7	160	232	8	240

In this survey, agriculture and trade were the main stated occupations, with nearly half (49.6 per cent) and over a quarter (28.75 per cent) of respondents engaged in these respectively. Tailoring was the third most common occupation, with 8.3 per cent of respondents engaged in this occupation; with 5.4 per cent in other artisan jobs and only 2.9 per cent in service (ie regular employment) mainly in the private sector. Relatively few were wage labourers.

Foreign labour migration appears in these data to be marginal involving less than 1 per cent of those surveyed. It is certain that since these data were collected, foreign labour (and remittances as a major source of income) will have increased among the Muslim communities of both the hills and the *terai,* but these data are possibly misleading, even for that period.

Indeed, in a more recent study, hill *janajatis* had the highest proportion (31 per cent) of household members working overseas (ie not in India), but Muslims were second (22 per cent). Among those receiving remittances, this source of income accounted for about a third of annual household income; among Muslim households, who on average had among the lowest average per capita incomes, those receiving remittances received a slightly higher proportion of household income from remittances than other groups. A shift out of agriculture, visible in most other groups, was taking place particularly among Muslims and *terai dalits,* with almost

53 per cent of *terai dalits* and 46 per cent of Muslims working outside agriculture. The share of Muslims in higher return occupations had apparently declined (Bennett et al 2013: 26-27).

In 2009, the differences between the rural hills and the rural *terai were* striking. In the hills, just over 40 per cent (42.5 per cent) were in agriculture, whereas in the *terai,* it was over half (53.1 per cent). As for trade, just over half (52.5 per cent) of those in the hills were engaged in trade, but less than 20 per cent (16.9 per cent) of those in the *terai.* The situation was quite the opposite for tailoring and other artisan jobs: nearly 20 per cent (18.75 per cent) of respondents from the *terai* were engaged in such jobs, but less than 5 per cent (3.75 per cent) of respondents from the hills. No respondent from the hills was in service, government or private.

There were also interesting differences between the situation in the rural areas and the towns. In the 2009 survey, unsurprisingly, more respondents from the rural areas were engaged in agriculture than in the district headquarters: nearly 70 per cent (69 per cent) of rural respondents were engaged in agriculture but fewer than 30 per cent (28 per cent) of the urban respondents. The situation was just the reverse in relation to trade: 45 per cent of the urban respondents were engaged in trade but only 12.5 per cent of rural respondents; 8 per cent of the urban respondents were engaged in artisan jobs, but only 2.5 per cent of those in rural areas.

More Muslim males in the *terai* were engaged in agriculture than in the hills; but comparatively more Muslim males in the hills were engaged in trade than in the *terai.* Muslim males from the hills were ahead of those in the *terai* as regards the proportion in foreign job. However, more *terai* males were engaged in labouring, service, tailoring and artisan jobs. The diagrams related to these comparative situations are presented as below:

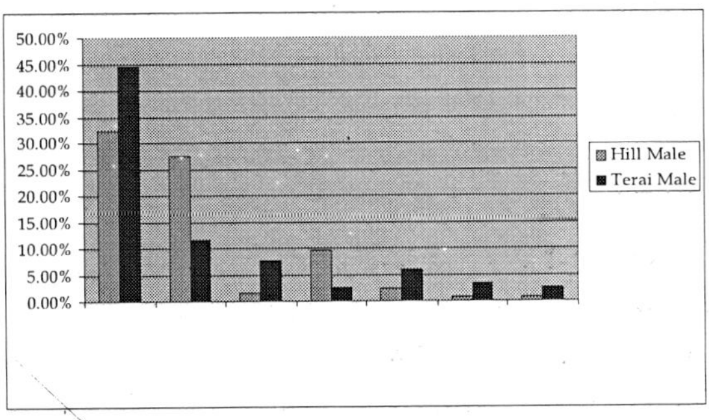

Diagram 1: A Comparative Occupation Patterns of Muslim Males of Hill and Terai Region

A comparison was also undertaken of the differences between the situation in the 'urban' areas of the district headquarters and that in the rural areas as a whole. These differences are presented in diagram 2 below, for males and females respectively, in the terai and in the hills.

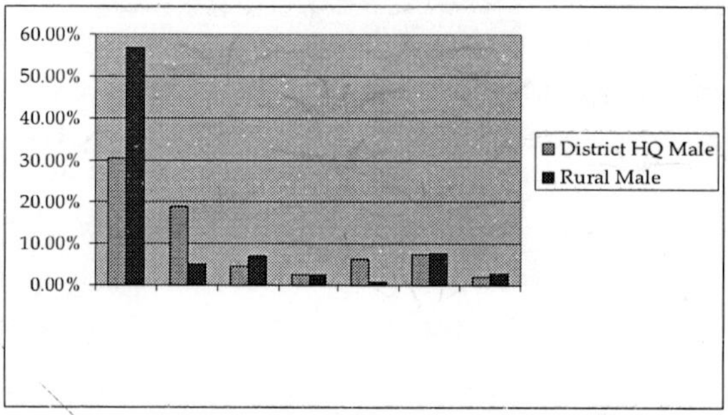

Diagram 2: Occupations of Muslim Males in District Headquarters and Remote VDCs (terai)

Agriculture and trade were the principal occupations of males in the *terai* region as a whole. Agriculture was the most important occupation of males in the rural *terai* (more than 55 per cent) and also in the urban areas (about 30 per cent). As regards trade, nearly 20 per cent (18.8) of males in the urban areas were involved, but only about 5 per cent in the rural areas. Other areas of their engagement were service, foreign employment, labouring, and artisan jobs. A significant number of Muslim males residing in the district headquarters were engaged in tailoring.

According to the 19 members of a focus group interviewed by NEMAF in Jaispur (Nepalgunj) in summer 2015, 'most Muslims are involved in agriculture and this is one of the main sources of income locally'. They estimated that 'maybe 80 per cent are involved in farming their own land or the land of others as tenants; some 10 per cent are labourers, in agriculture or other sectors. Very few indeed have regular employment; a few are plumbers or electricians. A small number are involved in business, but there is little encouragement from the government for Muslims in business. About 5 per cent go abroad to live and work'. This is interesting given that Dastider suggests that 'Nepalgunj is the only place in the whole of Nepal where Muslim traders are found in substantial numbers', drawing on the fieldwork on Cholraj that Sharma described in an unpublished paper (Sharma nd).

A focus group of 15 women and girls interviewed by NEMAF for this project in summer 2015 in Bachhupurwa (Nepalgunj), at the Aisa Madaratul Banat English Medium Girls School, also suggested that the majority were involved in farming: out of 100 Muslims in the area, some 65 per cent would be involved in agriculture, 26 per cent employed as labourers, 5 per cent would be in business, 2 per cent in regular employment and 2 per cent in foreign employment. They commented that very few Muslims were regularly employed in either the private or public sector. As regards business, they indicated that Muslims were mainly involved in 'traditional' and mainly small scale businesses, but that nowadays in Nepalgunj bank facilities and hospital facilities are improving gradually and business is relatively popular. People near the border can earn NRs 200 to NRs 300 per day.

According to this focus group, agriculture remained the most important source of income in Nepal. Most of the Muslims in agriculture farm the land of others. People who live in the towns now generally give their land to rent to village farmers, and when crops are ready, they divide the produce into two parts one is given to the owner and the other is kept by the tenant who does the farming. In this era of modern methods and equipment, still in Nepal the farmers tend to depend on traditional system inputs: seeds, cultivation and irrigation are the main elements of the local agriculture. Only very few Muslims in Nepalgunj own larger plots of land 10, 12, 15 *bighas*; most Muslim landowners having only 3 or 4 *bighas*; and most Muslims there do not own land at all.

By contrast, one of our key informants in Nepalgunj, Ms Mahmuna Siddiqui (Vice President and Acting Chair of Fatima Foundation Nepal, Board of Member of Sankalp Kathmandu, working as a member in Amnesty International Nepal and a member of the Trafficking Control Committee at the district level) suggested that Muslims were involved in five major occupations or economic activities for Muslims: business 30-35 per cent, salaried employment 15 per cent, wage labouring 25 per cent, agriculture 5 per cent and foreign employment 20 per cent.

As regards business, she said there were some businessmen in Nepalgunj who were successful, these included radio, TV and watch sellers/repairers. As far as regular salaried employment was concerned, this was relatively rare but might involve teaching, nursing, working in a bank, as an engineer or auditor or doctor, or with an INGO or NGO. But these privileged employees were generally from good families who were well off and were aware of the importance of education. Many Muslims were wage labourers; in the *terai* many, especially in the rural areas, were engaged in farming but very few owned their own land. In the villages, the women also worked.

Foreign employment had become more common; remittances improved economic conditions and the income from employment abroad helped families to fulfil their basic needs and improve the standard of living. If, however, the government could establish some factories, or industry in general, and the Nepali youth were engaged in these industries, then it would help to improve the county's economic condition.

Another key informant from the Nepalgunj area, Mohamed Faisal Ansari, a major business man, also suggested that agriculture was less important than others had stated. In his opinion, there were five major categories of sources of income to Muslims and these were, in order of importance: business (30-35 per cent), foreign employment (20 per cent), local wage labour (25 per cent), regular employment or 'service' (15 per cent) and agriculture (5 per cent).

Incomes

As far as incomes are concerned, the empirical data from studies and surveys show that Muslims as a whole tend to have relatively low incomes in comparison with other social groups, but as we have indicated earlier, in section 1, there has been a general improvement in respect of poverty incidence, although there also appears to be growing differentiation as regards wealth, incomes and poverty as between individuals, and to a lesser extent as between households.

Table 20: Average Monthly Per Capita Income by Caste and Ethnicity, Nepal, 2003-04

Ethnic Group	Average per capita income (NRS)	Average per capita income urban (NRS)	Average per capita income rural (NRS)
Nepal	**15,000.00**	**28,957.00**	**12,534.00**
Newar	26,100.00	36,600.00	14,460.00
Hill B/Chhetri	23,900.00	32,408.00	21,465.00
Terai B/Chhetri	16,000.00	34,678.00	13,625.00
Hill Janjati	13,500.00	26,448.00	11,987.00
Terai Dalits	13,200.00	20,460.00	11,927.00
Terai Janajati	12,700.00	14,106.00	12,719.00
Terai middle castes	11,300.00	12,736.00	11,212.00
Muslims	**10,200.00**	**11,563.00**	**10,126.00**
Hill Dalits	8,830.00	18,602.00	8,018.00

Source: DFID and World Bank, 2005 as cited in UNDP, 2009, from NLSS 2003-04

The study of Muslims undertaken in 2009 through a sample survey of selected districts in hills and *terai* (by Rana 2009) provides a snapshot of average incomes from different sources in the study areas at around the same time. This study indicates a significantly lower figure, especially for the *terai*, than the 'national average' provided by the UNDP. Incidentally, these data suggest that income levels among *terai dalits* whose Human Development Index was found to be lower even than that of Muslims (see section 1) are higher, not only than those of Muslims but also than those of hill *dalits* in terms of average per capita income overall; much of the difference being due to hill *dalits* in rural areas earning substantially less.

The average income for Muslims is generally higher in the hills than in the *terai*, particularly as regards income from trade and from wage labour; but small sample size means that one should be wary about over-interpreting these figures (in Table 21).

Table 21: Average Income of Muslims in Hills and Terai (Sample Survey 2009)

S.N.	Source of income	Hills (In NRs)	Terai (In NRs)
1.	Agriculture	6,729.56	3,703.99
2.	Trade	10,754.72	2,592.02
3.	Foreign Job	62.89	1,457.06
4.	Service	770.44	1,863.50
5.	Wage Labour	5,723.27	1,226.99
6.	Skilled Labour	251.57	789.88

This suggests that although the Muslims of both hill and *terai* districts were lagging behind the average per capita income level of the country, the economic condition of the Muslims in the *terai* was particularly poor. The per capita income of Muslims in the hills was NRs 24,292.45 whereas the total per capita income of those who live in the *terai* from all sources combined was only NRs 11,633.44. Strikingly, although agriculture is a major activity in the *terai*, agriculture contributed only NRs 3,703.99 on average to an individual Muslim's income. The data here for incomes from wage labour, skilled labour and even more so from foreign labour, suggest low incomes, and certainly as regards the last of these must be questionable.

The difference in income between the rural areas and urban areas (district headquarters) was also striking, if unsurprising (see Table 22).

Table 22: Average Individual Income of Muslims in Urban and Rural Areas (2009)

S.N.	Source of income	Hills		Terai	
		District headquarter (In NRs)	Rural (In NRs)	District headquarter (In NRs)	Rural (In NRs)
1.	Agriculture	**4,635.19**	8,729.51	1,467.03	**5,650.10**
2.	Trade	**17,639.48**	4,180.33	**3,890.11**	1,462.72
3.	Foreign Job	0.00	122.95	1,681.32	1,261.95
4.	Service	515.02	1,014.34	1,598.90	2,093.69
5.	Wage Labour	**5,278.97**	**6,147.54**	857.14	1,548.76
6.	Skilled Labour	0.00	491.80	1,252.75	387.19
	Total	**28,068.67**	**20,686.48**	**10,747.25**	**12,404.40**

The data reveal, not surprisingly perhaps, that Muslims residing in the district headquarters of hill districts were relatively better off, in terms of incomes (and probably overall wealth), the others. Per capita income in the hill towns was NRs 28,068.67. By contrast, per capita incomes in the *terai* towns were among the lowest of all at NRs 10,747.25 although not surprisingly they were leading other groups as regards income from foreign employment. Trade was the main source of income for the Muslims residing in the district headquarters of the hill regions and agriculture the main source of income for those living in the hill rural areas. The earnings from trade for Muslims in the hill district headquarters were NRs 17,639.48, on average, whereas the average income from agriculture for a rural hill Muslim was only NRs 8,729.51.

We saw from Upadhyay's 2012 study of a Muslim hill village in Tanahun District, that those earning NRs 8,000 a month were among the better off, and that about half of all households were earning considerably less than Rs 8,000, with 42 per earning less than NRs 4,000 and 23 per cent (over a fifth and nearly a quarter) earning less than NRs 2,000. In the *terai,* a Muslim residing in the district headquarters was earning most from trade, but his income from trade was still just

NRs. 3,890.11 an absolute pittance but still more than the poorer Muslims in the rural hill areas.

The Muslims of the rural *terai* were earning most of their total income from agriculture; but the average income from this source was only NRs. 5,650.10. Although Muslims in the *terai,* both in the district headquarters and in the rural areas were earning a considerable amount, relatively, from service and foreign employment, the contribution of these was not enough to raise their incomes overall to equal those of Muslims in the hills. The contribution to the average income of a Muslim in the urban *terai* from service and foreign employment was NRs 1,681.32 and NRs 1,598.90 respectively and for the rural *terai,* it was NRs 1,261.95 and NRs 2,093.69 respectively. The comparison of income as between Muslims in different contexts urban/rural and hills/terai is instructive, but even perhaps even more so is the comparison of income in relation to expenditure, which gives some idea of the structure and dynamic of household budgets and the extent to which income meets demand and need.

The amount of the annual expenditure per individual Muslim in the study area of the project was calculated on the major headings such as food, education, *madrasa* education, clothes, health, festivals, agricultural and other prominent areas of expenditure. The expenditure of Muslims in study area was compared with their per capita income to assess their economic status. Findings of this analysis are presented below:

Table 23: A Comparison of Unit Income and Expenditure (2009)

S.N	Study area	Unit income (NRs)	Unit expenditure (NRs)	Saving (NRs)
1	Hill District HQ	28,068.67	16,239.84	+ 11,828.83
2	Hill rural	20,686.48	11,068.13	+ 9,618.35
3	**Hill average**	**24,292.45**	**13,571.76**	**+ 10,720.69**
4	Terai District HQ	10,747.25	13,005.02	- 2,257.77
5	Terai rural	12,404.40	13,760.73	- 1,356.33
6	**Terai average**	**11,633.44**	**13,419.84**	**- 1,786.40**
	Total	15,783.51	13,443.41	+ 2,340.10

The data indicate that, overall, average per capita income across all groups was NRs. 15,783.51 and their unit expenditure was NRs. 13,443.41, showing small a surplus or savings of NRs. 2,340.10. Hill Muslims generally showed a significant surplus of income over expenditure (NRs.

10,720.69). The surplus of Muslims residing in district headquarters of hill region was on average NRs. 11,828.83 and that in rural areas was NRs. 9,618.35. Since the per capita income of Muslims of hill area in total, district headquarters and rural areas were NRs. 24,292.45, NRs 28,068.67 and NRs 20,686.48 respectively, it seems they were able to secure a margin of more than 40 per cent of their income, despite the fact that their income was below national per capita income

Generally, however, among Muslims in the *terai,* expenditure exceeded income, implying an overall negative balance. The average household income and expenditure of Muslims in the *terai* as a whole were NRs. 11,633.44 and Nrs. 13,419.84 respectively, giving rise to a gap of NRs. 1,786.40 per year. The Muslims in the urban areas appear to have faced an even greater problem, with a gap of NRs. 2,257.77, compared with those in the rural areas,with a gap of NRs. 1,356.33 per year. This may represent a large burden of debt, but also possibly an element of borrowing for investment purposes. This is an area that requires further investigation. As to the items of expenditure, it is clear that food was the major item of expenditure, with more than 40 per cent of income going on this item alone. This is pretty standard for lower middle income groups in Nepal as a whole going on this item along (see Diagram 3).

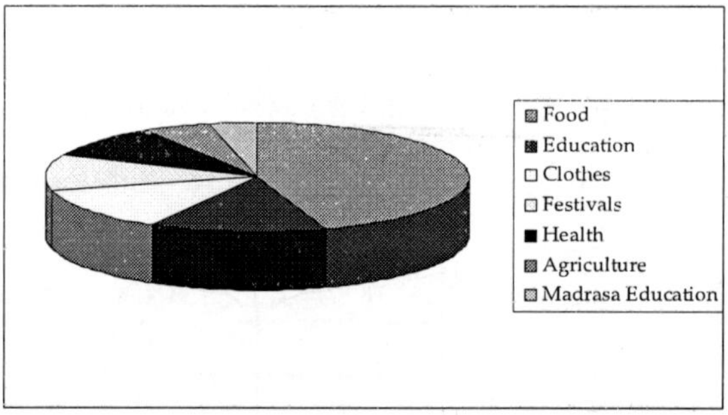

Diagram 3: Overall Expenditure Pattern of Muslims in the Study Area (2009)

Other major headings of expenditure according to their importance were education, clothes, festival, health, and agriculture. Interestingly, about a sixth (16.45 per cent) of income was going on education, most of which (82.5 per cent) went on mainstream private or government schools with much less (the remaining 16.4 per cent) on *madrasa* education.

The situation was somewhat different as between the hills and the *terai.* While food was the major item of expenditure in both hills and *terai,* the Muslims of hill region were spending about 20 per cent of their income on mainstream education, while the *terai* Muslims were spending only about 10 per cent less than their expenditure on some other items, such as clothes, festivals, health etc. Muslims in both areas were spending relatively little on *madrasa* education (in about equal proportion); it should be remembered, however, that *madrasa* education in generally free or takes only a nominal amount of money as fees to the *maulana* or *imam*.

It is rare for statistical data on incomes and expenditure and occupations to reveal the full complexity of the underlying class structure and relations, but we can begin to get an idea from these data and from a variety of other sources. One key informant at least in the Janakpur area indicated in 2015 (to the NEMAF team) that Muslims in the Dhanusha and Mahottari districts tended to be more 'middle class' and better off, and to be predominantly Barelsis, but how far this indication can be sustained as a generalisation, is not clear.

Unfortunately, it has not been possible to access the disaggregated data directly from the published volumes (statistical reports) of the NLSS 2010-11 to produce information for an up-to-date picture of incomes and income distribution, and for income and expenditure patterns, for Muslims, for comparison with other groups. It is hoped that the basic data could be obtained or accessed from the CBS at some time in the future as part of a further research project.

Foreign Migration and Remittances

The one area that seems under-reported and understated in the data considered above is that of labour migration and remittances, particularly foreign labour migration and remittances from abroad. It is known from more general studies that over the last decade or so, that the number and proportion of those from the *terai* migrating abroad to live and work has risen dramatically, to the point where some *terai* districts are more involved than are the hills districts of the west, the far west and the east of Nepal. Districts in which Muslims constitute a significant proportion of the total population, such as Dhanusha, are among those sending the most migrants abroad, mainly to the Gulf. The District Development profile for Dhanusha District, for example, indicated that some 25 per cent of the male population was living and working abroad in 2012. Investigations in Dhanusha during 2014 suggested that this district is one of those now sending the most migrants abroad, mainly to the Gulf, and Muslims are among the highest-sending groups.

This is not too different a picture from that found in Raghunathpur in Dhanusha District in early 1999, when Dr. Ganesh Gurung undertook fieldwork there on behalf of one of the pioneering studies of foreign labour migration (Seddon, Adhikari & Gurung 2001: 130-136). At this time there were just under 10,000 (9,870) people in the village and a total of 1,286 households, of which 6.5 per cent were Muslims. A significant minority (40 per cent) of the households, including most of the Muslims, were landless and 75 per cent owned less than 1.5 *bigha* of land. Nearly 10 per cent of the households (and 1.3 per cent of the total population) had a household member earning an income from outside agriculture, with 215 people working in India and 276 people in the Gulf about 10 per cent of the total male population. Of the nine wards in Ragunathur, foreign labour migrants were concentrated in three; 177 or 67 per cent of the total in the Gulf (mostly in Saudi Arabia) were from these three wards, which contained a significant proportion of Muslims.

At that time, migration to the Gulf was relatively novel and it seems that it was Muslims in this area who pioneered this development. Despite painful stories of some who had suffered mishaps and misfortunes, it was generally regarded as a good option, with relatively high wages there enabling a worker to send back NRs 4,000 to NRs 5,000 a month. Most had gone through manpower agencies in Janakpur, but some had been recruited by the small number of informal agents from Kathmandu based companies, who were making good money out of sending Nepali workers to the Gulf. In all, 419 people (4.2 per cent of the total population from roughly 33 per cent of households) were working abroad, although the work in India was mainly seasonal, mainly agricultural and mainly in the Punjab. A news report in *The Kathmandu Post* (28 April 1998) stated that 50,000 able-bodied people, mainly men, travelled from Dhanusha District every year to the Punjab/Haryana for about three months to harvest wheat or rice there.

Few, however, of the rapidly growing number of studies on foreign labour migration distinguish the level and nature of foreign migration by caste and ethnicity in such a way that one can distinguish Muslims from non-Muslims. This again, is an important area for further research. The impression we have, albeit based on only anecdotal evidence, is that Muslim communities are now very highly involved in foreign labour migration, particularly from the *terai*, and particularly to the Gulf. One of the key informants from the Janakpur area interviewed during this project during 2015, Vijay Kumar Dutta, a member of the Border Area Development Program and founder of Public Youth Campus, Janakpur, remarked that 'the present economic condition of the Muslims community has changed, mainly due to the income from remittances'. Having said that, he also commented that

> 'Muslims are mainly involved in the low prestige occupations like house building, vegetable selling, umbrella and shoe repair mending, tailoring and many low graded works. Those working in Gulf or in other countries are generally working in lower status jobs. (On the other hand) ... 'most of the Muslim houses were in the past thatched and made of mud but this is changing day by day due to remittances from the Gulf. Now there is a change in habitation and they build good houses and invest in social status too. Most of the youth are now going to the Gulf, so that the economic status of Muslims is relatively good at present. Economically they are prosperous; but socially they are in very bad condition. In spite of having the changes in economic condition there is lack of toilets in the Muslim community. Also, women are more victimized than men in the Muslim community'.

It is not evident from this that being Muslims helps these Nepali migrant workers to secure better conditions than their non-Muslim fellow migrants from Nepal.

6

Agriculture and Employment

Landownership

In 2000, Dastider stated that 'the lack of proper statistics does not enable us to estimate land holdings of Muslims and their role in agriculture' (2000: 767). This still remains broadly the case; but a study undertaken in 2009 (Rana et al 2009) in a number of hill and *terai* districts provides a snapshot of the survey respondents as regards their involvement in agriculture and the importance of agriculture in everyday life (see Table 24). Firstly, as regards landownership, a significant proportion (39 families = 16.25 per cent) of Muslims in the study area were landless.

Table 24: Land Holdings by Muslims in the Terai and the Hills

Area of land	Hill families			Terai families			Grand Total
	District HQ	Rural	Total	District HQ	Rural	Total	
Landless	0	1	1	35	3	38	39
Less than 1 Bigha	13	11	24	29	37	66	90
1- 3 Bigha	26	26	52	12	28	40	92
3-6 Bigha	1	2	3	2	11	13	16
6-9 Bigha	0	0	0	0	1	1	1
9-12 Bigha	0	0	0	2	0	2	2
Total	40	40	80	80	80	160	240
Average	1.57 Bighas	1.66 Bighas	1.62 Bighas	0.86 Bighas	1.64 Bighas	1.25 Bighas	1.32 Bighas

Most of these, however, were in the *terai* and most were in the urban areas: in fact, the vast majority (89.7 per cent) of all landless were living in the *terai* district headquarters. By contrast, all of the families residing in the hill district headquarters, like those in the hills more generally, possessed some land. One local informant, interviewed as part of the IDEA/NEMAF project in the *terai* during the summer of 2015, suggested that 53 per cent of Muslims are landless; 22 per cent are farmers; 12 per cent work as agricultural labourers; 40 per cent are engaged in wage earning. The average land holding is around 9 *katthas* per family.

According to the 2009 survey, besides landless people, there were two categories of small landowners: 37.5 per cent of households had less than one *bigha*, and about the same proportion (38.3 per cent) had 1 to 3 *bighas*. These could be regarded as small landowners and producers, whose engagement in agriculture would be predominantly subsistence oriented. It is generally considered that 1.5 *bighas* is just about enough for subsistence purposes for the average family. So, the former would be unable to survive on the produce from their own land, and would also be labourers on the land of others, or bring in incomes from elsewhere; and many of the latter would also struggle to keep their heads above water from the produce of their own farm. Only 7.9 per cent of all households were larger landowners with more than three *bighas* of land and most of these (84 per cent were in the *terai*).

Muslim families in the 2009 study area possessed only a very little nonregistered land. Their average possession of nonregistered land was about three *katthas* (1 *kattha* = 338.6 sq metre). Only 30 families out of total 240 families (12.5 per cent) possessed nonregistered land and only one family had possessed more than three *bighas* of nonregistered land.

Forms of Tenancy

This study also attempted to analyse the tenancy situation of the land owned by the Muslims of study area. A small proportion (26 out of 201 12.9 per cent) of Muslim families in the study area had rented out their land to tenants on different conditions. As can be seen in Table 24, the total landholding of all Muslim families in study area was 240 *bighas*. Only a small proportion of this (just over 10 per cent) was rented out to other people for farming. The average area of land given to other people for farming was roughly similar in the all parts of the study area. On average, 0.16 *bighas of* land was given to share croppers (see Table 25).

Table 25: Land Rented Out

SN	Area of land	Hill Families			Terai Families			Grand Total
		District HQ	Rural	Total	District HQ	Rural	Total	
1.	Less than 1 bigha	5	2	7	2	1	3	10
2.	1- 3 bigha	2	3	5	3	6	9	14
3.	3-6 bigha	0	0	0	2	0	2	2
	Average	0.16	0.17	0.17	0.20	0.16	0.18	0.16

It was found that only a few Muslim landowners rented out land and the vast majority of these rented out 3 *bighas* or less. Roughly three quarters (73 per cent) of the land rented out was let under sharecropping arrangements; a quarter (24 per cent) was given to rent and one family let out its land under both arrangements (Table 26).

Table 26: Conditions of Tenancy

SN	Condition	Hill Families			Terai Families			Grand Total
		District HQ	Rural	Total	District HQ	Rural	Total	
1	Share cropping	4	4	8	7	4	11	19
2	Contract/Rent	2	1	3	0	3	3	6
3	Both	1	0	1	0	0	0	1

Sharecropping is often taken as an indication of the existence of 'semi-feudal' relations of production and farming systems, but when asked why they gave out land in this way, most respondents stated that the land was not enough to provide full support for them; they had to be engaged in other jobs and they could not spare time for farming. As a result, they were forced to give their land to others for farming. This seems to be a general phenomenon of increasing significance across Nepal, and is related both to the increasing attraction of employment outside farming and the increasing difficulty of maintaining even small farms as viable entities. It is not necessarily, therefore, an indication of the prevalence of 'semi-feudal' relations.

Having said that, it is also the case that there is a small number of large Muslim landowners in most districts of the *terai*. Our focus group in Bachhupurwa (Nepalgunj) at the Aisa Madaratul Banat English Medium Girls School suggested that 'only very few Muslims in Nepalgunj own larger plots of land 10, 12, 15 *bighas*; most Muslim landowners have only 3 or 4 *bighas*; and most Muslims do not own land'. Dastider refers to one locality where there were large landowners, as if this was a real exception: 'Koder Betwa village near Krishnanagar (Kapilvastu District) has the distinction of having only big Muslim landlords Abdul Waheb Khan is one of them, who now owns only 28 *bighas* (as permissible) under the Nepal Land Reform Act of 1964), while his ancestor was initially given 600 *bighas* of forest land at a very nominal price by the then Rana ruler at the end of the 19th century (narrated to the author by Abdul Waheb Khan)' (2000: 769).

There has clearly been significant change as regards landownership, class relations and forms of tenancy, and the nature of farming over the last few decades. It is, however, quite possibly the case that the general description provided by Dastider only 15 years ago still obtains: 'a caste based hierarchic social structure is inevitably linked with feudal land relations where low caste people usually constitute the lowest economic strata and have little or no influence on the society and economy of that country' (2000: 767). What is true, for sure, is that 'barring the few shopkeepers and small traders and even fewer landlords, the overall economic condition of the *terai* Muslims matches their inferior social status'.

Crop Production

Farmers remain highly dependent on cereal crops, notably rice, wheat and maize. Paddy was the main crop produced by the sample households in the 2009 study, with an average output of 8.9 quintals per year. Wheat was in second place, with an average production of 2.5 quintal per family. Maize and millet were other crops, with average output respectively of 2.3 quintal and 1.4 quintals per family. The production of pulses, oilseed and vegetables was 0.4 quintal, 0.3 quintal and 0.24 quintal on average per family. In broad terms this meant that the average household was producing 15.9 quintals of crops per year.

Table 27: Crop Production

Crops	Yearly production (quintals)						
	Hills			Terai			
	District HQ	Rural	Total	District HQ	Rural	Total	Grand Total
Paddy	419.8	301.8	721.6	459.6	949.6	1409.2	2130.8
Wheat	161.6	202.9	364.5	110.7	126.02	236.72	601.22
Maize	252.65	276.8	529.45	0.5	17.55	18.05	547.5
Millet	147.8	186	333.8	0	0	0	333.8
Pulses	39.9	10.2	50.1	11.7	26	37.7	87.8
Oilseed	26.1	31.3	57.4	2.9	11.5	14.4	71.8
Vegetables	5.55	13.7	19.25	0	37.8	37.8	57.05
Total	1053.4	1022.7	2076.1	585.4	1168.47	1753.87	3829.97
Average	26.33	25.56	25.95	7.31	14.60	10.96	15.95

However, as we have seen, the majority of farmers (75.8 per cent) were small and medium farmers with less than 3 *bighas* of land per family: 16.25 per cent were landless; and fewer than 8 per cent had land of more than 3 *bighas*. Consequently, the majority of Muslim families produced less than they needed; but even so, some felt or were obliged to rent or sharecrop their land in order to make a better income in other ways, outside farming. Average production was 25.95 quintals per family in the hills, but only 10.96 quintals per family in the *terai*. Paddy and wheat were the main crops in the terai, while the Muslims of the hills produced maize, wheat and millet along with the paddy.

An essentially qualitative field study was undertaken by Abdul Khan in 2010, in three wards of Mohammadpur VDC in Bardia District, selected for the preponderance of Muslims in the VDC (52 per cent of the population were identified as Muslim, 40 per cent as Hindu and 8 per cent as Christian). He used focus group discussions and other similar techniques, including semi-structured interviews. He does not state the gender of his interviewees but it would seem that all were adult males. Three quarters (73 per cent) of his respondents had been resident in the VDC for more than two generations, but the remainder (27 per cent) were more recent arrivals.

Of his 100 interviewees, 64 per cent were illiterate, 21 were literate, 11 per cent had been to primary school (to 5th grade) and 4 per cent to secondary school. Two thirds (67 per cent) were farmers and a quarter (25 per cent) were labourers, of the rest, 5 per cent were in 'service' (government employment) and 3 per cent were businessmen. Two thirds were landowners and one third owned no land. Of the former, 32 per cent owned 1-10 kattha, 64 per cent 1-4 *bighas* and 4.5 per cent (three people) owned five or more *bighas*.

Most farmers produced relatively small amounts of cereal (ie less than 40 quintals a year), but a few (about 10 per cent) produced a good deal more. Those producing the smallest amounts of cereal also produced lentils (*masoor* and *arhar dal*) and mustard.

Table 28: Production from Agriculture

Food Quantity	<10 quintals		11-20 quintals		21-40 quintals		41-60 quintals		> 60 Quintals		Total	
	n	%	n	%	N	%	N	%	n	%	N	%
Rice	10	24.6	14	21.5	17	26.5	10	15.4	8	12.3	65	100
Wheat	54	88.5	5	8.2	0	0	2	3.3	0	0	61	100
Maize	54	94.8	1	1.8	2	3.5	0	0	0	0	57	100
Masur Daal	63	98.4	0	0	1	1.6	0	0	0	0	64	100
Mustard	59	100	0	0	0	0	0	0	0	0	59	100
Rahar Daal	51	98.1	1	1.9	0	0	0	0	0	0	52	100

Source: Field Survey 2010

Food Security

Only 10 per cent of respondents said that the crop produced on their land was sufficient to cover their yearly requirements; the remaining 90 per cent admitted that their production was insufficient to meet their yearly food needs. In the hills, 13.25 per cent were self-sufficient while the remaining 86.75 per cent said that output was insufficient for yearly needs. In the *terai,* only 8.12 per cent responded positively to the question of food self-sufficiency and the remaining 92 per cent agreed that it was insufficient for their yearly needs.

The respondents were also asked about the months of sufficiency of the food produced by their land. Among the total families, 32.25 per cent said that it was sufficient for three months only; about same number of respondents (32.08 per cent) said that it was sufficient for them for 3 to 6 months; 18.33 per cent said that it was sufficient for 6 to 9 months; only 10.83 per cent felt that the crop produced from their land was sufficient for them as food for 6 to 12 months.

Table 29: Food Sufficiency

Sufficiency	Hill Families			Terai Families			Grand Total
	District HQ	Rural	Total	District HQ	Rural	Total	
Yes	7	4	11	4	9	13	24
No	33	36	69	76	71	147	216
Total	40	40	80	80	80	160	240

Diagrams 4 and 5 presented below indicate the number of months of self-sufficiency in food from the crop production of their own land in the hill and *terai* districts. This clearly indicates that there are more months of insufficiency of foods for the people in the *terai* than in the hills, and indicates the generally weaker economic status of Muslims in agriculture in the *terai*.

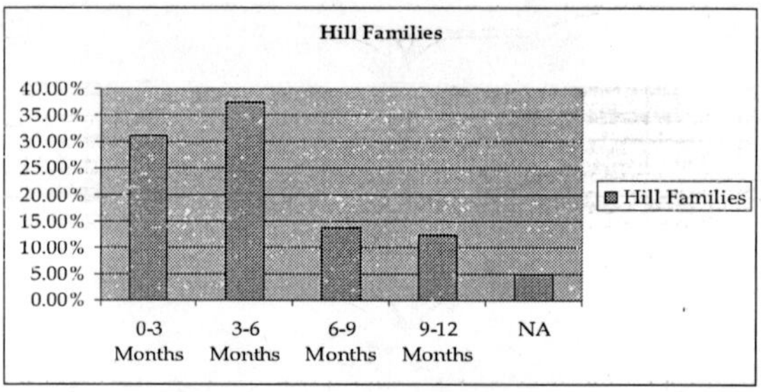

Diagram 4: Months of Food Sufficiency (Hills)

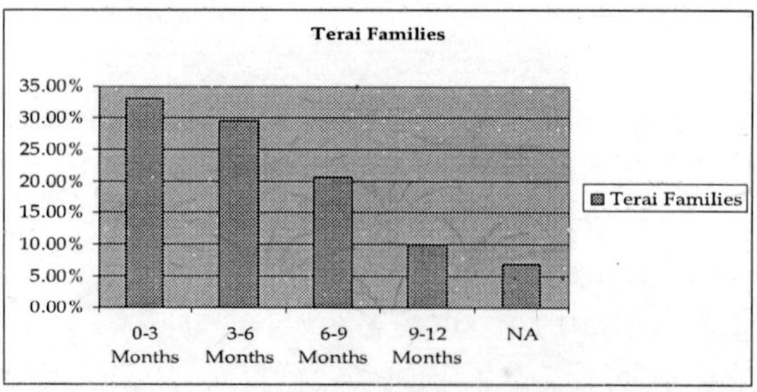

Diagram 5: Months of Food Sufficiency (Terai)

The respondents of hill and *terai* regions were also asked about their strategy to overcome the insufficiency of food. Among the 214 families who did not produce sufficient food from their land, 57.4 per cent said that they try to cover the deficit by buying food, 31.0 per cent said that they worked in return for payment in grain and the remaining 11.6 per cent said that they overcome it by labouring for cash. So, this is the other side of the sharecropping phenomenon: there are nearly three times as many who receive grain as payment for their labour as receive cash. More (40.8 per cent) in the rural *terai* relied on the sale of their labour, while more in the hills (86.95 per cent) relied on the purchase of food suggesting they had additional or alternative sources of income.

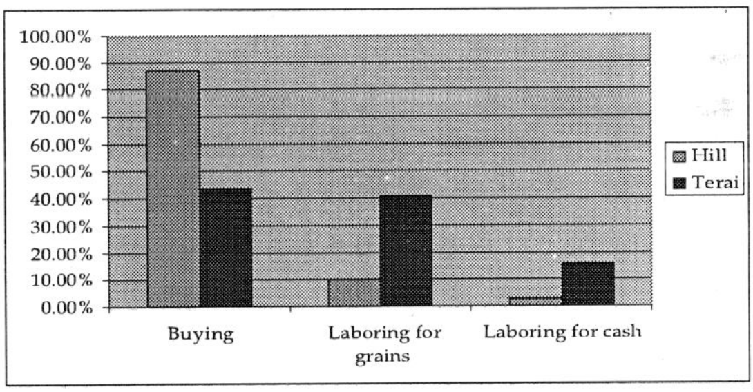

Diagram 6: Strategy to Overcome Food Insufficiency

These findings suggested that more than half of the Muslim families sought to buy the food to overcome its insufficiency from production, but about 40 per cent had to engage in labour to meet their requirement. The vast majority were employed in the private sector.

Employment

Perhaps surprisingly, in the study undertaken in 2009 (Rana et al), only 16 per cent of Muslim households had family members in full time regular employment. The proportion was lower in the hills than in the *terai:* in the *terai*, 20 per cent households had family members employed, whereas in the hills it was only 7.5 per cent of households. Again, perhaps surprisingly, more households in the rural areas had employed household members than those residing in the district headquarters: 23.45 per cent of households in the rural *terai* had family members in paid employment; in the rural hills it was 12.50 per cent of households. By contrast, the percentage in the district headquarters of the *terai* and hills were 16.25 per cent and 2.5 per cent only. Only 12 families out of 240 households (5 per cent) were engaged in government jobs; only 7.5 per cent had family members in private employment and 3.33 per cent) were engaged in job as freelancers

The jobs obtained in the private sector tend to be for the most part low level jobs: office assistant, helpers and *maulvis*; those in self-employment were tailors, mechanics, private clinic and health volunteers. Access to higher-ranking and higher paid employment was limited. Similarly, the public sector jobs accessible to Muslim families included: Auxiliary Health Worker, teacher, police force, health post, VDC secretary etc. All these jobs were related to the lower levels of the civil service. Access for Muslims to the public sector overall is highly constrained.

In 2004, UNDP (2004) reported that the Muslims had a very low share of civil servants and public sector employees compared with their share of the overall population.

Table 30: Share of Muslims Among Gazetted Third Class Officers of Nepal

Year	1990/91	1992/93	1994/95	1996/97	1998/99	2001/02
Percentage	0.9%	0.6%	0.4	0.2%	0.5%	0.5%

Source: UNDP, 2004.

This remains the case a decade later, despite the introduction of quotas for 'disadvantaged groups' after the implementation of the Interim Constitution of 2007, in which jobs in the civil service are 'reserved' for identified minorities for the appointment of different post of government. The relevant ordinance provided for the reservation of 45 per cent of posts in the civil service to women, *adivasi janajatis, madhesis, dalits,* people with disabilities and those living in backward regions, while filling vacant posts otherwise through free competition.

In recent years, public agitation, demonstrations and other forms of intense pressure caused the government to modify the Nijamati Service Ain, so that 45 per cent of 'reserved seats', to be fulfilled by open competition, were provided for women, *dalits, janajatis, madhesis,* handicapped people and members of so-called 'backward communities'. The Civil Service Bill issued on 3 August 2007 provided for a more nuanced reservation of jobs in the civil service. It made it mandatory to allocate 33 per cent of the 45 per cent of 'reserved' places to women, 27 per cent to *janajatis,* 22 per cent to *madhesis,* 9 per cent to *dalits,* 5 per cent to people with disabilities and 4 per cent to people from 'backward regions'. In somewhat the same way, the 12th amendment to the Nepal Police Regulation issued on 8 November 2008 utilised a formula for the distribution of reserved quotas on the basis of 32 per cent to *janajati* (indigenous minorities), 22 per cent to *madhesis*, 15 per cent to *dalits*, 20 per cent to women and 5 per cent to those from 'backward regions'.

However, these quotas and job 'reservation' measures did not identify 'Muslims' as a distinct category (UNDP, 2009). Muslims find it hard to secure employment on the administration or in the armed forces, and very few Muslims are in the police or governmental jobs. The number of secretaries and assistant secretaries in government ministries, of members of the Bar Association, the Human Rights Commission, the Public Service Commission, the National Planning Commission, the Akhtiyar Durupyog Anusandhan Aayog, and the Dalit Commission, remains zero from the Muslim community. This has diminished the self-confidence of the Muslim community as a whole and of individual members of the Muslim communities and has a negative impact on the ability of Muslims to acquire influence and status in the wider Nepalese community.

7

Education

In part, poor access to public sector employment and indeed the relatively poor economic and social status of Muslims generally is to an important degree the result of poor levels of education and lack of qualifications. Muslims in general are considered to be one of the most educationally disadvantaged groups, with an education attainment ratio of 0.238 compared with 0.421 for Nepal as a whole. This is despite the emphasis on the value of education given in the Quran and the Sunna the first word of the Quran is 'Read!').

Almost all of the key informants and focus groups interviewed during the field work in the *terai* undertaken during May-July 2015 by NEMAF (some of them *maulanas* or head teachers) referred to the problem of education as a major issue, and expressed the hope that in future girls as well as boys would receive a proper education. The data collected by this project, as well as earlier information available from secondary sources, indicates that this optimism is not at the present time substantiated by actual practice.

Schooling and Literacy

Before the 1940s, Muslims, like many other 'low caste' groups, were not allowed to attend the schools provided for other children. The majority therefore were confined to local Quranic schools or *madrasas.* While Sanskrit education has long been recognized, education at the *madrasas* has not, until recently. A Muslim primary school was opened in Kathmandu during the Rana period. It is still running as a *madrasa*, situated in the Nepali Jame Mosque, near Trichandra Campus, but the number of students is very limited in number, according Samima Siddika (1993), cited in Khan (n.d.). There may well have been other *madrasas* elsewhere in Nepal.

After 1960, there was no restriction on opening of *madrasas,* and the number of these grew rapidly. Even now, many Muslim parents prefer to send their children (and particularly girls) to *madrasas* rather than to state schools, for cultural-religious reasons and for reasons to do with the negative attitude towards girls' education generally. The *madrasa* system can in fact now take students up to the equivalent of SLC and even College level, but it lacks the appropriate institutional framework, for example for setting examinations; much of the curriculum is derived from Indian schools, and text books are lacking and teachers are scarce.

Nepal as a whole has made remarkable progress in education over recent decades. Literacy, for example, which was only 39.6 per cent on average in 1991, had grown by 14.1 per cent to reach 53.7 per cent by 2001. But the literacy rate for Muslims, which was 22.4 per cent in 1991 had only reached 34.7 per cent by 2001; this in comparison with a national rate in 2001 of 53.7 per cent, according to the 2001 census.

Table 31: Comparison of Population, Literacy and Poverty (2001)

Population groups	Population Percentage	Literacy percentage	Human Poverty index
All Nepal	100	53.70	0.325
Brahman Hill	12.91	74.90	0.441
Newar	5.49	71.22	0.447
Thakuri	1.48	63.39	n.a.
Chhetri	15.98	60.11	0.348
Gurung	2.49	59.79	0.299
Rai	2.83	58.19	0.299
Limbu	1.62	58.12	0.299
Tharu	6.58	47.12	0.313
Tamang	5.63	45.04	n.a.
Yadav	3.70	40.83	0.313
Muslims	**4.27**	**34.72**	**0.239**

Source: Census, 2001 UNDP, 1998.

The general literacy rate for Muslims was around 35 per cent in 2001 (2001 Census 2001, Parwez 2009) as compared with the national average of 52 per cent (54 per cent according to the CBS 2001), with Muslim men around 62 per cent, but Muslim women only 27 per cent, as compared with national figures of 81 per cent and 54.5 per cent respectively. Adult literacy was lower than general literacy for all Muslims (at 30.32), suggesting that things had improved over recent years, although mean years of schooling remained a miserable 1.60.

A survey carried out in the districts of Banke, Rautahat and Mahottari in the *terai*, in 2004 (by Parvez), suggested that only 23.4 per cent of household heads were literate 13.4 per cent from the *madrasas* and 10 per cent from state schools. Of these, the overwhelming majority (62 per cent) had been educated only up to primary level, if that. A more recent study in a reasonably well-off community in Kapilvastu (Khan p. 31), however, suggested a literacy rate of over 40 per cent, with males four times more like to be literate than females; but rates were much higher in those under 35 years of age than those over 35, again suggesting an improvement in recent years. In the Kapilvastu case, 156 out of 161 (97 per cent) who were literate had attended a *madrasa;* only five (all aged 10-14) had attended another kind of school and all of those had been to a private school, not the public mainstream primary which was in the village only five minutes' walk from most of the Muslim homes.

Women's literacy is particularly low in Muslim communities, with only 27 per cent of Muslim women literate as compared with, say, *dalits* as a whole (35 per cent), although *dalits* in the *terai* have a slightly less good literacy rate (17 per cent). Muslim men, by contrast were reported as 97 per cent literate, whatever that may mean (DHS data 2006).

Mozamille Haque remarks that the 2001 Demographic and Health Survey indicated that Muslims had one of the lowest rates of primary school enrolment of all groups with only 32 per cent attendance. Even *terai* dalits had higher rates at 37.5 per cent and all other groups were over 45 per cent with most over 70 per cent the average rate of primary school enrolment for Nepal as a whole was 73.5 per cent in 2001. As for secondary school attendance, Muslims were slightly better than *terai* dalits in 2001, 7.9 per cent as compared with 7.2 per cent but there is little in it. The average, for Nepal as a whole, was 30.9 per cent.

Generally, only 10 per cent of Muslim men were reported to have completed primary school, compared with a national average of 8 per cent but 42 per cent had no education, compared with the national average of 18 per cent. This is a striking figure. For Muslim women, the figure was 78 per cent with no education as compared with a national average of 53 per cent. Some 42 per cent of Muslim children of primary school age were enrolled in *madrasas* and only 18 per cent in mainstream schools, public and private; the remaining 40 per cent were not in school.

Some 42 per cent of Muslim children drop out of school during their primary education; and, according to the statistics of Human Development 2006, the percentage of Muslim students obtaining the secondary certificate was 25.5 per cent (for boys) and 12 per cent (for girls). The FRP study, *Access of Muslim Children to Education: Phase II, 2004* reported that only 18.1 per cent of all Muslim primary school age children (6-10 years) was studying in the mainstream schools, i.e. government and private schools; 41.22 per cent of this age group were studying in *madrasa;* and 41 per cent of total Muslim children belonging to this age group were out of any type of schooling. The main causes of the low participation of Muslim children in mainstream schools as reported by this study were: lack of religious education in the mainstream schools, lack of Islamic environment, language of instruction different from local language and lack of awareness of parents, co-education, absence of female teachers, *purdah* system, and conservative thinking of parents etc. (CERID, 2004). But it is also the case that, in addition to these specific constraints and barriers, government schools are few and far in between, and their paucity is particularly noticeable in localities where the Muslim communities are located.

According to Haque, 'the most critical and pitiable situation of Muslim is understood as backwardness in education. And the reason behind the illiteracy is poverty and lack of proper awareness towards the education though Islam has made it compulsory for every Muslim men and women to get education. Most of them are leading the life under extreme poverty and below the poverty line' (Haque 2009).

Ten years later, the 2011 Nepal Department of Health survey found that literacy rates among Muslims were exceptionally high, but that 37 per cent of Muslims had no education at all (Pandey et al 2013: 42). Among men aged 15-49, that is, males who were no longer of school going age, 37 per cent had no education at all had never been to school significantly higher than all other social groups with the exception of *terai/madhesi* dalits of whom 57 per cent had no education at all; 20 per cent had completed primary school; 37 per cent had completed secondary school; and 9 per cent had gone on to higher education. Interestingly, this last figure is significantly higher than for *dalits* as a whole (3 per cent) and even higher than for *janajatis* as a whole (8.8 per cent), but slightly lower than for *terai/madhesi janajatis* (10 per cent).

Islamic and 'Mainstream' Education

Islamic education and the teaching of the Arabic language are not offered in government schools. Muslims have their own education institutions in the form of the *madrasa* and *maktab*. Mosques and Quranic schools and colleges (*madrasas*) are places for meeting, for religious and educational purposes. The vast majority of *madrasas* serve local Muslim communities in rural and urban areas as primary schools. These are, in effect, local 'neighbourhood' and 'community' Quranic schools operating throughout the country, offering a basic education for Muslims. It is not known how many *madrasas* there are in Nepal, but the density of madrasas is greater in the *terai* than in the hills and even in Kathmandu, largely because of the concentration there of demand (because the vast majority of young Muslims live in the *terai*).

A FRP study entitled *Access of Muslim Children to Education: Phase II, 2004 reported* that 41 per cent of all primary school-age Muslim children (6-10 years) in the study area were studying in *madrasas*. Only 18 per cent of this age group was studying in mainstream (i.e. government and private) schools. Some 41 per cent of all Muslim children belonging to this age group were out of any type of schooling. The main causes of their low participation in mainstream schools, as reported by this study, were lack of religious education in the mainstream schools, lack of Islamic environment, language of instruction different from local language, lack of awareness of parents, co-education, absence of female teachers, traditional *purdah* system, conservative thinking of parents etc. (CERID, 2004).

Rana et al (2009) suggest that *madrasas* were only established in the 1940s (the first one being in 1941); it seems more likely, however, that they existed before this time but were not recognised as 'schools' by the government. According to Shamima (1993) and Bista (1996), Muslims were not in fact allowed to attend Nepalese state schools until the 1940s. The HLNEC (2055 BS) was the first commission to give explicit consideration to the education of 'backward communities', such as backward castes, language minorities, caste minorities (*dalits)* and economically backwards groups, and suggested special provision to increase their access to education.

A study in 2009 (Rana et al) carried out in a number of districts (Saptari, Rautahat, Kapilbastu, Banke and Tanahun) but which distinguished between the *terai* and the hill areas of Kapilvastu and Tanahun districts explored the issue of education among Muslims in some detail. It found that the Muslim communities and households in 'the hill areas' were generally better off than those in the *terai* and that they were investing considerably more in the education of their children and tended to favour the state schools rather than the *madrasas,* much more than in the *terai* areas. The significance of this for their children's literacy and level of school education was clear. To what extent this was a function of a more generally difference between hill and *terai* communities is not entirely clear.

The tendency for Muslim children generally, but particularly in the *terai*, to attend the *madrasa* rather than the public school indicates their unwillingness to send their children to state schools, but at the same time, studies have indicated that parents were not fully satisfied with the education provided by the Muslim institutions, which do not include 'modern' subjects in their curricula but concentrate on culture and religion. This encourages further marginalisation and separation of young Muslims from their peers and reduces their capacity to compete effectively later in life in the wider economy and society. It tends to increase social exclusion, which leads to the segregation of this community from national mainstream. Local Muslims are aware of this. According to one key informant in the Janakpur area interviewed during the fieldwork for the IDEA/NEMAF project, Tahir Nadaf,

> 'a number of *madrasas* are operating throughout Nepal, but they are unable to produce the skilled personnel and professionals that could match the country's demand. So, the products of such *madrasas* are unable to get any job in the government sectors and hence they are bound to do jobs in the *maqtab* (small local *madrasa*) or in the mosque as Imam (one who leads the prayer) or *muezzin* (one who calls the Muslims to prayer by reciting the *Azan*)[1].

The Nepal Government has not ever given attention to bringing Muslims in the mainstream. They do not support the *madrasas* which play a significant role in the uplifting of the Muslim community either financially or morally.

In Nepalgunj ward 8, it was estimated during fieldwork by NEMAF in 2015 that the population consisted of about 300 Muslims and 200 Hindus, of whom the majority were some 60 per cent female and 40 per cent male, as a result of foreign labour migration. The level of education was generally poor with only about a quarter of girls going to any school, but some 85 per cent of boys.

Gender and Access to Education

Only 3 per cent of Muslim men in 2009 had completed secondary school or gone beyond secondary school level, compared with 20 per cent on average in Nepal as a whole; for women the comparative figures were 2 per cent as compared with 9 per cent. In 2011, 9 per cent of Muslim men had completed higher education and 37 per cent had completed secondary school (Pandey et al 2013: 42). This suggests a significant change in terms of male education in recent years.

It remains the case, however, that Muslim boys and even more so Muslim girls tend to be poorly represented in 'public' state schools, and a larger number are to be found in specifically Muslim *madrasas,* where they learn Islam, mathematics, and other subjects according to a basic traditional Islamic curriculum, often derived from India and usually taught by a local cleric (or *imam).* There is an opportunity for a very small minority to pursue their Quranic studies at a higher level in College, in one of the main cities of the *terai* or in Kathmandu, or abroad.

The majority of girls only ever go to the *madrasa.* There has been progress in the education of girls, but still Muslim girls are discriminated against, both by their own parents and by the wider society, and have low enrolment levels at primary and even more so at secondary school and in higher education. According to one of the key informants interviewed as part of this project during 2015 in the Janakpur area, Vijay Kumar Dutta, education is not regarded as a priority for girls:

> 'The parents in the Muslim community still think that co-education is not suitable for their daughters as regards learning their culture, character and other knowledge. So, they mainly prefer a *madrasa* education for their daughters in comparison to what they prefer for their sons.

Also, he suggests that

> 'Due to the parents' working in the gulf countries, the trafficking of girls is increasing in the Muslim community. Most of the educated girls are being trafficking. It's creating a great problem in the muslim community nowadays. It is also disturbing the

> environment of society. Due to these types of problems, parents are hesitating to send their daughters to the schools and colleges as well as outside of the home. So, the number of girls getting education is limited, due to the aforesaid reasons. It's unbalancing the education system of the Janakpur area'.

A recent small investigation in Dhanusha district in 2014 found that in one ward, of some 300-400 Muslim households, no girls had received an education beyond the *madrasa*. A recent study in Kapilvastu found that 'there was no single Muslim girl found who was studying in the mainstream secondary school or college level, but there are a large number of girl students studying in religious schools in higher level' (Khan p. 28).

There is a particular problem relating to the education of girls and the lack of separate educational facilities for them, given the reluctance of many Muslims to allow their daughters and sisters to be taught within a co-educational system. One of the key informants from Nepalgunj, Ms Mahmuna Siddiqui (Vice President and Acting Chair of the Fatima Foundation Nepal, a board of member of Sankalp Kathmandu, working as a member in Amnesty International Nepal, and a member of the Trafficking Control Committee at the district level) remarked that, 'custom demands that Muslim girls and women must dress according to Islamic rules and regulations Islamic costumes are obligatory for Muslim girls and women. But most schools (whether public or private) do not permit Islamic dress, and so an unfriendly and hostile environment is created. Muslim parents, girl students, *maulanas*, the wider muslim community and even non-Muslim teachers, agree it was acknowledged that an unfriendly environment combined with an inappropriate curriculum and co-education (with boys) are the major causes for Muslim girls not to go to, or else to drop out of, mainstream schools'.

Ms Khan explained that 'in Islam there are 73 *firka* (sects) these include Wahabi (Deobandi), Sunni (Barelwi), Ahl-e-Hadis, Dawete Islamiya, etc. *Firka* means a group whose members follow the Islamic rules and regulations in one particular way. All firka are equally valid and accepted in Islam'. She had a generally positive outlook on the situation of Muslims in Nepal:

> 'In the old days Muslims people were little educated, as were other groups. But now the number of literate Muslims is significantly increasing. We can see that in every sector Muslim

> candidates are appointed. But even so, most Muslim families do not agree to send their daughter into school. Still they think 'what is the use of study?' Most Muslims are backwards in education in our country, Nepal. They believe more in running their own business than in taking a job through which they can fulfill their one basic need (meal).

Finally, in this regard, a report in *the Himalayan Times* of 9 November 2016 suggests that in Rautahat District at least there is a systematic move towards supporting education for girls:

> 'Breaking with tradition, the Muslim community in Rautahat District has started sending daughters who were earlier confined to household chores, to school. Haji Ikur, a local Muslim leader, said they had realised the value of education for women: 'Our sons and daughters should be equally educated. Everyone must avoid following irrational traditional beliefs that deprive their daughters of education', he said.

Many Muslim girls from Bara, Parsa, Mahottari and Sarlahi districts are studying in Jamiya Khadijatul Kubra School in Rajpur Pharhadawa VDC in Rautahat District, and have been doing so for the last five years. Muslim girls from many parts of India also study at this school, free of cost. School Principal Kari Sahubuddhin reported that around 400 girls were studying at the school, while 150 girls were residing in the school hostel. He said that Urdu was the major subject, while Nepali and other subjects were optional at the school. He added that the school was being operated with funds collected from the local community and young men working abroad. 'If the government helped us, we would be able to provide education to hundreds of other Muslim girls'.

Shekh Bakil, a guardian, said the Muslim community felt more comfortable sending their daughters to the Khadijatul Kubra School as it is the only one in Rajpur Pharhadawa that has a hostel for girl students. He added that guardians were also motivated to send their daughters to school their as the school had a 'girl-friendly' environment.'

Past Government Policy

As far as government policy towards *madrasas* is concerned, this source indicated that 'the major educational commissions in the field of education were the NNEPC, the ARNEC[2] (2019 B.S.) and NEPS (2028

BS), all of which focused on Nepali speaking sections of the population and discriminated against non-Nepali speaking people, in so far as Nepali was the medium of instruction'. Gaige (1975: 108) confirms that 'the first effort to organise a national education system began in 1954 with the appointment of a National Education Planning Commission, which produced its report on *Education in Nepal* in 1956. Exclusively from the third grade on, and as much as possible in the first two grades. No other languages should be taught, even optionally, in the primary school because few children will have need for them, they would hinder the teaching of Nepali' (NNEPC 1956: 104).

Publication of this report contributed to the development of what Gaige has called 'the language controversy' of 1956-58 and to protests throughout Nepal but particularly in the *terai,* where there was a strong movement to have Hindi in particular accepted as a language of instruction (Gaige 1975: 109-115). In October 1957, the Department of Education issued a Directive confirming that all schools would be required to adopt Nepali as the medium of instruction, but in January 1958, the Ministry of Education issued a second directive which gave up attempts to carry out this requirement at the primary school level and even conceded that in middle and high schools 'instruction shall be imparted through the medium of such language as decided by the Board of Directors for the time being and till another arrangement is made' (cited in Gaige 1975: 114).

In early 1961, a National Education Commission was set up to submit suggestions for a national system of education. Its report, produced that year, recommended that Nepali be the medium of instruction for all grades. The Report was followed by the Education Code later in the year and the Education Act in 1962. Article 5 of the Code put into law the Commission's recommendation regarding the medium of instruction and the Education Act confirmed it (Gaige 1975: 124). The National Education System Plan (NESP), first promulgated in 1971 and which was 'primarily aimed at counteracting the elitist bias of the inherited system of education by linking it more effectively to productive enterprises and egalitarian principle' included Urdu, Arabic as optional subjects in its curriculum. But no single teacher of these subjects has been appointed up until now

The constitution of 1990 adopted a multilingual policy in the field of primary education and in 1991, the World Bank's Basic and Primary School Education Project (BPEP), which was implemented in 40 districts as part of the Master Plan for Primary Education for 1991-2001, put Muslims, for the first time, into the category of special focus group. The National Education Commission was set up in 1992 and its report in

1998 emphasized the need for the education of disadvantaged or deprived groups. But its recommendations did not identify a special need for Muslims. Today the National Muslim Commission states, on its website, that

> 'Most of the Muslim community ... are severely backwards and under poverty line. In comparison, Muslim peoples are more uneducated and unemployed than other peoples. (The) mosque education system is not yet managed properly. It is necessary to promote and organize the historical mosque education. There is a requirement for effective programs for maintaining the national standard of mosque education and equivalency to the formal education and procedure. It is deemed necessary to keep the record of the religious-importance-bearing Masjid, Madarsa, Edgah, Majahar, Karbala, Kavresthan as well as (to) establish land rights and ownership'.

The example of one larger *madrasa* outside Kathmandu, given in the article by Mozammil Haque, is enough to understand the potential significance of *madrasas* for Muslim children Al-Jamiatul Islamia Al-Islah Madrasa (school) is situated in Sunsari District in the village of Bhutaha. Here, the level of education is up to Aalimiat (Intermediate). Several subjects are taught as Nepali, English, Science, Geography, Social Science, and Mathematics which are quite similar to the national curriculum. Students are able to sit for district level examinations and for SLC. Their performance is generally good. The total number of students in this school is around 2,200. Mozammil Haque, whose views on the status and condition of the Muslim community in Nepal was cited extensively at the beginning of this book, was a student of this *madrasa.*

But, he points out, 'the Government has failed to bring any programmes to aid such *madrasas,* whose financial condition remains always vulnerable, to flourish and there is a real need to introduce such programmes to uplift the situation and quality of education being given in such *madrasas* and to encourage Muslim children to attend school' (2009). There is still no overall strategy to integrate *madrasas* into the mainstream of primary education, although the Government of Nepal has declared it will register *madrasas* as primary school institutions, and they will be registered as 'free of cost'; but initiatives in some districts have been undertaken, largely as a result of foreign donor initiatives, on a piece meal basis.

The BPEP II (1999), for example, implemented an incentive scheme for Muslim children in three VDCs in Rupandehi district; but the money apparently did not reach the target group. UNICEF Nepal has appointed some mainstream subject teachers in *madrasas* in Kapilvastu district, and has provided stationery for some *madrasas*. The UNICEF programme is on a trial basis. Another initiative was the Banke UNESCO Club.

The Banke UNESCO Club

In Banke, the Banke UNESCO Club formed a network of *madrasas* in the Nepalgunj area in 2005, called the *'Madrasa Islamia Sangh'*. There followed a campaign for local *madrasas* to be registered at the district education office, but there were issues around the issue of whether *madrasas* were obliged to adopt the curriculum of Government of Nepal. The establishment of the Banke UNESCO Club was itself a struggle. In Chaitra 2063 (2005), the BUC, with the support of the Islami Sangh and local *maulanas*, managed to 'lock' the DEO office. Despite being charged with batons by the police, the *maulanas* were able to enter the office and lock the rooms. Some of the staff were locked inside the rooms, although the DEO senior officer and some other high ranking officials were outside.

In Jetha 2064 (2006), the Nepal Government officially recognized 70 madrasas in Nepalgunj. The BUC then started to work with the *madrasas*, with financial support from Save the Children International; the madrasas of Banke were among the first to be registered in Nepal. In 2006, 70 local *madrasas* were registered. The BUC supported those *madrasas*, helping them to join the mainstream as official recognised educational institutions. A monitoring committee was formed by DEO in 2011 August to monitor the registered *madrasas and* discovered that 10 out of them had no children, but were still receiving all the facilities from the DEO Office.

Today, 118 (or 119) *madrasas* out of a total of 154 in Banke are registered in the District Education Office and all of these have adopted the curriculum of Government of Nepal along with the Urdu and Arabic language teaching. BUC is currently implementing a programme (the Mainstreaming for Quality Education project) in 15-20 *madrasas* of Nepalgunj municipality and nine of the surrounding VDCs with the financial and technical support of Save the Children. There is a Per Child Fund (PCF) for 35 children and this holds Ns 68,000 annually for teachers. There is no overall support from Nepal Government to *madrasas* anywhere in the country because there is no coherent policy for the *madrasas*. Rahat Kota holds Rs 1,700 per month for *madrasas.* Normally teachers get paid NRs 2500/3000 per month.

In this project, BUC proposes to collaborate with different stakeholders using a participatory approach to mainstream *madrasas* into the formal education strategy for quality education. The stakeholders are: the District Education Office (DEO), the Madrasa Management Committee (MMC), Parent/Teachers Associations (PTA), teachers, *maulanas,* mothers' groups, children clubs, youth clubs, resource persons, the District Development Committee (DDC), the Village Education Committee (VEC) and other district and local level stakeholders. Community mobilization is the main strategy to sustain the impact of this project for a long duration by making madrasas accountable. BUC will mobilize mothers' groups in particular to increase the attendance rate of girls; the mobilization of children's clubs, youth clubs and mothers' groups during the enrolment campaign will help to increase the enrolment rate, including out-of-school Muslim children, into to the formal education system. Currently, the level of learning achievement is estimated at 58 per cent in grades 3 and 5; the 'survival rate' is 48 per cent according to the baseline data.

'Capacity Strengthening' will be another strategy of this project to provide quality education to Muslim children in child friendly learning environment. Under this project BUC will provide different training, orientation and other capacity strengthening activities to improve the quality of education in all *madrasas*. BUC will provide Literacy Boost Training and ATL training to the teachers and *maulanas,* SSA/SIP training to the MMC/PTA,teachers and *maulanas*, Social Audit Training to the teachers, *maulanas,* MMC and PTA for the capacity building of *madrasas. This* project will support primary level children by providing ATL training to the teachers and *maulanas* to create child friendly learning environment in *madrasas*. Teachers will develop instructional materials at local level using the local resources during their ATL mobile meeting after receiving ATL Training. This project will also enable school children to draw up their own code of conduct through their own participation. BUC will provide some renovation support for the class room management.

Also under this project, LWF orientation, gender sensitization training and School Health and Nutrition (SHN) training will be provided to the teachers and *maulanas* to strengthen their capacity. A SHN kit box will be provided after the SHN training in all project madrasas. The project will also conduct health check-up of the children and provide de-worm tablets every 6 months to improve the condition of health and nutrition among Muslim school children.

This project will also assist the different national and local level campaigns related to the education theme. BUC will mobilize the community people, teachers, *maulanas* and other stakeholders during campaigns like the National Enrolment Campaign, in coordination with different education related stakeholders. CEMIS orientation will be given to collect and update the educational information of the madrasas' catchment area. Out of school Muslim children identified through CEMIS will be enrolled in *madrasas* during enrolment campaigns.

College Level Education

If the number of Muslim students in state schools is small, and their performance poor, it is even less impressive in colleges and universities. The number of Muslims receiving higher education is negligible. There are at least four substantial mosques in Kathmandu and a number of central Qur'anic schools or *madrasas*, such as the Jankbur Daham School, which was set up in 1386 AH. This is a centre producing Da'awa activists. But most of those going on to college level education move into the public sector.

But the census of 2001 showed the number of Muslims obtaining first and post-graduate degrees as just over 4,000 (4,067). Their numbers were particularly low in professional courses like Medicine and Engineering. The cost of higher education is one problem, but lack of basic qualifications and hence the ability to successfully pass the highly competitive examinations and tests of admission to higher education programmes is another. This is reflected in the small number of Muslim professionals in the country. There are fewer than 200 Muslim doctors, and only a handful of these hold a postgraduate degree.

The *madrasas* evidently play a very significant role in the education sector and produce hundreds of educated Muslims who are able to work in a variety of capacities and economic positions within Nepal and outside thereby contributing to the development of the country as a whole. But these *madrasas* have their own problems, lacking state support and relying on donations collected from individuals, non-government organisations and external sources. Lack of recognition and the formal affiliation of the *madrasas* and their certificates within the Nepalese education system as a whole has created barriers to the effective integration of those attending the *madrasas* within the wider Nepalese economy and society, and reduced their potential contribution to its development and prospering.

One of the key informants from Nepalgunj in the 2015 study by NEMAF and IDEA, Ms Mahmuna Siddiqui (Vice President and Acting Chair of the Fatima Foundation Nepal, a Board of Member of Sankalp Kathmandu, working as a member in Amnesty International Nepal, and a member of the Trafficking Control Committee at the district level), remarked that an additional problem for continuation after primary school was that the government and universities have not recognized *madrasa* qualifications. Furthermore, there is no Muslim university in Nepal. That is why so many Muslims, and particularly girls, finish their studies at the primary level. Boys do least have the choice to study either at state or private school or *madrasas*, while by tradition most of the girls can only go to *madrasas.*

Recent Government Educational Policy

As regards recent educational policy, the Interim Constitution of 2006/7 provided clear guidelines for the policies to be adopted by the state which would formally ensure the right of Muslims to education and other social welfare benefits provided by the state. Article (17) regarding 'educational and cultural rights' ensures the right to basic education in the mother tongue. It also ensures that every citizen should have the right to free education up to secondary level. It also ensures that each community residing in Nepal should have the right to preserve and promote its language, script, culture, cultural civility and heritage.

The provision made in the Education Act (7th Amendment) for the use of mother tongue in primary classes can be considered as a positive step towards addressing the instructional needs of indigenous and linguistic minority children across the country. The Interim Plan (July 2007 to July 2010) has also developed policies and programs to address the directives of the Interim Constitution with a view to ensuring the 'social inclusion' of marginalized groups. It has prepared policies to provide education in the mother tongue, has adopted a three language policy and has also recommended the development of a system for the accreditation of the traditional education provided by Gurukuls, Madrasas, Ashrams and Gumbas to ensure equivalence, as regards levels of achievement, to what is provided by regular formal education.

In line with the three-year interim plan, the School Sector Reform (SSR) Core Document (2008) developed different plans and policies to address the educational and cultural needs of marginalized groups. In the chapter on the socio-cultural context of this program, it has stressed that cultural diversity is one of the Nepal's national treasures. It has admitted that historically, some communities were not equally benefited by development interventions, mainly because of their limited access to educational opportunities. A number of minority groups and ethnic communities had faced 'marginalization'. Disadvantaged groups (such as women, *dalits, madhesis*, people with disabilities and ethnic minorities - *janajati)* had low levels of participation in schooling. This document admitted that raising the participation of these groups was a key challenge for the government.

In 2007 (circular issued 30 Kartik 2063), the Ministry of Education (MoES) launched a programme to register *madrasas* officially with the local authorities as primary schools, as requested, as long as their registered student numbers and physical facilities satisfied clause 77 of Education Rule 2059, and information regarding their funding sources were provided. If the number of students was too low, they would be allowed to conduct alternative schooling according clause 52 of Education Rule 2059. The *madrasas* officially registered as schools would be eligible to conduct the examination for Grade 5 themselves, and to organise district level examinations through the District Education Office (DEO) or Resource Centres.

For 'alternative schooling', the DEO is supposed to arrange for grade-wise examinations through a registered local school, based on the learning achievements of each grade. The DEO is supposed to provide the pass/fail certificate based on the examination taken by that school. (Circular of DoE dated 30 Kartik 2063). According to the Department of Education, registered *madrasas* were to be provided with a sum of Rs. 12,000 per fifty students as a SIP fund. This fund could be spent for educational materials. It was also planned to provide teachers for these Madrasas under Rahat quota. The most recent information (2012) suggests that the government now allocated Rs 26,000 ($300) to each registered *madrasa to* cover teachers' salaries.

This initiative received a generally positive reaction from the Muslim community – although some Muslim leaders criticised the policy as discriminatory, citing the difficulty of the registration process and general lack of resources from government but many *madrasas* all-over the country were registered as primary schools, based on the above-mentioned provisions. According to *Flash I Report (2064*), by late 2007, there were altogether 214 registered *madrasas* in Nepal, now running as primary schools (DOE, 2007). According to more recent information provided by the Department of Education (and reported in the 2012 *International Religious Freedom Report on Nepal*) approximately 835 madrasas are now registered with district education offices. The Department of Education prepares curricula for the registered *madrasas*.

The registration of *madrasas* has raised a number of issues. According to CERID (2008), although parents and students were generally enthusiastic, Maulvis had specific concerns about the possible erosion of the cultural and religious environment of *madrasas*. They claimed that *madrasas* are above all Islamic institutions, established with the purpose of providing cultural education to Muslims. Formal registration by the state, and particularly the responsibility for the curriculum held by the Department of Education, might adulterate their cultural and religious significance, leading to a need to 'top up' the official curriculum with religious and other material considered of importance by the teachers.

It was in fact found that many *madrasas* were now teaching both the full Islamic and mainstream courses, which overloaded both teachers and students. Those responsible were very confused as to how to maintain a proper balance of their courses. They were looking for proper guidance from MOES (CERID, 2008). According to CERID (2008), the great challenge was related to the assurance of quality education: proper curricula, financial constraints, lack of physical infrastructure, skilled teachers etc. were considered the major hindrances to quality education.

Educational Outcomes

According to the 2001 census, the average literacy rate of Muslims was about 35 per cent. Ten years later, it was nearer 45 per cent. Male literacy is around 50 per cent but female literacy remains extremely low at about 38 per cent. Of those who are literate, somewhat less than 30 per cent (28.1) are *madrasa* literate; only 15.9 per cent of adults are *madrasa* literate. The literacy rate among *madrasa* literate males is 28.8 per cent and females 27.4 per cent. The percentage of those literate from attending mainstream schools is only 15.6 per cent.

A study undertaken in 2009 (by Rana et al) provides a snapshot five years ago of Muslim education in selected districts, mainly in the *terai* but also in the hills.

Table 32: Educational Status of Survey Respondents

Level of education	Hill			Terai			Total		
	M	F	T	M	F	T	M	F	T
Illiterate	2	1	3	51	4	55	53	5	58
Only literate	5	0	5	35	1	36	40	1	41
Primary	28	0	28	7	0	7	35	0	35
Lower secondary	17	0	17	8	1	9	25	1	26
Secondary	20	0	20	11	0	11	31	0	31
Higher	4	0	4	8	0	8	12	0	12
Islamic	3	0	3	33	1	34	36	1	37
Total	79	1	80	153	7	160	232	8	240

Among those surveyed, nearly a quarter (24.2 per cent) were illiterate and 17.1 per cent barely literate; 14.6 per cent had received education up to primary level, 10.8 per cent were educated up to lower secondary and 12.9 per cent up to secondary level. Only 5 per cent were educated up to higher level.

According to Tahir Nadaf, a political leader who belongs to Nepali Congress from Dhanusha district, a well-known businessman in Janakpur and a reputed person in his local community as well as in Janakpur city, 'the educational condition is very poor in our community even in comparison to the Dalits. According to the census of 2058, educated Muslims amounted to only 27 per cent. People go to the Gulf countries to earn their living but their children misuse the money sent to them in the name of study and other expenditure. If we consider those appearing in the SLC students' list we find only 3 per cent of Muslim students - which shows the real educational condition of our community' (interviewed in Janakpur in 2015).

Tahir Nadaf also commented that the *madrasas* have played a very significant role in the education sector and produced hundreds of Muslim intellectuals each year who are now working in several sectors within the nation and outside the nation, contributing to the economic development of the nation in spite of it lacking proper care. But these *madrasas* have their own problems, lacking assistance and means and exhibiting dependence upon funds collected from donations by individuals, organizations and the nation as a whole this is also a great problem. Lack of reorganization and affiliation of the *madrasa* and its certificates have created a strong bar for the products of the *madrasas* to work and serve the nation, being involved in the mainstream of the nation. There is also a woeful lack of separate educational facilities for females, as Muslim women feel a hesitation to be involved in the co-education system'.

It is not just a lack of state support, however; there is also a social and cultural problem within Muslim communities themselves.

> 'In addition to the state's disregard, many Muslim women are uneducated and unaware of the rights provided them by the Holy Quran. Since the Quran has traditionally only been available in Arabic or Urdu, its meaning can be interpreted and expressed only by the *maulana*, which leads to some communities being exposed to a very narrow view of the teachings. A large number of *maulanas* many of whom come from India, where societal norms are even more conservative than in Nepal have a limited education.
>
> Nepali society is naturally patriarchic, with men having authority and control over women. Women are rarely assertive. The common interpretation of Islam in Nepal is that the male leads, that the husband "owns" the wife, and that a father or husband has the right to treat a woman as he sees fit. Traditional norms and the religious leaders that regulate Muslim society in Nepal create an environment in which women are extremely dependent upon men for economic support. Employment and educational opportunities for Muslim women, which are often already severely limited by the impoverished conditions in which many live, are further restricted by community traditions'.

According to Tahir, the educational status of Nepali Muslims is the most important reason behind their backwardness.

Of those surveyed in the 2009 survey mentioned above, only 15.4 per cent had been educated in Islamic schools. Although only a few respondents were female, their educational status indicated the low educational status of women than male in Muslim community; of the eight female respondents, five were illiterate, one barely literate and one educated in the Islamic stream. Only one was educated up to lower secondary level. The meagre number of female respondents was not enough to justify the conclusion that their educational status is lower than that of males, but the data are probably indicative.

Significantly, there was a great difference in the educational status of respondents from the hill and from the *terai* districts. Among the respondents of the former, only 3 out of 80 (3.75 per cent were illiterate, whereas, among the respondents from the *terai*, 34.4 per cent were illiterate. In the hills, only 3.75 per cent of respondents were educated in *madrasas, whereas* in the *terai*, the figure was 15.4 per cent. Another source suggests that

> 41.2 per cent of Muslim children of primary school age are studying in *madrasas*
>
> 39.8 per cent of the boys and 42.6 per cent of the girls of primary school age actually enrolled at school are studying in *madrasas*
>
> 18.1 per cent of primary school age Muslim children are studying in mainstream schools
>
> 42 per cent of school age Muslim children are out of school
>
> Out of school children are mainly engaged in basic labouring work.

Training and Skills Acquisition

Access to employment and income generating opportunities in the private sector are more directly related to skills, including those acquired through the passing on of 'traditional' skills, informal and more formal apprenticeships, and formal training and education.

Formal education, however, is not the only way in which people, young and older, may obtain qualifications and skills, although a basic education is perhaps a prerequisite for many better or higher paid jobs. Training and informal skills acquisition can also provide a basis for employment and income generation. A skilled worker has generally better employment opportunities and opportunities for income generation than someone without skills.

A study undertaken in 2009 (Rana et al 2009) looked, among other things, at skills possessed by Muslims in a sample survey in selected hill and *terai* districts. This suggested that relatively few of those surveyed had what were identified as specific skills) although definitions of what is a skill may vary considerably). In this study, 76 out of a total of 240 families (32 per cent had a family member with a particular skill. However, in the *terai* the proportion was greater (42 per cent); of these, the families residing in the district headquarters were more skilful (67.5 per cent of families had a skilled family member); in the hill areas, only 11 per cent of families had a skilled member.

Table 33: Possession of Skill by a Member of the Family

Responses	Hill Families			Terai Families			Grand Total
	District HQ	Rural	Total	District HQ	Rural	Total	
Yes	9	0	9	54	13	67	76
No	31	40	71	26	67	93	164
Total	40	40	80	80	80	160	240

Table 34: Learning a Skill

Responses	Hill Families			Terai Families			Grand Total
	District HQ	Rural	Total	District HQ	Rural	Total	
Yes	7	0	7	23	7	30	37
No	33	40	73	57	73	130	203
Total	40	40	80	80	80	160	240

Sewing was the skill most widely possessed by Muslim families: 41 per cent of families had one member at least who was skilful at sewing; 15 per cent were mechanics and 13 per cent were masons. Embroidery, painting and barbering were other skills possessed by Muslims in the study area. It was also found that some members of Muslim family were learning skills. The largest number of Muslims currently learning a skill was among those living in the district headquarters in the *terai*; among the families of this area, 29 per cent of families had members who were learning a skill. Some members of hill district headquarters of hill region and rural areas of *terai* were learning skills. No member of any Muslim family residing in the hill rural areas was learning a skill.

According to the respondents, the main purpose for learning a skill was related to securing employment or starting their own business; very few were doing so for purely personal interest. Most were learning sewing; other skills being learnt included painting, embroidery, mechanics, masonry.

8

Gender & Women

General Status of Muslim Women

If the status of the Muslim community as a whole, and of the different Muslim communities, requires particular attention, it is also the case that Muslim women face distinctive problems of their own. They have a distinct identity and status in terms of religion, ethnicity, culture and ritual and have historically faced multiple forms of discrimination: first, as women; second, as Muslims; and third, as Muslim women. Poor, elderly and/or disabled women and girls face even more constraints. Much of this emanates from within the Muslim communities, families and households, although the failure of the state to change the conservative, patriarchal attitudes and behaviour that prevail inside Muslim communities, families and households, is also a matter of concern.

Gender inequality pervades all areas of economic, social, cultural, political and personal life. Discrimination against girls starts before birth and has a significant effect on morbidity and mortality in infancy, childhood, adolescence and early adult-hood, with 'missing girls' in childhood and high levels of maternal death in childbirth. Restrictions on education, early marriage, the dowry system, limited involvement in household decision-making, purdah, easy divorce by husbands, the unequal inheritance system, and other practices contribute to subordination of Muslim girls and women through most of their lives. Formal rights available in theory to Muslim girls and women are rarely exercised because of local community and family constraints, customs and traditions. Some poor Muslim women in the *terai* work as agricultural labourers, but mostly in their own villages, and generally they are confined to the house and its immediate surroundings, if it has a courtyard and to largely domestic economic activities.

If discrimination begins even before birth, then limited access to education may be the single most debilitating restriction. Literacy rates among Muslim girls and women are among the lowest in Nepal; studies have also revealed very low rates of even primary school attendance for girls, with high dropout rates as they age. There is very little access to reproductive health care and education, due to cultural barriers and constraints. An analysis of the 2006 Demographic and Health Survey shows only 17 per cent of Muslim women had knowledge of family planning, the lowest among all groups in Nepal.

There is widespread lack of knowledge among Muslim about their legal rights, due to lack of education, and lack of co-operation regarding, if not active withholding of, information and documents relating to citizenship, birth and marriage certificates, death certificates of their husbands, on the part of male relatives and wider family groups. There is little or no support for women seeking to exercise their rights. Activism is discouraged. Even so, on occasion, Muslim women have been prepared to act. *AsiaNews.it* reported on 12 January 2008 an incident in which Muslim women in Nepalgunj had taken to the streets the previous November to protest against 'talak' or Islamic divorce'. The article by Kalpit Parajuli stated that

'Hundreds of divorced Muslim women demand the same rights as men during two days of protest against 'talak'. Islamic divorce allows husbands to repudiate their wives, throw them out of the house without any support. In Nepalagunj, 236 (mostly rural Muslim women) have been through this experience. Destitute, they are forced to go back to their original family; some are even forced into prostitution'.

She cited *Kathmandu (Asia News)* which apparently had reported that 'hundreds of Muslim women along with their supporters took to the streets of Nepalgunj, a town in western Nepal, to protest against '*talak*' or Islamic divorce. The demonstrators, including 465 divorced Muslim women, human rights activists and about 100 Muslim men, marched on 26 and 27 November 2007 to demand immediate compensation from the women's former husbands as well as equal division of assets after divorce.

'Many Muslim women said that after divorce they were left with no support. Some said that they had to go back to their original families or find shelter at human rights organisations. "Muslim men release (*talak*) their wives from the marriage, i.e. divorce them, but then no one thinks about them," said Sima Khan, president of the Muslim Awareness Federation, one of the protest groups that organised the demonstration. "Women don't get any of their husbands' assets, or any support. This has increased the incidence of divorce in the Muslim community. We must achieve equal rights for these women," she added.

"My husband divorced me five years ago. Now all my children are with him and I live with my parents," said Roni Ansari, 39, who marched in the front of the demonstration. "I don't have anything except a small job for my basic needs. Where will I be if my parents did not allow me to stay with them in my old age?" Homelessness is in fact a problem for many Muslim women. Some are driven out of their parents' home once the latter pass away.

"I escaped when my husband and mother-in-law tried to burn me with kerosene," said Shano Khan, 17, who divorced three months ago. "Now I am staying with my parents who are not that happy for me to live with them. I don't have a job. What can I do?" "Many women go hungry or get into prostitution to make ends meet after divorce," explains Nitu Haluwai, a Muslim human rights activist. "The existing divorce law does not respect our religious precepts," said Nazrul Hassen, president of Nepal's Muslim National Federation. "We have a different system and therefore do not consider it [the national law] as binding on us."

The situation is due to the fact that Nepali Muslims do not adhere to the country's divorce law which requires both parties' consent. Instead, under *talak* if a woman wants to divorce she must ask for her husband's permission, and then pay him a certain sum. However, Muslim leader Maulana Abdul Jabbar said that *talak*, which is based on the Qur'an, has been badly interpreted over the years. "Divorce proceedings ought to take place in accordance with the law but without transgressing religious values," he said'.

There are also several Muslim women's groups and NGOs, including the Fatima Foundation, which are active in support of Muslim women in Nepal (see Appendix 1 for a list of those we have been able to identify).

Muslim women's rights activist and President of the Nepal Muslim Women's Society, Kausar Shah, says that, 'in Islam, there is no discrimination between son and daughter or men and women; but in practice, there is.

Women are not allowed to go outside'. According to Shah, there are really positive provisions in the Qur'an relating to Muslim daughters/ women. It says that both sons and daughters should be given education or trained equally; if that is not done, it is a sin; the Qur'an vehemently opposes dowry. Despite this, educational inequality and 'the dowry' persist in practice. 'In order to empower Muslim women', she says, 'the new Constitution must recognize difference and diversity, and while dealing with women, the Constitution, its laws, policies and programmes and provisions should clearly outline and support the different needs of Muslim women and women from other disadvantaged groups'.

It is not just a matter for the Muslim community itself, either. 'As there is no recognition of the Muslim community as such and limited representation of Muslims in any sector, namely, bureaucracy, health, employment, politics, etc., you can imagine the status of Muslim women', says Shesh Chandtara, Chair of the National Women's Commission. 'There are only a handful of educated Muslim men, while there are hardly any Muslim women. Thus, Muslim women lag far behind'. She, however, adds that, "slowly, there have been positive changes in recent days. Muslim daughters are going to school and attending programs. Even so, Muslim women have been deprived of education and also from going out of home due to the misinterpretation of the religious books by their religious leaders'.

Notes on The Status of Muslim Women (from a Presentation by Mohna Ansari)

- Very little access to participation in political and civil life for Muslim women;
- Lack of encouragement, non-conducive environment, and negligence by the political parties block Muslim women's access to political participation
- Very weak social status, lack of empowerment and lack of safety for Muslim women
- Social/cultural norms of patriarchal Muslim society, lack of education, employment and empowerment programs and absence of safety net/welfare scheme/help mechanism make the Muslim women a highly vulnerable population

Household Expenditure and Household Decision-Making

The study undertaken in 2009 (Rana) to explore the characteristics of Muslim communities in selected hill and *terai* districts, also considered decision-making within households and families, as part of its consideration of gender relations. Decision-making in regard to seven domestic matters were selected: purchase of valuable assets, child education, participation in social activities, selling household produce, agricultural activities, buying essential commodities and cultivation. It was found that male members of the family dominated in all family related matters.

Males dominated particularly in those decisions related to buying valuable assets, participation in social activities, buying essential commodities, and cultivation. In these areas, male members of the family took 83 per cent, 82 per cent, 73 per cent and 72 per cent of decisions respectively. Females had a better share in decision-making regarding the sale of household produce, buying essential commodities, and agricultural activities in which female's share in decision-making was 17.5 per cent, 15 per cent and 15 per cent respectively. However, all of these areas were also male-dominated. Decisions related to the children's education were the main area in which both men and women participated; 24 per cent of decisions of this area were taken by both males and females, although again men dominated the process of decision-making.

By comparing the hill and *terai* data, it was found that there was not much difference in the proportion of decisions related to buying valuable assets, participation in social activities and children's education as far as men were concerned, but women in the *terai* lagged behind in these areas in comparison to females of hills: with 5 per cent 7.5 per cent and 14 per cent of decisions involving hill women but only 2 per cent, 1 per cent and 2.5 per cent of women in the *terai* involved. Women in the hills enjoyed greater freedom in many areas of decision making such as selling household produce, agricultural activities, buying essential commodities and cultivation: 40 per cent, 40 per cent, 42 per cent and 39 per cent of women were engaged in decision making in these areas respectively.

Women in the *terai* enjoyed a very limited role in household decision-making. The area in which they shared the largest share of decision-making was that of selling household produce, but even here only 6 per cent of decision making involved women. In other areas, less than 5 per cent were engaged in the processes of decision-making. The only area in which women in the terai had a significant share in decision-making was with regard to their children's education: 29 per cent of decisions related to children's education were taken by both male and female. In conclusion, it was found that male members of the family take most of the crucial decisions in domestic matters.

Even as regards such crucial decisions as contraception, family size, access to midwifery and other health services, household expenditure (on food, education of children, etc.), Muslim women generally deferred to men. This is the product of unequal gender relations and has profound implications for family size and composition, infant and maternal mortality, child mortality, sex ratios, education patterns and future gender relations.

Table 35: Decision Making in Family Matters

Areas of Decisions	Decision in percentage								
	Hills			Terai			Grand Total		
	M	F	B	M	F	B	M	F	B
Buying valuable assets	83.75	5.00	11.25	83.13	1.88	15.00	83.33	2.92	13.75
Child education	71.25	13.75	15.00	68.75	2.50	28.75	69.58	6.25	24.17
Participation in the social activities	80.00	7.50	12.50	83.13	1.25	15.63	82.08	3.33	14.58
Selling household product	52.50	40.00	7.50	75.00	6.25	18.75	67.50	17.50	15.00
Agricultural activities	37.50	40.00	22.50	83.75	3.13	13.13	68.33	15.42	16.25
Buying essential commodities	47.50	42.50	10.00	85.63	1.88	12.50	72.92	15.42	11.67
Cultivation	47.50	38.75	13.75	83.75	2.50	13.75	71.67	14.58	13.75

Very similar patterns were found by Khan as regards women's role in household decision making. Even among Muslim women who earned cash, a significant proportion (15.5 per cent) reported that it was mainly their husbands who made decisions about how cash earnings were to be used. The majority (52 per cent) said it was jointly decided, but only a quarter (25 per cent) said that the decisions were mainly theirs. As regards decision making on other matters, only 31 per cent said that they participated fully in all four of the main areas of decision making own health care, major household purchases, daily purchases and visits to her family or relatives. Only 48 per cent usually made decisions about the purchase of everyday items on their own or jointly with their husbands; only 43 per cent were involved in decisions about visiting her family or relatives; only 41 per cent were involved in major household purchases, and a staggeringly low proportion, (36 per cent) were involved in making decisions about their own health care. Of the groups living in the *terai*, Muslim women had the highest percentage (47 per cent) reporting no participation in any of the four areas of decision-making. Khan reports that there 'even food items are decided by male members' (Khan p. 29).

Upadhyay reports that his field survey showed that over 12 per cent of women in Miya Gaon, Hukka in Tanahun District, in the western hills, had no role at all in household decision making and 17 per cent had only 'a partial role'. Just over half (55 per cent) had what he calls 'an advisory role' and only 16 per cent had a determining role. He adds that 'the vital decisions related to money matters and all crucial issues are dealt with by the senior males of the family' (2014: 97). He links this with the division of labour, in which the women's role is generally to undertake the domestic labour, and argues that the stricter the gender division of labour the less role there is for the women in decision making.

As regards parental responsibility towards children (0-19 yrs.), a study undertaken in 2010 in Bardiya District in the western *terai* found that two thirds of those interviewed (a sample of 100 in all) said that parents should ensure their children went to school, 19 per cent said that they had the responsibility of seeing them married and 11 per cent said they should help them go abroad to earn better.

Table 36: Parental Responsibility

Particulars	Frequency n=100)	Percentage (%)
Responsibility of parents towards 1-19 yrs children		
Send to foreign country	11	11
Send for education in school	66	66
Engage them in wedlock	19	19
Don't know	4	4

To raise the family status, nearly 70 per cent said that both sons and daughter should be educated and 19 per cent said female education should be given priority; only 12 per cent gave priority to the son.

'Most Women Stay at Home'

Some poor Muslim women in the *terai* work as agricultural labourers, but mostly in their own villages, but generally they are confined to the house and its immediate surroundings, if it has a courtyard and to largely domestic economic activities. The analysis of occupation pattern of Muslim females (in the Rana 2009 study) indicated that more than half of them (51.2 per cent) were engaged in household chores and over a fifth (22.6 per cent) did not mention their occupation and many of these were students or not employed. About a quarter (26.2 per cent) was engaged in occupations which directly generated income: 15.2 per cent in agriculture and 9.2 per cent in trade; the other occupations included labouring, service and tailoring (1.0 per cent, 0.7 per cent and 0.14 per cent respectively).

The analysis of occupations of males and females revealed that agriculture and trade were the main sources of income. Most women, however, remained within the home; and only a quarter were engaged in income generation. A very small number of Muslims altogether were engaged in service, in which very few females were involved. Foreign employment was another source of income but only about 5 per cent of Muslim males were engaged in this activity; no female was reported to be engaged in foreign employment.

The comparative analysis of occupation patterns of females of the hill and *terai* regions also revealed differences between the regions: females in the *terai* were more housebound than those who live in the hills.

The above diagram shows a great difference in the number of Muslim females in relation to their engagement in household chores. More Muslim females residing in the *terai* were engaged in household chores than in the hills: 58.3 per cent as compared with 36.7 per cent. More Muslim females were engaged in agriculture in the *terai* than in the hills; but the involvement of Muslim females in the hills in income generating was greater than of the females of the *terai* and more hill females were engaged in trade than in the *terai.*

This study also attempted to analyse comparative situation of occupations of Muslims females in districts headquarters and remote VDCs of the *terai region*. The findings are presented below:

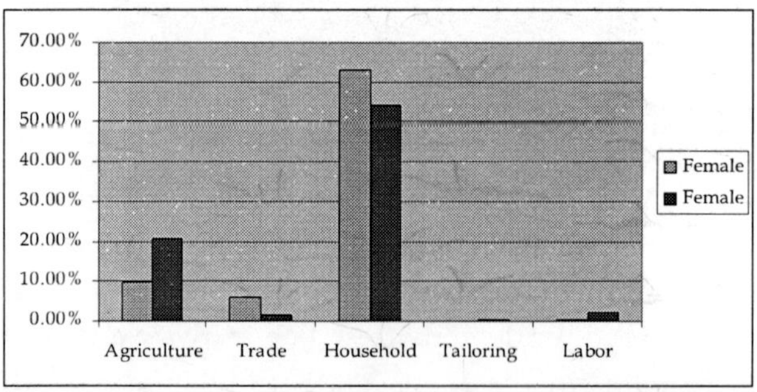

Diagram 7: Occupations of Muslim Females in District Headquarters and Remote Terai VDCs

Most Muslim females, whether in district headquarters or rural areas of the *terai,* were housebound and involved in household chores: more than 60 per cent of Muslim females in district headquarters and more than 50 per cent in rural areas. Only a few women in both town and country were engaged in income generating occupations; of these, a far larger percentage of females residing in district headquarters were engaged in trade and more females residing in rural areas were engaged in agriculture.

Upadhyay's study of a hill village in Tanahun District in the western hills, however, suggests that in this case, the gender division of labour was relatively strict and women worked for longer hours than men at different tasks (cooking food, gathering wood, agricultural work, child rearing for women and wage labouring and farming for men and more 'public activities'). Even if women are also involved in agriculture and labouring, their household and domestic duties take priority and appear to be defining of the gender relationship (2014: 97-98).

Sex, Marriage, Divorce and Inheritance

According to one of our key informants in Janakpur, *nikah (marriage)* is *sunnat* (proper, sacred) for all Muslims. Islam does not accept sexual and other relation between boys and girls without *nikah*. Only after *nikah are* a husband and wife *paak* (pure) for a physical relation that is *halal. Nikah mehar* is most important for bride in marriage. Without offering *mehar* (literally a kindness, dowry) as indicated in the *nikah* to his bride, a groom should not touch his wife. But he can request that it be on the basis of a promise, if he does not have the necessary amount; he can touch her when the permission is granted with an understanding of future 'payment'. In Islam, *nikah* is a contract and *mehar* is the name of that 'right' which a wife gets from her husband.

The preference for marriage in Muslim communities is between cousins, although in reality this is not always possible. There is some evidence to suggest that in some areas, particularly in the hills where the total Muslim population is any one area may be extremely limited, that there are problems about finding suitable marriage partners. Sometimes hill Muslims marry *terai* women but this can create difficulties because of language and other differences. A man can marry four women if he can fulfil all the requirements of his wives equally.

The prevalence of the *mehar* or dowry system in which the family of the bride is required to provide a dowry to accompany the young woman into the marriage in the *terai* generally, and among the Muslim communities of the *terai* as well, indicates that women are not valued as much as men (in the sense that a dowry is required effectively to 'top up' the value of the women). It also constitutes a major burden on the family of the young woman who are required to find the wherewithal for the dowry. There is evidence to suggest that the amount of the dowry has been increasing rapidly in the last few years, not only in monetary terms but as a proportion of the total marriage expenditure for the bride's family. The prospective burden of the dowry constitutes an additional reason for a family to welcome the birth of a girl less than that of a boy, contributing thereby to the general gender discrimination that is all too visible in the demographic statistics.

It is not clear whether the Muslim communities of the *terai* are any more prone to this aspect of gender discrimination than other communities (caste or ethnic groups), but the general attitude towards females in broadly speaking at least equally and probably more discriminatory in so far as women are more carefully guarded and precluded from participation in activities outside the home, from education onwards, than among most other groups. There are indications of a strong preference for early marriage for girls and young women, and this shows relatively little sign of changing.

Several key informants interviewed during the fieldwork in Janakpur area drew attention to the prevalence of the *talak* system of divorce, which they implied enabled men to divorce their wives relatively easily, whereas the reverse was not the case. One of the key informants in the IDEA/NEMAF study in 2015, Tahir Nadaf, for example, remarked that

> 'There are no laws specific to religious doctrine and the *shari'a* (religious law) is not recognized by the state. However, some of the most restrictive customs, such as 'triple *talak*', which is the tradition of unilateral divorce by saying the word "*talak*" three times in a row, and the denial of alimony, are still commonly practiced within the Muslim community. Successive Nepalese governments have done little to protect women's rights beyond the drafting of unenforceable laws. The state has avoided taking a position these Muslim practices, but justifies this as non-interference with the cultural identity of minorities. This passivity reveals a lack of commitment to women's rights as guaranteed in the Nepal Constitution.

> 'This is not confirmed by other information and it would be important to find out more about the extent to which arbitrary divorce by uttering the 'I divorce thee' three times is in fact practised. It is clearly, however, another aspect of the extreme discrimination against women that is an integral part of Muslim society in the *terai*.'

In August 2007, *Irin News* published a major article on divorce, suggesting that, in the Nepalgunj area at least,

> 'Women in Nepal's minority Muslim community are increasingly contesting through the courts the divorce settlements imposed on them by their husbands. The women say they are the victims of an abuse of Islamic law by their husbands.'
>
> "All he did was say *talaq* on the telephone and I was threatened never to return home," said Kausar Jahal Idrisi, a 32-year-old mother of two who now lives in extreme poverty in the town of Nepalgunj on the western edge of the *terai* region in southern Nepal. For the last 15 years, since the divorce, Idrisi and her children have been living in a shack. They cannot afford to buy enough clothes or food and the children have been unable to attend school. Her husband, Sahim Ahmed, refused to provide any support. She complained that men were misusing Islamic Law, which has a procedure called *talaq* for ending a marriage. A Muslim husband in Nepal can divorce his wife by repeating the word *talaq* three times. However, Idrisi has finally broken her silence and gathered the courage to fight for justice. With the help of local Muslim lawyers, she took her husband and his family to the district court in Nepalgunj to win her right to a share of the family property. The case is taking time to resolve, but Idrisi hopes she will win the legal battle.
>
> "Muslim women want to end the misuse of religion that is victimising them," said lawyer Mohna Ansari, who has been helping women to fight for their rights. She said men often divorced their wives for trivial reasons. "Many Muslim husbands divorce their wives in a fit of temper or for trivial reasons. This is an insult to our religion," Maulana Tabar Banjari, a prominent religious leader in Nepal, told IRIN. Without mutual consent such practices should stop, Banjari said." The problem is that *talaq* has been used to get an easy divorce," said local Muslim intellectual Iqbal

Iraqi." Our religion respects marriage and preaches that *talaq* can be said only when there is constant bickering between husband and wife; then they can divorce by mutual consent," said another intellectual, Nazimo Ansari.

'According to a local non-governmental organisation (NGO) called the *Nepali Muslim Samaj Bikash Chetna Kendra*, which works on raising social awareness among Muslim women and vulnerable groups, there is a very high divorce rate in the Muslim community. A study it carried out in 2006 in Nepalgunj found over 235 cases of women whose marriages had ended after their husband invoked *talaq*. The NGO pointed out that there could be hundreds more such divorces in the villages, where rural Muslim women lack access to legal advice. "The problem of *talaq* is very serious in the villages; Muslim women have been victimised," said the NGO's president, Mohammed Sher.'

'Nepal's Family Law, amended in 2006, provides for equal division of assets upon divorce. It stipulates that divorce is permitted only if one partner's infertility is certified by a government-recognised medical board. One-sided divorces without mutual consent are illegal in Nepali law." Nepali laws that protect women's rights are strong weapons to help these poor victims and they are now increasingly becoming aware and empowered as well," said Laxmi Poudel, a prominent lawyer in Nepalgunj. Over the past year, the number of court cases of *talaq* victims has been increasing, according to local women's rights groups. "Many are nowadays seen approaching the courts and this is an inspiring sight," said lawyer Abdul Ajij Musalman, who added that Muslim women had gradually lost all fear of being socially ostracised. "We have to make this a national campaign so that more Muslim women are aware of their rights and able to protect themselves," he said.'

'The violations against Muslim women should be actively protested. Wrongful use of our religion is only hurting poor women and their children," said Mohammadi Siddi, president of the Fatima Foundation, a local organisation leading a campaign to protect the rights of Muslim Nepalese women. Although the misuse of *talaq* continues, the movement against misuse of the practice is gaining momentum, as evident from the increasing number of Muslim women who are now speaking out for their rights, according

> to the Fatima Foundation. "We want to end this exploitation practiced in the name of religion," said Butul Khan Pathan, who filed a case at Banke District court against her husband who divorced her to marry another woman. Pathan fought successfully to get half of her husband's property and now serves as an example to others'.

According to Islamic law, women can inherit property but a daughter receives only half of the share received by a son. But, in Nepal, generally even this has not been considered practicable and the Nepalese law has long been based on Hindu law in which only an unmarried daughter above 35 years of age can inherit her father's property. As the Asian Womens Resource Exchange (AWORK) noted as long ago as 1997, 'Section 16 of the Chapter on Partition of the existing National Code of 1963 provides that a daughter is entitled to inherit parental property if she is unmarried and is 35 years old. Once she gets married, she has to return the property to the family less the marriage expenses. A son, on the other hand, is heir of the ancestral property upon birth. In reality, few women inherit property'.

There were several attempts during the 1990s and early 2000s by various NGOs representing women's interests to have this changed and eventually the law was altered by parliament so that womens' inheritance rights were strengthened. Daughters would be regarded as rightful heirs, wives were given stronger rights of access and ownership to their husband's property, and widows and divorced women were given full inheritance rights. In reality, in Muslim communities in Nepal, these legal rights are relatively rarely exercised, as women are reluctant to go against long standing custom and practice.

Another major issue for women is the practice of *purdah,* whereby women are not allowed to leave the house unless veiled or 'properly covered up' and accompanied by a male member of their family. With so many husbands away from home in foreign parts, this makes life difficult for the women left on their own, who need to make purchases in the market and participate to some extent at least in public life. One effect of this seclusion is that Muslim women seem less involved than women from other communities in agriculture or other more public income generating activities (such a petty trade or other service activities).

9

Politics & the Muslim Community

The Panchayat Era

The 1950s

The constitutional developments of the 1950s (eg the Constitutions of 1948, 1951 and 1959, and changes introduced in the 'Muluki Ain' etc.) especially the establishment of Panchayat system in Nepal from the beginning of the 1960s effectively integrated the question of the status of social and religious groups in Nepal into a political process. More specifically, although no special legal provisions were introduced to protect the rights of various groups, the Panchayat system in a sense, expanded the scope of political participation. On the one hand, Muslims were given right to profess Islam but at the same time they were prevented from spreading Islam, especially in terms of conversion, within the territory of Nepal. One can find the origin of this kind of restriction in the 'Muluki Ain' itself.

This new 'right to religion' created space for the growth of Muslim institutions to propagate Islamic teachings within the community, something that also had clear political implications. According to Iqbal Iraqi, the first Muslim parliamentarian of Nepal and a core member of Rashtriya Janatantrik Praja Party, in the 1950s and 1960s, the king encouraged an informal system of representation by which the 'elders' of different 'communities' were given some kind of political responsibility for maintaining cordial relationships among different groups. Iqbal himself was nominated to participate in various international conferences, as a representative of 'Nepalese Muslims', and later was nominated to the National Parliament. This informal mechanism provided a specific political status to the community and effectively recognized the status of Muslims as a sociocultural (and religious) group within the wider political system (Int. Iqbal Iraqi, Dec. 2009).

It also encouraged Muslims to establish social and religious networks and associations to assert and promote this distinctiveness. The first major Muslim organization to be formed in Nepal was the All Nepal *Anjuman Islah (*All Nepal Reform Council), which was first established in 1953, for the social and economic development of Muslims. Upadhyay (2014) suggests that this was a 'committee appointed by the late King Mahendra to resolve communal problems', although in reality there had been little indication of such 'problems' before this time. This organisation merged with the *Jami'atul Muslim (*Muslim Council) in Rautahat District and the *Idare Tamire Millat* in Banke District, factions of which then broke off and merged to form the All Nepal *Anjuman Islah* (ANAI) in 1958 (Sijapati 2011: 27).

The All Nepal *Anjuman Islah* worked 'for the social and economic development of Muslims in Nepal', and used methods such as radio broadcasting, starting in 1955 on Radio Nepal, to raise awareness through special programmes on the eve of Muslim holy festivals. In 1957-58, it petitioned the Department of Education in 1957-58 to include Urdu and Persian as alternative subjects to the mandatory elementary Sanskrit in the high school qualification examinations for all Muslim pupils (Dastider, 2007, 153). This underlines the fact that the introduction of the right to religion, even in its restricted form, effectively paved the way for an identity-based Muslim politics of some kind, with a concern first and foremost for formal language recognition (which was, interestingly, historically a matter of major importance in the development of a Nepalese identity see Pratyoush Onta on the role of the Nepali language in the formation of Nepalese national identity).

Gaige (1975) notes that there were two Muslim parliamentarians in the first (1959) elected national assembly in Nepal (of 109 members). However, there was only one representative (out of a total of 125) from the Muslim community in the National Panchayat which was formed after the dissolution of the elected National Assembly this was Iqbal Iraqi. Through the first two decades of the Panchayat period, until 1979, the maximum number of Muslim representatives at the national level was five. During this period, National Panchayat members were not directly elected by the population as a whole or by voters in constituencies, but were elected by the elected bodies at local (district) level.

The 1960s

Nepal's status as a Hindu nation continued to be a defining characteristic of successive Constitutions. For example, in the 1948 Constitution, Lord Pashupatinath, one of the most revered deities of Nepal whose temple in Kathmandu still enjoyed a special status, was specifically mentioned in the preamble. The 1959 and 1962 Constitutions respectively very clearly pointed out that King had to be a Hindu, and that Nepal was a Hindu state. However, the most significant development as regards minority religions and religious groups was the official enshrinement of the 'right to religion'. The 1962 Constitution allowed all the citizens of Nepal, including those belonging to the non-Hindu religious communities, to practice their traditional religions.

As Upadhyay remarks, '(the king) replaced the 1853 old legal Code with a comparatively more modern new Code in 1963, which provided equal citizen status to the Muslims' (2014: 33). This was the first time that the 'right to religion' had been constitutionally recognized, though non-Hindu religious communities, including Muslims, had already been practising their religion along with other elements of their 'traditional' customs and practices and laws for many centuries.

Reflecting on the question of the significance of the 'right to religion' in the 1962 constitution, Tahir Ali Ansari, the only Muslim Judge of the Supreme Court of Nepal, argued that this 'right to religion' should be seen in the context of the time. From the time of his intervention in Nepalese politics and the dissolution of the elected government and political parties in the early 1960s until the new Constitution of the early 1990s, the King remained the supreme authority, and there was no tradition of 'claiming rights' whether political, social or religious. The rights 'given especially the right to the practice of non-Hindu religions were merely a legal sanctioning of already established sociocultural practices. Furthermore, as Upadhyay comments, 'although the new Code allowed Muslims to practise their religion freely, the ban on conversion or the dissolution of marriage etc. remained as it was in the 1853 Code. Any attempt to convert people religiously remained a punishable offence with three-year imprisonment' (2014: 33).

Nevertheless, according to Iqbal Iraqi, the protection given to Muslim social groups during the Panchayat era actually played a crucial rule in their subsequent politicization (interview, Iqbal Iraqi, Dec, 2009). Economically powerful Muslims who had some kind of political connections with the inner circles around the king started mobilizing resources either to form new religious/social organizations or to establish control over the numerous localized religious institutions, which were already functioning. These initiatives were encouraged by the powers that be precisely because such institutions were supposed to operate within the constitutional and political framework, and at the same time, could provide a kind of ideological and political dynamic to the new partyless Panchayat regime.

It is suggested by Shamima Siddika, that 'many Muslims got elected as Pradhan Panch of their village panchayat in the 1960s. Some were nominated as central and zonal level offices also'[1]. The former is very likely; the latter unconfirmed as yet. At the local level, Muslims were certainly involved in politics during the Panchayat era, but they tended to be involved mainly through their local village and, much more rarely, district panchayats although a nationwide conference of Nepali Muslims was apparently held in Jokaha village in Rautahat District in 1963. Resolutions were passed to amend the national legal code to allow 'blood relation marriage' (cousin marriage is a common marriage preference among Muslims in Nepal as elsewhere – see for example Seddon 1981 for the case of Morocco), and also to annul the edict requiring government permission to construct a mosque[2]; while in 1966, a Hajj committee was formed, to facilitate the travel of Nepali Muslims undertaking the pilgrimage to Mecca, so that they would no longer have to go through India.

Gaige shows that in a sample survey of *terai* districts in the late 1960s, Muslims already figured, albeit in a small way, in local panchayat councils. In Mahottari-Dhanusha district, where they constituted some 7 per cent of the total population, they had some representation as members and even chairmen of the village panchayat 5.9 and 4.9 per cent respectively in 1967 and as members of the district assembly 2.6 per cent. In Jhapa, where they constituted an even smaller percentage of the total population, they were still represented 2.8 per cent of members of village panchayats and 2.2 per cent of chairmen of the district assembly.

In Bara district, where they constituted a significantly larger proportion of the total population (13.7 per cent), they managed to account for 7.1 per cent of all village chairmen and 1.9 per cent of district assembly members. But in Kapilvastu, where they amounted to 18 per cent of the population as a whole, they managed to secure 19.1 per cent of village panchayat members and 18.5 per cent of village chairmen in 1967, and 12.3 per cent of district assembly members. In none of these districts, however, did they manage to break through to become members of the district panchayat or local council.

The 1970s

The 1970s were marked by the growth of Muslim associations specifically concerned to promote a sense of Muslim identity within Nepal and to develop greater confidence among Muslims as such. The *Millat-e Islamiya* was established in 1971, 'to facilitate the Islamic environment and Islamic awareness throughout the whole country'. In its early years, it forged links with overseas Islamic organisations and obtained assistance from the International Islamic Federation of Student Organisations in Kuwait and the World Assembly of Muslim Youth, based in Saudi Arabia, and translated a number of Islamic books and brochures. It established an Islamic library in Ghanta Ghar (in central Kathmandu near the clock tower) a well-known 'Muslim area') and aimed to facilitate the establishment and running of *madrasas* in the hill regions of Nepal, addressing the concern of many Muslims of reform orientation that in the hills, at this time (and even during the early 1980s), 'Muslim inhabitants did not even pronounce Kalimah'[3] (Sijapati 2011: 29).

The organisation was originally called the *Jami'at Millat-e Islamiya* and was established with financial support from the Saudi Embassy in Bangladesh where one of its founders and later presidents, Imran Ansari, was studying in medical school. This allowed the organisation to purchase prime real estate on Raj Path. The organisation continues to have its headquarters there, and to run an Islamic library with over 10,000 titles in English, Urdu, Hindi, Nepali and Arabic. The *Millat-e Islamiya* works with the *Islami Sangh* and the National Muslim Forum, renting part of its space to the former. As of summer 2008 there were plans for the *Islami Sangh* to establish its own space outside the Ring Road (Sijapati 2011: 29); but its current address is still at the corner of Durbar Magh and Kamaladi Road.

The *Muslim Sewa Samiti,* registered in 1974, set as its objectives the cultivation of Quranic study and knowledge, Arabic language instruction, the translation of the Quran into Nepali (the Bible had been translated into Nepali by the mid-19th century). It also was concerned to promote the improvement in the economic and social conditions of Muslims. The Samiti even apparently played a role in facilitating Muslim overseas labour employment in the Gulf and education in Saudi Arabia. Sijapati suggests that 'these institutions represent the beginning of religious group consciousness at the national level that asserted 'Muslim identity' in resistance to the state's programmes of Sanskritisation and nationalism'.

The *Muslim Sewa Samiti* was, however, a staunch supporter of the panchayat system and organised a nationwide meeting in 1979 in which Muslims unanimously voted for a continuation of the panchayat regime. It was argued that the king 'respected the voice of Muslims and their specific religious goals and needs' (Sijapati 2011: 28). After all, he had intervened when in 1971 there was serious inter-communal conflict in Bara and Rautahat districts, triggered by the killing of a Muslim accused of 'cow slaughter'. The two districts were affected for two weeks and it was only when the king, returning from a trip abroad, marshalled armed police and suppressed the disturbances. Upadhyay comments that 'this use of state machinery for their protection seems to have augmented the Nepali Muslims' confidence in the Hindu monarch and state' (2014: 34).

The Samiti even organised a 'Quran competition' with the full cooperation of the government, which provided a hall in the Police Club in Kathmandu; during the recitation of the Quran all the statues of the Hindu gods and goddesses were covered with cloths, so as not to cause offence.

The 1980s

In 1981, the system was changed (under the Constitution of 2019 BS) in favour of direct elections to the National Panchayat. In the Panchayat elections, 14 Muslims contested seats (12 from the *terai* and 2 from the hills) although only two (1.8 per cent of total elected members) were elected to the national legislature - Ismail Ansari from Mahottari and Sheikh Siraju from Rautahat. During this period, these two Muslims, both from *terai* districts, were elected to the national assembly, and one other was appointed by the king.

Also, in the course of time, especially in the 1980s, the social and cultural networks that evolved out of the charitable, social welfare and cultural institutions began to contribute to the making of a distinct Muslim political and cultural identity. For example organizations like the *Islami Sangh Nepal* was established in Kathmandu (in January 1985) by a handful of Muslims from the *terai* towns of Krishnanagar, Nepalgunj, Birgunj and Biratnagar as a *da'wat* grassroots organisation promoting

Islamic social values and practices and conducting social work among Muslims in Nepal as a whole. Others, like *Millat-e-Islamia* and the *Muslim Seva Samiti* slowly began to emphasize the distinct and distinctive religious aspect of Muslim identity in Nepal.

These institutions turned out to be the sites where political and social discourse was constituted. This process was continued into the 1990s, particularly after the promulgation of the new Constitution and the 'opening up' of Nepal to a greater plurality of voices and to demands for the effective representation of a greater variety of social groups, notably *janajati*. Muslims had, historically, been poorly represented in the political life of Nepal a problem that continues even today.

Multi-Partyism and Minorities

The 1990s

The Constitution of 1990 was the first important landmark in this regard, for although it was based on the idea of Nepal as a Hindu monarchy, it also introduced significant clauses relating to religious minorities. For example, it was clearly pointed out that the state should treat all its citizens equally (Article 11 and 12 of 1990 Constitution). In addition, all the citizens will be free to profess and practice religion. Article 19 says that 'every person shall have the freedom to profess and practice his own religion as coming down to him hereditary have due regard to traditional practices, provided that no person shall be entitled to convert the religion of any person. Every religious denomination shall have the right to maintain its independent existence and for that purpose to manage and protect its religious places and trusts. The introduction of these clauses marks an interesting contradiction, especially from the point of view of Muslims.

The constitution of Nepal as rewritten in the early 1990s, like the previous constitution of 2019 BS, still declared Nepal to be a Hindu state with a Hindu King. This effectively discriminated against other religions eg Buddhism, Islam and Christianity and against those who followed these other religions. Modern political and religious identities, of the kind claimed, or rather reclaimed since the early 1990s, had not been constituted at this point and group consciousness of the need to claim rights was limited. In this context, the newly assigned 'rights' did not change or transform the existing cultural and social practices and it was not permissible for any social group and/or political party to mount any organised protest against the status quo.

Ansari explains that at this time, Islamic *shari'a* (Islamic law) was merely the doctrine by which Muslim communities were governed internally. However, interestingly because of the contrast with many 'secularised' Islamic states where family law is the bastion of *shari'a* matters of dispute over property, polygamy and divorce had to be settled according to the established Nepalese legal code. All religious communities were subject to these legal provisions (Int. Judge Tahir Ali Ansari, July 2009). The Muslim community was not recognised as an entity with its own distinctive cultural, social and religious characteristics and its own rights as such.

The rise of multi-party democracy from the 1990s onwards encouraged all kinds of social groups to participate in the political process, which was dominated by the various existing and emerging political parties. Muslims also now joined these political parties. The Nepali Congress and the United Communist Party of Nepal (UCPN) in particular distributed tickets to Muslims as part of their larger mobilization drive. According to the official data, 31 Muslim candidates fought elections in 1991, out of which five Muslim Members of Parliament (MPs) were elected to the Lower House (the largest number and proportion of the total ever achieved up to this point).

In the 1991 elections, according to Dastider (2007), Muslim MPs elected to the Lower House of Parliament, the House of Representatives or Pratinidhi Sabha, were Khalil Miya Ansari (NC), Sheikh Idris (NC), Salim Miya Ansari (CPN-UML), Mirza Dilshad Beg (NSP) and Sayed Meraj (NC). In this way, the Muslim representation in the legislature had increased in percentage terms, from 1.8 per cent in 1959, 0.8 in 1978, 1.8 per cent in 1981 (excludes nominated members) to 2.3 per cent in 1991 (lower house 2.4 per cent and upper house 1.7 per cent). Muslims now also occupied important political posts such as Cabinet Minister and leader of the Lower House of the Parliament for the first time. One Muslim out of a total of 60 was elected to the Upper House.

The major political parties also encouraged Muslims to form their own pressure groups. This development later paved the way for the establishment of 'Muslim wings' in almost all the major political parties. Despite this momentum, the results of the National Assembly elections in 1994/5 (2051 BS) and 2000 (2056 BS) were not encouraging and showed clearly that no 'breakthrough' had taken place. Only four Muslims were represented in the 205 member parliament of 1995; and in the next election, in 2000, this number was halved to two.

In the 1994 election, Salim Miya Ansari was elected to the Pratinidhi Sabha as the candidate of the Communist Party of Nepal (Unified Marxist-Leninist) from the Bara-4 constituency. Ansari won with 20,148 votes against 16,145 votes for Pharmulaha Mansur of the Nepali Congress. Ansari served as Minister of Forest and Soil Conservation in the CPN(UML) government formed in 1994. When the CPN(UML) was divided in 1998, Ansari joined the Communist Party of Nepal (ML), and later became Minister of Tourism in the coalition government. When the CPN(ML) and CPN(UML) reunited, Ansari again became a CPN(UML) leader. In December 2002, Ansari left CPN(UML). He was then a Central Committee member of the party. He subsequently formed the Samajbadi Party Nepal. In July 2005, Ansari was appointed Minister of Forest and Soil Conservation by King Gyanendra. On January 30, 2007, Ansari was arrested following riots in the *terai*. He was released on February 18, 2007.

Originally hailing from the region of Gorakhpur in Uttar Pradesh, Mirza Dilshad Beg came to Nepal in the 1980s and joined the Nepal Sadbhawana Party; later he resigned to join the Rashtriya Prajtantra Party and won two consecutive terms, in 1994 and 1999, as the representative of Kapilvastu in the House of Representatives. He subsequently held ministerial portfolios in two governments. He was shot dead on 29 June 1998. There are various theories as to why, but his long association with criminals in Mumbai and his links with the Pakistani secret service provide at least two reasons.

Farmulha Mansur was elected to the (lower) House of Representatives (Pratinidhi Sabha) in the 1999 elections to represent the Nepali Congress Party. Mohamed Aftab Aalam was also elected as a Nepali Congress Party representative in the lower house; so too was Salim Miya Ansari. Under the 1990 Constitution, this House consisted of 205 members directly elected by the people. It had five-year terms, but it could be dissolved by the king on the advice of the prime minister before the ending of its term. The Pratinidhi Sabha was dissolved on January 15, 2007, and substituted by an interim legislature. The new interim legislature is largely composed of former Pratinidhi Sabha MPs, but does not include Farmulha Mansur.

The general grievances of the Muslim community, as well as their overall status in Nepali society were apparently recorded in a working paper ('Socio-economic status of Muslims in Nepal') for the Second National Muslim Conference, held in Kathmandu in August 1996. I have not been able to find this document. It would be a valuable complement to the more recent concerns expressed (see Appendix 2). The idea of a specific Women's Caucus in parliament, to lobby for women's interests and rights, was considered as early as the late 1990s. For on 28 April 1998, Maryam Montague, Representative of the National Democratic Institute for International Affairs in the USA, sent a paper for discussion on 'The Objectives and Structures of Women's Caucuses' to the women members of parliament who were planning to form a Women's Caucus. It is not thought that at this time there were any Muslim representatives in the Women's Caucus. It was not, however, until 2002 that the Women's Caucus was actually established.

The Early 21st Century

Even at the beginning of the 21st century, when various social groups (eg women, *dalits, madhesis, adivasi janajatis*) had been clearly identified as requiring special attention and support for the purposes of 'social inclusion' (the term that had by now come to dominate the debates about democracy and human rights in Nepal), 'Muslims', although clearly a religious minority, remained without such a privileged social and political identity, and were effectively marginalized as indeed are many other 'minorities' unrecognized and ignored by the 'social inclusion' project of the 'donors' and, increasingly, of the government.

According to the Asian Development Bank, 'data from 2005 show that females, *dalits, janajatis, madhesis* and Muslims were under-represented in almost all organs of state and society'; it added that 'as a result, these groups are lacking in voice, agency and influence necessary for removing barriers and increasing access to development opportunities that will result in improved livelihood status' (ADB 2012: 9). Given this situation, self help seemed the best way forward; and so, towards the end of September 2004, the *Islami Sangh Nepal* brought together 55 Muslim social workers, intellectuals and religious leaders to discuss the situation in Nepal in general and the challenges faced by Muslims in particular this led to the formation of the National Muslim Forum, which was registered in June 2005 and held its first annual meeting in Kathmandu the following December. The aim of the Forum was to help Muslims find a unified Nepali Muslim voice, representing the common interests of the Muslim population, to establish a political platform for articulating Muslim needs to the government.

Megan Sijapati has devoted a whole chapter in her book on the *Islamic Revival in Nepal* to the National Muslim Forum (chapter 5 'towards a unified voice'), so there is little point in discussing in detail its aims, objectives and achievements. But she at least sees the Forum as crucial in articulating notions of Muslim collective identity within a framework of minority rights and identity politics in Nepal. She makes the point, however, that unlike many other groups in Nepal, this identity was not an ethnic identity or that of an indigenous nationality, but was that of a political and sociocultural entity defined largely by its religious beliefs and practices. At the same time, it also emphasised the importance of shared national concerns and citizenship what Sijapati calls 'shared national belonging' (2011: 79) and within that, a sense of 'shared hardship', associating the Muslim community clearly with other disadvantaged groups in Nepal.

Muslims, in other words, were to be considered as constituting a community (*millat or qaum*) within a country, defined both geographically and politically (ie *desh* and *muluk*) (Sijapati 2011: 81) as 'a Nepali community'. At the same time, the Forum recognised the internal differences and even divisions sectarian, ideological, political, social and economic within this Muslim 'community', and expressed its concern about the 'Ahmadi threat', posed by the relatively recent arrival (a decade ago) of the Ahmadis a distinctive Muslim sect regarded as heretical by most Nepali Muslims and defined as such by the Forum.

We have already discussed some of the Muslim associations that were formed during the years between the 1950s and the 1990s. Most of these were intended to promote various aspects of Muslim culture and religion in a predominantly Hindu country. More recently, following the end of the conflict that resulted from the Maoist insurgency between 1996 and 2006, there have been further efforts to promote the education and political advancement of Muslims, by Muslim groups and associations, both as part of the re-assertion of the status of 'minorities' more generally (including *janajatis, dalits, adhivasis* etc.) and as a specific case of a religious minority. But, as indicated above, there are important divisions within the Muslim community as a whole, which militate against an inclusive and coherent strategy for Muslim advancement in general; but there are also some individuals and organisations (including many of those listed in Appendix 1) that devote themselves to overcoming these divisions in the interests of this wider community.

A Time of Hope

The 'Rise' of Secularism

The 2006 Peoples' Movement propelled the marginalized communities to the forefront and also higher up the national agenda; this gave at least some visibility to the Muslim communities and there was some positive effect as regards that status and position of Muslim women as well. Until 2006, Nepal was a Hindu kingdom where conversion to another religion was a punishable offence. After the pro-democracy movement of 2006, however, the new interim parliament proclaimed the country 'secular', thereby intending the encourage freedom of religious belief and practice. In November 2006, the Maoists and the seven-party alliance reached a historic settlement through the Comprehensive Peace Agreement which made it possible, within a relatively short while, to form an interim government, an interim legislature and make some further progress towards the restoration of democracy and re-assertion of human rights.

The Pratinidhi Sabha (House of Representatives) was dissolved on 15 January 2007, and substituted by an interim legislature. This was largely composed of former Pratinidhi Sabha MPs, but did not include the Muslim, Farmulha Mansur, who had been a representative of the Nepali Congress Party since the elections of 1999. It did, however, include Rizwan Ansari, nominated by the UML, who was to become state minister for Home Affairs in 2009. On 7 February 2007, the Prime Minister, G. P. Koirala, promised 'federalism' and 'an equitable electoral system' that would recognise the rights of all of the peoples of the *terai* - 'the Madhesis'. Two months later, an interim government was formed.

There continued, however, to be considerable political turmoil in the *terai* as different political groups fought, under various banners, to mobilise the highly differentiated population of the region to ensure greater representation in the new emerging political dispensation. This had the effect not only of unifying certain groupings but also of increasing tensions and the potential for conflict. Muslims in the *terai* in particular were unavoidably caught up in this turmoil, in which some political activists demanded greater recognition of the rights of 'Madhesis' as a whole, while others, e.g. some Tharus and many Muslims, emphasised the rights of more specific disadvantaged minorities. For the Muslims in particular, it was important that 'secularism' was not interpreted as meaning 'atheism', but tolerance and freedom to pursue the religion of one's choice without the imposition of rules derived from the dominance of Hinduism. But, not only were there Muslims in the hills as well as the *terai*, so that Muslims could not be subsumed into the category of 'Madhesis' without substantially dividing the Muslim community, but many Muslims in the *terai* were not prepared to abandon their Muslim identity in favour of the broader, Hindu-dominated majority of Madhesis.

The Interim Constitution and Secularism

The Interim Constitution of 2007 pledged to accomplish the restructuring of the state in order to solve the problems arising from inequalities and divisions of class, ethnicity, religion and gender in Nepalese society. It expressed its full commitment to democratic values and norms, including the competitive multi-party democratic system of governance, civil liberties, fundamental rights, human rights, adult franchise, periodic elections, complete freedom of the press, independent judiciary and concepts of the rule of law; implicit in this was freedom of religious belief, expression and practice. It went on to state explicitly, that 'the sovereignty and the state authority of Nepal shall be vested in the people of Nepal' and that, 'having multi-ethnic, multilingual, multi-religious and multi-cultural characteristics with common aspirations and being united by a bond of allegiance to national independence, integrity, national interest and prosperity of Nepal, all the Nepalese people collectively constitute the nation.

This is what was meant by a 'secular' state. No laws specifically affecting freedom of religion were, however, changed. On the other hand, as regards the Muslim Community, the Interim Constitution for the first time ever incorporated provisions for uplifting the marginalized communities, by adopting an inclusive policy in state mechanism and agreeing quotas for many marginalised communities i.e. women, *dalits*, *janajatis*, people from remote regions, *madhesis* and 'others'. The 2007 Interim Constitution was the first time in Nepal's history that Muslims were officially mentioned but then only once. Furthermore, it did not recognize Muslims explicitly as a minority group, nor did it reserve a quota for them specifically; they were included under 'others'. Adhikari and Gellner have argued ('New Identity Politics' in *Modern Asian Studies*) that 'the original intention of the Interim Constitution of 2007 was for the 30.2 per cent 'others' category to include minorities not covered by any of those explicitly mentioned (eg Muslims). But it was quickly taken to constitute a quota or entitlement for the larger categories that were not Dalits, Janajatis, and not Madhesis in other words for Bahuns, Chhetris, Thakuris, and Sannyasis' (p 21).

Significantly, the day after its promulgation, Upendra Yadav of the Madhesi Janadhikar Forum was arrested for setting fire to a copy of the Interim Constitution because it failed, in his view, to provide specifically for the interests of the people of the Madhes (a relatively new umbrella term for the peoples of the plains area of the *terai*). The day after that, 17 January 2007, a protest movement erupted in the *terai,* as people who saw themselves as Madhesis demanded 'their rights'. Although there can be little doubt, particularly in retrospect, that the Madhesi movement was a genuine popular reaction (albeit one orchestrated by a minority of political leaders with a view to self-advancement) both to the evident opening up of the political process to groups hitherto effectively marginalized, including the *adhivasi janajatis* and, potentially, the various peoples of the *terai,* and also to visible attempts by the 'hill elites' to exclude 'Madhesis' from the new republican political arena, it was also fuelled by Hindutva tendencies.

A key figure in this movement was Yogi Adityanath acting head of the *Gorkahnath Math* and a leader of the BJP, MP in the Lok Sabha and national president of the Indian chapter of the *Vishwa Hindu Mahasangh* (VHM), which maintained its headquarters in Nepal, and founder of the extremist *Hindu Yuva Vahini,* which was considered the BJP and even the militant *Vishwa Hindu Parishad* (VHP) to be moderate who argued that 'the unifying force in Nepal, like the soul that unites the body, is the Hindu king and Hindu culture'. Why he asked, referring to the decision of the restored parliament in May 2006 to declare Nepal a secular state - was secularism imposed there (*yeh secularism kyon laad diya waha pe*)? He supported the Madhesi movement, but did not wish to see a separate Madhes: 'what we want', he said, 'is a unified Nepal as a Hindu state'[4]. He was virulently anti-Maoist, in part because of their alleged atheism.

Indeed, during the 2006 UP assembly elections, one of his key campaign planks was to oppose the links between the Nepalese Maoists and all the Indian left parties. Just before the 2007 Madhesi 'uprising', he had hosted a meeting of Madhesi leaders, to encourage them to start anti-Maoist agitation. He was also extremely suspicious of Pakistan's intentions in Nepal and in the Lok Sabha he had often raised the issue of ISI-sponsored *madrasas* in the Nepalese *terai* and UP. He was also at the forefront of the opposition to abolish the Hindu character of the Nepalese monarchy.

Sijapati has remarked that 'when King Gyanendra Shah yielded to mass protests organized by the seven political parties and the Maoists in April of 2006 and a Constituent Assembly declared Nepal a secular nation, Hindu organisations based in India and Nepal decried the country's change from a Hindu monarchy to a secular state. They claimed that Nepal was obligated to retain its Hindu essence and not fall prey to secularism. Reports in 2007 indicated that a new alliance of Hindu groups, called the Nepal Armed Hindu Morcha, had formed with the objective of returning Nepal to its status as a Hindu state through any means, including violence...' (2011: 135-36). This was part of the backlash against progressive moves, in the name of 'secularism', to begin to recognise the rights of minority groups, such as Muslims. It was also a direct threat to the Muslim cause.

Towards the Constituent Assembly

On 28 June 2007, it was reported in *Gorkhapatra*, that the Intellectual Muslim Association of Nepal (IMAN) demanded a 10 per cent reservation in the constituent assembly (CA) from the Muslim community, according to a press statement by the organisation. Stating that the government's mind-set towards Muslim community was discriminatory, the IMAN said that the community should be represented in the CA through a proportional electoral system. 'The CA without proper representation from Muslim, Dalit, Janajati, and Madhesi communities would not be proper for mapping New Nepal', the statement read. Ijaharul Hak Makrani, the president of IMAN, claimed that 'without Muslims being represented, the spirit of the Constituent Assembly would be totally defeated'. The election to the Constituent Assembly was at that time scheduled for November 22 2007. 'But', commented the newspaper, 'how the leaders of the ruling Eight Party Alliance (EPA), under the leadership of Prime Minister Girija Prasad Koirala, react to the demand of the Muslim populace who have always been ignored in the political setup is not known yet'.

At around the same time, the Muslim group *Awam Sahara Nepal* declared that it would organize street protests if the government did not meet its demand to set aside seats for its community in November elections. 'If the government does not address our demand we'll be forced to come to the street and protest for it' said ASN leader Mohammed Nizamuddin. The popular movement (Jana Andolan II) of 2006 had shown how street protest could generate new momentum for progressive change and led to the Interim Constitution of 2007, which then expressed a commitment to the election of a broadly-based and inclusive Constitutional Assembly to draft a new Constitution for Nepal. On the other hand, protest could easily lead to violence.

In September of 2007, for example, what Sijapati describes as 'a tragic episode of sustained violence' occurred between Muslims and Hindus in the *terai* district of Kapilvastu, prompted by the murder of Abdullah Mohut Khan, a leader of the Madhesi Mukti Morcha Party and formerly a member of an anti-Maoist resistance group. Dozens were killed and hundreds more victimized in tit-for-tat inter-communal violence; hundreds fled the area. The government, however, failed to respond adequately during the several weeks of conflict, despite the fact that the preamble of this Interim Constitution guaranteed the basic rights of the Nepalese people to frame a Constitution for themselves and to participate in the free and impartial election of the Constituent Assembly in a fear-free environment.

The preparations for the elections to the Constituent Assembly involved the adoption of a mixed form of election system, including both FPTP and proportional representative (PR) systems elect legislators. The winning candidates under the PR system would be decided by the proportion of votes secured by the political parties across the country as a whole (Election Commission, 2008/2065 BS). It was argued by the Muslim protesters supported by other groups that the FPTP system did not provide an opportunity to the smaller political parties, or to various minority groups, to express their concerns through direct representation in the National Assembly. For this reason, a mixed system of election was adopted.

Under the new system the Constituent Assembly would comprise a total of 601 members, of which 240 candidates would be elected under the FPTP system and 335 under the PR system with the remaining 26 being nominated (UNDP 2009). There was a provision for the nomination of an equal number of male and female candidates to ensure stronger representation of females in the Assembly. There was also a provision, as in the Interim Constitution, to include 37.8 per cent *adivasi janajatis*,

31.2 per cent *madhesis,* 13 per cent *dalits,* 4 per cent from 'backward regions' and 30.2 per cent from 'other caste' groups. This provision was made to ensure the representation of minorities in the constitution assembly (Election Commission, 2065 BS).

During fieldwork in the *terai* in the summer of 2015, for this project, various political leaders were interviewed. Mr. Asgar Ali, ex-Deputy Mayor of Janakpur and a leading politician in the Ra-Pra-Pa (Nepal), remarked that

> 'The public agitation, demonstrations and intense pressure also caused the government to modify the Civil Service Act and 45 percent of seats was reserved to be filled by women, janajatis, madhesis, dalits, disabled people and members of backward communities. But (he argued) Muslims should also get separate reservation in the civil service, as they are among the most backward social groups. Muslims still have no representation in ministries at secretary level, in the Bar Association, the Public Service Commission, the National Planning Commission, the CIAA and other state apparatuses. Muslims of Nepal (he suggested) have a great desire to serve the nation in all respects, and believe that their reorganization and the establishment of general religious rights will create more love towards the nation and ensure that they may be able to contribute in a better way. Therefore the government should bring them in the country's mainstream'.

Yet again, there was still no provision for Muslims as a distinct and separate category. In so far as they figured at all, it seems that they were included in the quota for *madhesis,* given that the majority of Muslims live in the *terai* (*madhes*); but this failed to recognise their distinctive status and situation even in the *terai,* and ensured that no Muslims could stand as a candidate in the hill constituencies. Yet again, in effect, they were excluded.

Notes

1. Shamima Siddika; op. cit., pp. 239-40.
2. There was no restriction on opening a *madrasa* or local Quranic school
3. Kalimah are the 'words' of the Qur'an
4. See Prashant Jha's *Battles of the New Republic,* page 111-114

10

Muslims in the New Republic

The Constituent Assembly

In February 2008, a second *Madhesi* movement heterogeneous in many ways yet unified in demanding greater recognition of Madhes broke out, resulting this time in an explicit agreement by the Interim Government to recognise a Madhesi province, to integrate *madhesis* into the Nepal Army (NA) and to ensure the proportionate and inclusive representation of *madhesis* in the organs of state, joining the *adivasi janajatis* and others as recognized minorities. Many ethnic groups, notably the Tharu, objected to being characterized simply as *madhesis* and demanded specific recognition as a 'minority' after all, the Maoists had recognized a Tharuwan National Liberation Front as well as a Madhesi Liberation Front as early as 2000-2001 and had proposed a Tharuwan Autonomous Region in the western *terai* as well as a Madhes Autonomous Region in the central and eastern *terai.* Muslims also became more vocal in their demands that *madhesi* leaders and the interim government *not* categorise them as madhesis, alleging that the *madhesi* parties were trying to co-opt Muslim members and 'deny them their rights' (Sijapati 2011: 136).

Nevertheless, six Muslim candidates won seats in the Assembly under the FPTP system, ten were elected under the PR system a total of 16 and one was nominated. The number and proportion of Muslims in the Constituent Assembly of 2008 proved to be the largest ever, up to that point (http://www.election.gov.np). As Sijapati remarks, 'in the summer of 2008, National Muslim Forum members were proud to point out to me that seventeen of Nepal's Constituent Assembly members were Muslims' (2011: 135).

Sadrul Miya Haq won the Saptari-5 seat in the 2008 Constituent Assembly election as an independent candidate and won the seat with 10,603 votes. Muhammad Okil, of the Madhesi Janadhikar Forum, was elected from the Rupandehi-7 constituency, winning 8,121 votes. Mohammad Estiyak Rai, belonging to the Madhesi Janadhikar Forum, was elected from the Banke-2 constituency, winning 19,396 votes. Mohammed Aftab Aalam, who had been elected to the Pratinidhi Sabha in the 1999 election on behalf of the Nepali Congress, was the NC candidate in the Rautahat-2 constituency for the 2008 Constituent Assembly election[1]. Salim Miya Ansari was the NC candidate in the Rautahat-2 constituency for the 2008 Constituent Assembly election.

Farmud Nadaf was a member of the Dhanusa District Development Committee during the early 2000s. He joined the Communist Party of Nepal (Maoist) after the peace process had begun. He was sworn in as a Constituent Assembly member, along with Ram Kumar Paswan, on August 6, 2010 as a representative of the Unified Communist Party of Nepal (Maoist) after two Maoist CA members (Matrika Prasad Yadav and Jagat Prasad Yadav) had been expelled from the Assembly after having split from the Maoist party. Nadaf's appointment caused protests amongst Maoist cadres in Dhanusa. The local party organization had suggested Tara Mahato (widow of a Maoist martyr). After Nadaf was sworn in, 75 members of the Mithila Madhes State Council resigned.

Salma Khatun Mikrani was a Proportional Representative member of the first Constituent Assembly, representing the Madhesi Jana Adhikar Forum, Nepal party. The party later split into two, and she joined the Jaya Prakash Gupta group, who launched a new political party under the name Madhesi Janaadhikar Forum, Republican in May 2011. Before the second Constituent Assembly election of 2013, she left the Madhesi Janaadhikar Forum, Republican, and joined the Tarai-Madhes Loktantrik Party in a programme held by Chairman Mahanth Thakur in Janakpur in August 2013. She was the only representative of the Mikrani community in Nepal's parliament.

The Constituent Assembly elected in 2008 was supposed to draft a new Constitution. The composition of the CA was exceptionally broad and the outlook seemed propitious as it began its business for a progressive and inclusive Constitution. In 2008, of the 329 members of the Interim Parliament, only four were Muslim much lower than the 4.2 percent in the overall population, but at least a voice. In the new Constituent Assembly, by contrast, Muslims were better represented than they had been previously.

Table 37: Representation of Muslims in National Assemblies

1991	5 (2.45%)
1994	1 (0.50%)
1999	2 (0.99%)
2006	4 (1.22%)
2008	17 (2.83%)

Even in 2008, however, when for the first time in the history of Nepal, under the Proportional Election System which was part of the system adopted for the elections to the Constituent Assembly, which would draft the new Constitution women, *madhesis, dalits, janajatis,* 'backward sectors' and others were given a fixed percentage representation in the elections, Muslims were not given the same opportunity to exercise their political rights. They were included with the *madhesis and* only by achieving nominations as and by voting for Muslims as *janajati* or *madhesi* candidates in the various political parties could they achieve any degree of representation in the Constituent Assembly.

The total number of Muslims represented in the first CA was seventeen (2.83 percent of the total CA members). Out of those 17, six were directly elected whereas the remainder were represented proportionally or else nominated. The CA members directly elected to the first CA were Mohammed Aftab Alam from Rautahat-2 (Nepali Congress), Mohammad Rizwan Ansari from Sarlahi-2 (CPNUML), Karima Begum from Parsa-1 (MJF), Md. Istiyak Rai from Banke-2 (MJF), Md. Okil Musalman from Rupandehi-7 (MJF) and Sadrul Miya Haq from Saptari-5 (Independent). Of these six directly elected candidates, three were from the Madhesi Janadhikar Forum (MJF), a political force that emerged from Madhes movement of 2007 and had a crucial impact on Nepalese politics thereafter. All these elected candidates belong to *terai* districts' constituencies where the Muslims' demographic strength lies. Only one of the six was a woman, Karima Begum.

Out of the seventeen Muslim CA members, ten were elected through proportional representation, and one, Akbal Ahmad Shah from Kapilvastu, was nominated. Among ten proportionally represented candidates, seven belonged to the *terai* districts and three from non-*terai* districts Syangja (2) and Arghakhanchi (1), both in the western region. It is to be noted that the population of Muslims in these two districts was around 2,000, that is, about the half of the population of Muslims in districts like Kaski and Tanahun.

Table 38: List of Muslim CA Members (2008)

SN	Constituency/District	Name	Party	Elected/PR
1	Parsa	Eslam Miya Dhobi	CPN Maoist	PR
2	Sarlahi	Halina Khatun	CPN Maoist	PR
3	Syangja	Mohammad Safik Miya	CPN Maoist	PR
4	Rautahat-2	Md. Aftab Alam	NC	Elected
5	Banke	Mohammadi Siddiqui	NC	PR
6	Rautahat	Abdul Kalam Azad	CPNUML	PR
7	Syangja	Hashina Miya Begum	CPNUML	PR
8	Sarlahi-2	Muhammad Rizwan Ansari	CPNUML	Elected
9	Arghakhanchi	Nazir Miya	CPNUML	PR
10	Parsa-1	Karima Begum	MJF	Elected
11	Kapilbastu	Md. Akbal Ahmad Sah	MJF	Nominated
12	Banke-2	Md. Istiyaq Rai	MJF	Elected
13	Rupandehi-7	Md. Okil Musalman	MJF	Elected
14	Sarlahi	Salma Khatun Mikrani	MJF	PR
15	Kapilbastu	Sahlaudin Musalman	TMLP	PR
16	Nawalparasi	Alauddin Ansari	RPP	PR
17	Saptari-5	Sadrul Miya Hak	Independent	Elected

Source: www.weallnepali.com/about-nepal/names-of-601-constitution-assembly-ca-members-of-nepal

Only four out of the seventeen were women, one from the CPN (Maoist), one from the UML, and two from the MJF, and of these only one, Karima Begum, was elected under the first-past-the-post system (for Parsa 1 in the eastern *terai). She* was to become a deputy minister in the interim government in 2009 and Minister of State for Agriculture and Cooperatives in the government led by Madhav Kumar Nepal, and to prove highly controversial. Begum, who remains active in Madhesi politics, is now a central committee member of the Sanghiya Samajwadi Forum Nepal. Two, Salma Khatun Mikrani and Halina Khatun, were elected by PR from Sarlahi district, also in the eastern *terai.* The fourth, Hashina Miya Begum, who was one of the two representatives from the hill district of Syanjya, could read but not write Nepali and was assisted by her daughter.

Salma Khatum Mikrani was the only representative of the Mikrani community and was a member of the Madhesi Jana Adhikar Forum, Nepal. When the party later split into two, and she joined the Jaya Prakash Gupta group, who launched a new political party under the name Madhesi Jana Adhikar Forum (Republican) in May 2011. Before the second Constituent Assembly election of 2013, she left the Madhesi Jana Adhikar Forum (Republican), and joined the Tarai-Madhes Loktantrik Party in a programme organised by Chairman Mahanth Thakur in Janakpur in August 2013. She was born on 25 January 1976 at Kattarban village, in Rajdevi VDC, Rautahat District. Her father was Mohammad Shamsul Haque Mikrani, and her mother Jamila Begum Mikrani. She married Mohammad Azaz Mikrani, from Bhadsar VDC, Sarlahi, and lives with him in Bharsar-6, Sarlahi. She actively participated in the Madhesi movement in 2006 and 2007, and 'because of her bravery, sincerity, patience and courage' the party selected her to be the proportional representative of Sarlahi district.

Muslim Demands: the 10-Point Memorandum

Unhappy with their effective incorporation in political parties as *janajatis* or *madhesis*, a broad alliance of 31 Muslim groups submitted a 10-point memorandum to the CA in mid-April 2008, calling for the formation of a constitutional commission and a federation that recognized the Muslim community as an integral aspect of Nepali society. They also asked the state to adopt a policy of positive discrimination towards the community. The demands of Muslims were that the state should recognize their distinct identity and their right to equal treatment based on secularism, but that it should setup a separate Muslim commission to address the community's needs. Similarly, they also demanded a guarantee of proportionate representation for Muslims at all levels of the state government, recognition of *Madrasa* education and permission to enforce Muslim family laws and protection of mosques.

"We would really like to be able to build more mosques, expand our traditions and be able to publicly practice our faith without being fearful of repression," said Sadrul Miya Haq, a Muslim MP and coordinator of the National Muslim Struggle Alliance (NMSA). "Fundamentally, the Muslim demands are part of the need to create freedom of religion that does not keep Nepal only Hindu." The enforcement of family law, however, for one thing is controversial, as this allows Muslim men to marry as many as four women, which is against the national law and which women activists (including the very few Muslim women activists) argue would generate unacceptable discrimination against Muslim women if allowed and practised.

Women's Demands

Of the 601 members of the new Constituent Assembly, a record 197 were women. The Women's Caucus, which was originally established in 2002, was reformed on 2 January 2009 and now came into its own. The Women's Caucus in the Constituent Assembly also prepared a set of demands, with the help of International IDEA, entitled 'Women's Rights and Agenda to be Incorporated in the New Constitution' (www.idea.int/resources/analysis/upload/Women-s-Caucus-Book-Final-version-eng.pdf). The document provided a brief historical background to the women's movement in Nepal, in the context of a wider analysis of Nepal's political history, with particular emphasis on developments since 2006.

It referred to the fact that the Interim Constitution which originally had no women's representation but eventually, after protest, included four women in the drafting committee for the first time in the history of Nepal guaranteed women's rights constitutionally in separate headings under fundamental human rights. The document declared that 'Nepalese women's expectations are the similar to that (sic) of *dalits*, indigenous peoples, *madhesis* and people from backward regions regarding the inclusion of various issues such as equality, co-existence, representation, access and participation in the new Constitution'. It emphasised that 'the constitution must ensure equal opportunity, access and respect for all. It must also make special provision for previously marginalised and disadvantaged groups'.

As regards the Committee on Fundamental Rights and Directive Principles (one of the 14 committees of the Constituent Assembly, and arguably the most important) it was stated that 'the Constituent Assembly rules, 2065 (2008) lay down the jurisdiction of the Committee... as the identification of fundamental rights; grounds for the restriction of fundamental rights; provisions relating to the implementation of fundamental rights; directive principles and policies of the state; the provision of special protection for the rights and interests of women, children, youth, labourers, peasants, *madhesis*, indigenous people, *dalits*, people from backward regions, and all minority groups including disabled people and Muslims; provisions related to citizenship; and other essential matters related to the jurisdiction of the Committee'.

Note that mention of Muslims as a special group is made right at the end of a long list of so-called 'minorities', and after disabled people. This is despite the fact that despite the fact that several members of the Caucus were Muslim women and one of the co-ordinators, the Honourable Mohammadi Siddhiki, was also a Muslim. But, arguably, at least Muslims are specifically mentioned as a particular social group and as a minority requiring 'special protection'.

Muslims are also included in the list of those requiring 'special provision' under the heading of 'Right to Equality', although the list is different here, and includes an extraordinary number of social groups: 'women, *dalits*, indigenous ethnic tribes *(adiwasi janajatis)*, *madhesis* or farmers, workers, oppressed region (sic), Muslims, backward class, minority, marginalised and endangered communities or destitute people, youths, children, senior citizens, gender or sexual minorities, disable or those who are physically or mentally incapacitated and helpless people, who are economically, socially or culturally backward'.

Muslims are mentioned under the heading 'Right to Social Justice' as one of the groups 'having a right to participate in state structures on the basis of the principles of proportionate inclusion' and under 'Policy Related to Social Justice and Inclusiveness', to keep them 'participating in the state structure of the nation on the basis of the principle of inclusiveness and in public services on the basis of the principle of proportionate participation'. It is also stated that 'the guiding principle of public administration will be based on the appointment of staff on the basis of basic qualification and efficiency', but 'to provide for compensation to women, *dalits*, indigenous castes, *madhesis* and Muslims, based on human development index'. We have already seen in the previous main section that the human development index of Muslims places them at the bottom of all the social groups in Nepal, with the exception of *dalits,* specifically madhesi or *terai dalits*.

Muslims are mentioned in respect of elections both to the House of Representatives and to Provincial Assemblies and it is enjoined that all of the special groups listed (including Muslims) 'are equally represented on the basis of population and the closed list of the provinces'. They are not mentioned, however, in all of the lists of those requiring special protection or provision. For example, in the rights of women, specific mention is made of 'the proportionate representation of *madhesi* women, indigenous nationality and minority and *dalit* women will be made in all rights subjected to (sic = relating to) women'. Also, specific mention is made of the rights of *dalits*: 'the proportionate representation of all hill *dalits, madhesi dalits* and *dalit* women will be made in all rights received by the *dalit* community', but not of Muslims.

Muslims are mentioned under 'Judicial Rights', where it is stated that 'the persons of backward communities including women, indigenous castes, *madhesis, dalits,* Muslims shall be appointed as judges while appointing in accordance with such principle of proportional inclusion'. It is also stated that there will be special Commissions for *dalits, adivasi janajatis,* People with Disabilities, Minority and Marginalised Communities and People of Backward Regions (sic), for *Madhesis* and for Muslims. The document ends with a list of the 197 women members of the Constituent Assembly, including the Muslim women Halina Khatun Sokhin, Hasina Miya, Karima Begum, Mohammadi Siddiqi and Salma Khatun Mikarani.

Action by Muslims in the First Constituent Assembly

The adoption of a mixed system of proportional representation with first-past-the-post in the 2008 elections to the Constituent Assembly led to a historically diverse elected Assembly (CA). Of 601 members, some 17 were Muslim (2.8 per cent of the total membership). Of these, five were women, and a Muslim woman headed the National Women's Commission. For the first time in history, Muslim representatives both men and women - had an opportunity to reach the topmost decision-making level of the country.

The Muslim representatives in the CA were energised by this. They came together within the CA, formed a Muslim Caucus, and together made collective interventions in various thematic committees and in the main CA sessions, even though they were not represented at the main decision-making level within the CA." Our community's concerns and issues were never addressed in the history of Nepal's constitutions. Thus we had tried our best to include them," said Najir Miya, former CA member, nominated by CPN-UML. "Most importantly, we (Muslim representatives in CA) had raised the issues of recognition. If CA had brought the final constitution, we Muslim would have got at least some rights guaranteed in it."

As the deadline for Nepal's constitution approached, however, many contentious issues among Nepal's ethnic, caste, regional and political groups remained to be resolved. Analysts warned of further political instability unless a Constitution could be agreed upon soon, while NMSA said that it would launch a second phase of protests on 2 May 2008 to ensure constitutional guarantees for Muslims. In the event, the CA failed to meet its deadline, even when extended several times, and it was eventually dissolved. As in the case of many other minority groups, Muslims hoped that the final draft of the new Constitution would guarantee their rights, issues and concerns, and more importantly, it would recognize their distinct identity.

A certain amount of progress was made in 2008 in other spheres as well, particularly as regards the recognition of Muslim religious and cultural distinctiveness. The Kathmandu-based *Islami Sangh Nepal took* the initiative of getting the entire Quran translated into Nepali; the translated version was launched in May 2008 in a bid to spread the message of Islam among Nepali-speaking people. The five-year project was funded by the Al-Quran Academy in London, an international organisation engaged in Islamic research and publication. About 2,000 copies were printed in New Delhi and it was planned that these would be circulated in Bhutan and Myanmar as well, countries which have a sizeable Nepali-speaking population. Bookshops near the Kashmiri and Jama Mosques said there was a brisk sale of the Nepali Quran. Sales were expected to rise during the three-day celebrations marked by prayers and feasts.

On 9 December 2008, as the former Hindu kingdom of Nepal celebrated the holy Muslim festival of Bakr Eid, for thousands of Muslims there was an additional cause to rejoice as the government for the first time had announced a public holiday on the occasion. 'Prachanda' referred to the Bakr Eid as 'a source of inspiration' and hoped it would cement cultural and social harmony in Nepal." We thank the government for declaring Bakr Eid a state holiday," said Sheikh Ali Mirza, an Imam at Kathmandu's Kashmiri Masjid, one of the two main mosques in the capital. "It is also a matter of joy that the holy Quran is now available in Nepali so that people who do not know Arabic can comprehend the Prophet's teachings."

Nearly a decade later, when the government proposed a time extension for the second tranche of local elections, it initially chose the last day of Ramadan probably without thinking but after representations from the Muslim community, agreed to delay the elections by a few more days to enable the Muslims of Nepal and other Nepali citizens to celebrate the end of Ramadan and the Bakr Eid.

Slow Progress

But if the official situation appeared to be relatively positive, there were indications that some at least remained antagonistic to the Muslim communities. In early October 2008, for example, at least six people were injured when a powerful explosion ripped through a mosque in Hattimuda village in the vicinity of Biratnagar in Morang District when a bomb was thrown into the mosque by unidentified attackers. Nazrul Hassan, President of the Muslim Association of Nepal, called on local Muslims to exercise restraint. 'This is a deliberate attempt to disturb religious harmony. The government must act decisively against those behind this act', he said. The bombing came shortly after the release of an Indian security report based on confessions extracted during interrogation of members of the Students' Islamic Movement of India (SIMI), one of whom mentioned a Nepali student with whom SIMI interacted and who had discussed plans to launch attacks in Nepal. It was never made clear that there was, in fact, any link between this information and the attack on the mosque in Hattimuda village.

Another explosion occurred in April 2009 in the Rajapur area of Rautahat District. The UML candidate for Rautahat 3, Sailendra Shah, asserted that the explosion was carried out by NC candidate Mohammed Aftab Alam and that more people than reported were killed in the incident. Despite this, Aftab Alam was elected (with 1,266 votes against 776 votes of his nearest rival Mohammad Razi Haidar) as a member of the central working committee (CWC) of the Nepali Congress under the quota allocated for the Muslim community. Ten candidates contested the reserved seat.

Muslim Demands: The Six-Point Agreement

If Muslims as a whole tend to remain politically marginalised, there is also a tendency within the various Muslim communities themselves fail to make 'external' social, economic and political relations a priority and so in effect marginalize themselves. However, when the Maoist-led government announced a public service ordinance to provide 45 per cent reservations to marginalized groups in early 2009, various factions of Muslims launched agitations, at times in concert with other groups, and at times by themselves. In fact, in the beginning of March 2009, some Muslims, through the United National Muslim Struggle Committee (UNMSC), announced a series of protest programs together with other *terai* indigenous groups, like the Tharus, to demand amendments in the Interim Constitution and the ordinance. In particular, the committee demanded that the government's decision to categorize Muslims as *madhesis* be changed.

In addition, the Struggle Committee also demanded the formation of a Muslim Commission, proportional representation of Muslims in state bodies, a fresh population census of under-represented Muslims, Tharus and *adivasi-janajatis* with the active involvement of the communities concerned. Consequently, on 16 March 2009, the government and representatives of the Muslim community signed a six-point agreement agreeing to fulfil all the demands put forth by the Struggle Committee except for the implementation of *shari'a* law, on grounds that it was too complicated an issue to deal with within such a short period of time. This six-point agreement was a 'historic achievement for the Muslims', since it not only marked the government's concession to the demands of the Muslims but was arguably the first official indication that the Nepali state accepts its Muslim population as citizens with equal rights rather than as *mlecchas, or* 'foreigners'.

In this way, Nepal's first Maoist Prime Minister Pushpa Kamal Dahal ('Prachanda'), pledged to form a Muslim Commission for the 'uplift' or promotion of the Muslim community. The government also provided funding to help nearly 400 Muslims go to Saudi Arabia to perform the Haj. Despite his promises to the Muslim community, however, Maoist leader Pushpa Kamal Dahal 'Prachanda', whose government collapsed in May 2009, did not appoint a single Muslim to the cabinet. By contrast, Prime Minister Madhav Kumar Nepal, who succeeded 'Prachanda', expanded his Cabinet, adding five new ministers, and included two Muslims. Mohammad Aftab Alam, a Nepali Congress MP from Rautahat District in the Terai, was given Cabinet rank with Labour and Construction portfolios, while Rizwan Ansari, a member of the Nepal Communist Party (United Marxist and Leninist), was appointed as state minister for Home Affairs. This was the first time Muslims not have been brought into government since the elections to the Constituent Assembly the previous year.

In February 2010, Mohammed Aftab Alam made it clear in an interview in the *Nepali Times*, that he was not happy with the idea that the State Re-Structuring Committee had proposed to define the new federal states on the basis of ethnicity. 'This is totally wrong', he said, 'and is sure to invite more trouble. To designate provinces on the basis of either ethnicity or language is to wound the nation'. He suggested that 'restructuring should be on the basis of geography... looking at the model the committee passed, it seems as if the country is one of majority ethnicities, although no ethnicity has a majority here... State restructuring should not take place along ethnic lines, as those in the minority will be exploited'. He was clearly concerned that Muslims would lose out if the state restructuring involved the specific representation of 'Madhesis'.

Muslim Women: Various Initiatives

On 25 September 2009, IDEA posted an article on the Constituent Assembly's Women's Caucus, pointing out that

Nepal has become a source of inspiration to women in many countries where women's parliamentary representation is negligible. The Nepalese Parliament, for example, has 197 women out of 601 members a record of one-third representation. The 197 member Women's Caucus of the Parliament/Constituent Assembly (CA) has a 23-member Executive Committee. Honorary Dama Sharma from the Unified Communist Party of Nepal Maoist (the largest party in the Parliament/CA) is the coordinator of the Committee.

With members drawn from 19 of the 25 political parties represented in the CA, Ms. Dama believes that with this formal structure, the Women's Caucus, is playing a key role in ensuring women's rights in the new Constitution. Apart from advocating for women's rights and acting as a pressure group, the Caucus is also involved in studying important issues and analyzing them from the gender perspective. One of the features of the Caucus is its ability to work across party lines. The Caucus envisages having at least 50 per cent participation of women at all levels of the Nepalese state. It has already prepared a charter of women's rights and has submitted it to the CA so that it becomes the guiding principle while drafting the new Constitution, especially the chapter on fundamental rights.

Recently, two sessions with the Women's Caucus were held in Kathmandu. One session focused on the electoral system and quotas, and the other on fundamental rights. More than a hundred Women's Caucus members attended the event and recommended a joint action plan. The programme was supported by International IDEA and UNDP.

In 2009, the Prime Minister declared 2010 to be the year to combat gender-based violence (GBV) or violence against women (VAW). A study was undertaken in February-March 2015, by the Asia Foundation in association with DFID and Saathi (an NGO established in 1992 to address the challenges faced by Nepali women, notably violence against women, with offices in Kanchanpur, Banke, and Kapilvastu districts and a total of about 100 staff), and was published the same year. It conclusions were, broadly, that a great deal more work was required, not just to identify the scale and causes of violence against women but also to provide better protection and support for women victims of violence.

The Nepal Muslim Women's Welfare Society had been set up to serve the marginalised, disadvantaged and resource poor community of Muslim women in Nepal. It had a small core staff, but undertook a wide range of activities in some 12 districts, four in the eastern *terai* (Saptari, Siraha, Morang and Sunsari), three in the central *terai* (Parsa, Mahottari and Sarlahi), one in the western *terai* (Kapilvastu) and one in the mid-western *terai* (Banke).

In the winter of 2010, there were rumours that the National Muslim Forum had aspirations to become a political party. It had by this time come under the umbrella of the United Muslim National Struggle Committee, an organisation representing 24 of the country's Muslim organisations. In 2010, it was commissioned by the UNDP to work in partnership with the Muslim Women's Welfare Association, and to survey Muslim communities from ten districts across Nepal and prepare a report for the Constituent Assembly.

The *Islami Sangh Nepal*

In her discussion of the *Islamic Revival in Nepal*; Megan Sijapati refers to the *Islami Sangh Nepal* as having the longest history and greatest national reach of all the many Islamic and Muslim organisations in Nepal. 'Today', she remarks, '*The Islami Sangh Nepal* has a significant presence in the Kathmandu Valley, where its offices are located north of the Nepali Jame Masjid in the Ghanta Ghar area on King's Way'. The organisation has four branches: Al-Hira Educational Society, which aims to train scholars from the various parts of Nepal and coordinates the distribution of overseas scholarships for Nepali Muslims; The first Constituent Assembly struggled over several years to draft a new Constitution. It began in the mid-1980s; The Masjid Council, which overlooks mosque affairs, finding and the establishing of new mosques across Nepal; the Students Education Foundation, which overlooks Muslim student affairs at the local level; and the Health Services and Relief Association; which aims to provide health services among the Muslim population. It also helps to maintain the *Millat-e Islamiya's* Islamic Library a valuable community source housing materials for the study of Islam in many languages.

The *Islami Sangh* claims no explicit doctrinal affiliation and resists the attempts of others to associate it with one school of thought or another. Most of its leaders and senior members were educated in northern India. Many attended Darul Uloom Nadwatul 'Ulama in Lucknow, Jami'atul Falah in Azamgarh and Madrasatul Islah in Sareameer, all of which combine standard and modern curricula.

The First Constituent Assembly: Achievements and Failures

The original deadline for the promulgation of the new Constitution was 28 May 2011. In early April 2011, the magazine *Spotlight* ran a headline article in which it remarked that 'as May 28 draws closer, concerns over whether the new Constitution will be promulgated by that deadline are growing'. It pointed out that 'the many voices of difference and dissent coming from a range of political and ethnic organisations compound the problem'. It referred in particular to the concerns of *dalits* and Muslims:

> 'CA members Bishwendra Paswan and Sradural Miya Haq threw out the chair of the Constitutional committee when it rejected their amendment proposal to incorporate in the new constitution. "If the new constitution does not recognize the rights of Dalits and minority Muslims, we will burn its copies as soon as it is promulgated," said Paswan. "We will go for a long struggle against the state." Minority Muslim's rights should be recognized in the constitution, demanded CA member Sradural Miya. "If the CA ignores our demands, we will have no option other than to go for a rebellion," he said. These two smaller parties are not the only ones to challenge the future constitution. Other political parties and ethnic groups hold equally strong views'.

The next couple of years (2011-2012) were years of political infighting between the various major political parties and their leaders and there was little progress on any front. The Muslim Commission, promised by the then Prime Minister, 'Prachanda', in 2009, was not, for example, established for another three years. Securing basic rights for Muslim communities and individuals proved just one of the failures of the First Constituent Assembly, which was finally (and controversially) dissolved on 27-28 May 2012 because of the continual squabbling between the leaders of the main political parties and its successive failure to draft an agreed Constitution.

However, following the concerted efforts of the Muslim movement, a Cabinet meeting held on April, 5, 2012 eventually issued an order for the formation of a Muslim Commission with the mandate to conduct a study on the problems faced by the Muslim community and recommend the government to address them. The 11-member Central Hajj Committee, under the Ministry of Home Affairs, was another product of government recognition of the specific religious and cultural needs of the Muslim community. This Committee oversees and, together with various leading Muslim associations, organises the annual Hajj or pilgrimage to Mecca in Saudi Arabia, which is one of the five 'pillars' or requirements of 'good Muslim'. In 2012, the Hajj Committee helped send around 840 Nepali Muslims, both men and women, as pilgrims to Mecca. In 2013, the numbers sent as pilgrims exceeded 1,000. Also the Nepal Muslim Ettihad Organisation (NMEO), a specifically religious organisation, was established.

Muslim Demands: Another 10-Point Memorandum

In mid-April 2012, a broad alliance of 31 Muslim groups submitted a 10-point memorandum to the Constituent Assembly, calling for the formation of a constitutional commission and a federation that recognizes the Muslim community as an integral aspect of Nepali society. They also asked the state to adopt a policy of positive discrimination towards the community.

"We would really like to be able to build more mosques, expand our traditions and be able to publicly practice our faith without being fearful of repression," said Sadrul Miya Haq, a Muslim MP and coordinator of the National Muslim Struggle Alliance (NMSA). "Fundamentally, the Muslim demands are part of the need to create freedom of religion that does not keep Nepal only Hindu." As the deadline for Nepal's constitution approaches, many contentious issues among Nepal's ethnic, caste, regional and political groups remain to be resolved. Analysts warn of further political instability unless a constitution can be agreed upon soon, while NMSA says it will launch a second phase of protests on 2 May to ensure constitutional guarantees for Muslims'.

"Shortly afterwards, however, on 24 April, Muslim activists and politicians demonstrated at the District Administrative Office in Kathmandu, a prohibited zone that is off-limits to protesters, demanding that their voices be heard in the drafting of the constitution and their identity and religious background be supported; 23 were detained. Some in the community perceived this as a crackdown on Muslim activism and further action was threatened. As the deadline for Nepal's new Constitution approached, many contentious issues remained to be resolved. Muslim recognition and representation remained key issues for Muslim activists and NMSA stated that it would launch a second phase of protests on 2 May to ensure constitutional guarantees for Muslims".

The Muslim Commission

On May 3, in a pre-emptive 'strike', the government instituted the promised 13-member Muslim Commission, the officials of the Commission were nominated - one Chairman, one Member Secretary and eleven members - and the Commission 'activated'. Those nominated were 'people who were considered to have made a significant contribution to the development of the Muslim community'. Provision was made for at least one official per development region and their term of office was to be a maximum of four years.

The National Muslim Commission is a governmental organization of Nepal and its activities are to be undertaken in collaboration with the Ministry of Federal Affairs and Local Development (MoFLD), which provides limited support personnel and services. The Commission was set up to operate with a budget allocated to it by the government, but it was empowered to obtain grants or donations from any one or more of a range of sources (including foreign governments, international organizations, institutions, persons, national organizations, institutions, or persons). It has published a set of comments on the present status of the Muslim Community in Nepal, which go some way to recognising a number of key issues.

'Looking at the past, it seems that the state has not made as much of a contribution to the development of religious and historical sites on behalf of the Muslim community as they have for the Hindu and Buddhist communities. Until now, the mobilization of resources for the Muslim community has not been up to the expectation of its members. Most of the Muslim community are severely backwards and under poverty line. By comparison with other groups, the Muslims are more uneducated and unemployed. The mosque education system (of *madrasas*) is not yet managed properly and needs to be promoted and better organised. There is a need for effective programmes to maintain national standards in mosque education and correspond to the formal procedures applicable in the public or state sector. It is necessary to keep records of the major Muslim institutions (*Masjid, Madrasa, Edgah, Majahar, Karbala, Kavresthan*) as well as to establish land rights and ownership for these institutions.

In addition to academic scholarships, there needs to be provision for a separate quota for the Muslim population in the area of public service. Muslims are currently identified with *Madhesis*. For the effective social inclusion of the Muslim community (including the religious and community aspects), there has to be a provision for separate 'reservation'. Muslims live, not only in the terai but also in the hills and mountains, so it is not justified to label the Muslims as '*Madhesis*'. Even at the time of the elections for the second Constituent Assembly, there was no provision for the mandatory representation of the Muslim community, which shows the state's disregard towards this community.

Various national programmes for 'backward peoples' have yet to reach the Muslim community. Due to historical traditional values and beliefs, the women and girl children of the Muslim community are backward in education, health and nutrition and there are hindrances for them to receive adequate family, marital and social respect. It is important to design and implement programme to solve some of the problems faced by the members of this community. For example, there is no provision or permanent mechanism relating to the Huj house in Nepal, and no formal recognition of the Huj; also, there is no formal academic recognition of those Muslim students who have gained a higher qualification from foreign schools and universities; and, finally, Muslims identified as 'Madhesis' rather than having a separate identity.'

On 1 May 2012, IRIN reported from what it described as 'a tiny mountain village of 1,000 inhabitants on the edge of the Kathmandu Valley' the views of Sheikh Islam, a local community leader: 'we are Muslims, but we are Nepalis as well. We are a growing segment of society and we hope to have our voices heard as political leaders write a new constitution'. At that time, the Constituent Assembly was working to complete its task of drafting a new Constitution by 27 May its 5th deadline. 'Here in our village', remarked the Sheikh, 'we are struggling to make life tolerable and our community has hopes that Muslims will have a voice in the drafting process.' IRIN commented that 'his optimism does not appear to be widely shared among Muslims, who are under-represented in government'. 'In many ways, the Muslims in Nepal struggle like everyone else, but with the rising fear of Islam across the world, Nepalese remain scared of Muslims, which is why we are pressing for change' said Sheikh Islam.

Any hopes that Muslims may have had was frustrated as the Constitution-drafting process ended, as far as the first Constituent Assembly was concerned, on May 28 2012, without a constitution. At the end of May, the CA itself was eventually dissolved, after several years of inter-party wrangling about political positions in the government and a failure to draft the new Constitution, ending any hopes the Muslim community may have had that it would draft a Constitution in which Muslims were specifically identified and their rights fully recognised.

After the dissolution of the Constituent Assembly (CA) of Nepal in May 2012, many women representatives, including the Muslim women in the CA, expressed their regret at the failures of the CA, in particular as regards the position and rights of women, and as regards the status of Muslims.

Najir Miya, a former CA member nominated by CPN-UML, who believes that 'the main problem of the Muslim community remains their identity', argued that 'they have been historically marginalized and excluded so as their representation in politics, bureaucracy, and decision making level is dismal. Their literacy rate and human development index are both below those of the *dalits* and people from backward districts in the Karnali region'. Another former CA member nominated by Nepali Congress, Mohammadi Siddiqui, says, "As none of the six constitutions promulgated earlier addressed the issues of Muslims and Muslim women, it was really challenging and hard to make politicians and CA members understand who the Muslims are, and in the final new constitution. We however could include the concerns and rights in the constitution, but the CA ended without writing the Constitution." According to her, 'if the constitution had been promulgated, the Muslim wouldn't only have merely been recognized but many of their rights would be protected in it. But the sad fact is, it ended without bearing any fruit'.

The CA was not, however, was by no means entirely a failure, and several initiatives continued even after its official demise, including several relating to the Muslim communities of Nepal.

The National Madrasa Education Management Board

On 2 January 2013, the government instituted a 15-member National Madrasa Education Management Board, led by the Minister for Education. The Board has so far recognized 1,135 *madrasa* schools. The informal data has it that there are now nearly 3,000 *madrasas* in Nepal. This is significant progress, but Mohammad Nirdosh Ali, Chairperson of the new Muslim Commission, has said that 'the government must recognize the *madrasa* (religious school of Muslim), provide necessary resources as it does to the government schools, including school curriculum, teachers, stationeries and so on. Similarly, the government must recognize Muslims and ensure equal rights, as it did for other minority groups, whereby it should also guarantee proportionate representation of Muslims in all state mechanisms.'

The Nepal Muslim Women's Welfare Society

On 15 April 2013, it was reported in *Islamic Voice* that Nepalese Muslim women had come together to form the Nepal Muslim Women Welfare Society (NMWWS) to undertake advocacy for Muslim women's legal rights and political participation.

> 'According to Seema Khan, Secretary of the Society, 'Muslims constitute 4.4 per cent of the population of Nepal which is now a secular democracy. According to 2006 Census, literacy among Muslim women is 26.5 per cent'. Khan says, 'of the Muslims aged 20 and above, only two per cent people are either decently employed or hold positions in Government or are in the professional field'. Khan told this scribe while attending the International

Conference on the 'Status of Muslim Women in South Asia' held on March 6-8 in Hyderabad, that Nepal's democracy is still grappling with the problems of infancy and there is only a Constituent Assembly in the country. Of the 601 delegates in the Constituent Assembly, 18 are Muslims including five women. Surprisingly, the National Women's Commission of Nepal (set up in 2010) is currently headed by a Muslim woman, Sheikh Chand Tara. Of the four members in the commission, two including the Chairperson, are Muslim. The second of the two is Mohna Ansari, Nepal's only Muslim advocate (see below).

According to the Report on 'Gender, Caste and Ethnic Exclusion in Nepal', 48 per cent of Muslims have never been to school in comparison to 12 per cent Brahmans and Chhetris, the two upper castes who have traditionally ruled Nepal. The Report, by Lynn Bennett of the World Bank, puts Muslims among the most disadvantaged groups together with Dalits and Janajatis. Khan says the Muslim women suffer from early marriage, traditional culture and gender roles, dowry and high poverty. The NMWWS is conducting (a study programme) on 'Enabling Muslim Women's Access to Mainstream Politics in three Districts of Saptari, Rauthat and Parsa'. The Society website lists marital woes of Muslim women in Nepal among whom there are a large number of divorcees saddled with children'.

The NMWWS states that it is

'a non-partisan, non-profit and non- discriminatory organization serving the marginalized, disadvantaged and resource poor community particularly, to Muslim women of Nepal. The role of these non-government organizations has been witnessed to be pivotal in sensitizing and creating awareness among all sections of the society. Guided and motivated by this very phenomenon, a pragmatic team of social workers initiated the creation of this organization in order to complement and supplement the national plans, policies and priorities of the Government of Nepal'.

NMWWS has been serving the Muslim community by mobilizing the unused and underutilized resources (human and natural resources) available within the society. It has also undertaken significant activities that have enhanced the production and productivity of the economy as a whole. In the meantime, it has helped the society in creating awareness through advocacy, and strengthening the leadership capability of the hitherto excluded and disadvantaged groups. Socio-economic development and the empowerment of the Muslim women through their own participation have been the significant achievement of the organization so far.

With a view to achieving holistic development of community and especially to improving living of those targeted groups, NMWWS has been implementing multidisciplinary type of projects in partnership with donors and supporting organizations since its establishment. It has gained considerable understanding on root cause of the social issues and challenges, and knowledge and experience from its past experiences. The areas of expertise of NMWWS are advocacy, human rights, democracy, women's political participation, violence against women, non-formal education for adult women, skill training for income generation and community development activities'.

In the years following the demise of the first Constituent Assembly, International IDEA, which had been active in Nepal for many years, continued supporting the former Women's Caucus members in order to protect the achievements made in the CA on women's issues, and to ensure women's representation of at least 33 per cent in any new constitution making body. Former women CA members also continued to work for implementation of the Interim Constitution, through various agencies and in various forums, including that of the Nepal Women's Commission (NWC).

National Women's Commission

On 4 March 2013, Deepti Khakural of IDEA interviewed Mohna Ansari, a Member of the National Women's Commission since June 2010, and the first female lawyer from the minority Muslim community. Mohna Ansari herself is an example of what is possible albeit against the odds for a Muslim woman. She became the first member of her family to graduate from college and went on to become the only female Muslim attorney in Nepal, successfully arguing a landmark case for a woman to claim her legal right to family property. On 2 June 2010, she became a member (Commissioner) of the National Women's Commission. She left on 2 February 2014 to work with International IDEA and was instrumental in promoting and supporting this research project.

In the interview, she responded in detail to a number of key questions put to her:

Q. How do you see the status of Nepali women changing over the last decade? Who have been the agents of that change?

A. In Nepal, women have been facing social, cultural and legal barriers for a very long time. Women's movements in Nepal have always been demanding basic human rights such as equality, equal participation and recognition of women's identity. Some significant changes took place after the democratic movement of 1990 which brought about the new constitution and constitutional provisions on equality, nondiscrimination and ensuring some level of participation of women.

A decade long Maoist led peoples' war raised the questions of nondiscrimination and equality again. After the peace process and Jana Andolan II (second people's movement) in 2006, there were high expectations, but the political promises were not translated into actions by the different political parties. It seems that after every such popular movement, women's representation is always overlooked by the political parties. Women remain in a position where they are forced to request for their rights from men, who are always in the leadership position.

The Interim Constitution of 2007, which requires at least 33 per cent of women's representation in all state structures, is one of the major instruments regarding women's representation. This also applies to political parties too; but none of them have 33 per cent of women in their key positions. Similarly, the political parties have always denied the debate of women's equal citizenship rights and identity.

Every citizen in Nepal has been an agent of change. All the past and ongoing struggles and movements have created awareness within the different communities in our society. Today, not only political cadres but also youth, students, human rights activists, NGOs and to some extent the government are making changes in the society. However, women themselves are the real change makers since without their voices and perseverance nothing could have been achieved.

Q. Cases of violence against women have been much discussed recently in the media. Has the level of violence increased over the last few years or is the media just starting to report violence against women?

A. Our society has never been free from violence. Only that this topic finally interests the media. There are many FM radio stations and daily newspapers that are accessible to people. These days violence is often first reported in the media and then afterwards reported to the police. Women are more empowered now and their voices are also getting stronger because they do not want to tolerate violence any longer. However, with the increased reporting of the violence, the number of women getting justice has not increased. So I would conclude that the results are not satisfactory.

Q. What challenges does the National Women's Commission currently face?

A. Violence against women is the priority issue for the NWC. We have a mandate to work for the protection and prevention of violence towards individual women. If the police fail to listen to women's complaints, they come to NWC in order to get justice. After hearing individual cases we try to make the police pursue those cases.

At the NWC, we have scarce resources and no outreach offices in regional Nepal. We face many challenges including the ingrained unsympathetic government culture and remaining discriminatory laws. Our laws and policies are not victim oriented. We have provisions for penalties but not for compensation. However, we are working intensively with our given mandate.

Q. The new constitution prepared by the Constituent Assembly (CA) was supposed to establish women' rights and bring about equality. How do you see the dissolution of the CA from a women's perspective?

A. The fact that the CA ended without seeing a constitution adopted is a major loss for the women of Nepal. The CA was a unique platform where 197 women (almost 33%) were able to debate and advocate on their issues. At the moment we do not have any formal state level mechanism to provide for women's representation.

I am a bit sad though, that in spite of such a large number of women, the CA which was serving as Parliament too could not bring about more changes. Draft bills, such as the bill on witchcraft, on preventing sexual harassment in work places, on Truth and Reconciliation and on disappearances during the conflict, were not tabled and endorsed during the tenure of the Parliament, which I think was a lost opportunity for Nepali women.

Q. You are from the Muslim community, can you tell us something about your personal journey and experience in a leadership position.

Q. In our community women's leadership is not easily accepted. Our religion mentions equality, equal opportunity for education and even having the choice of marriage. In practice, however, due to cultural reasons, women leaders are not accepted by the society. I faced lots of challenges while I was going to school: at times my family was even asked why they were sending me to school.

People are not used to seeing Muslim women working in the public sphere. So many people commented on the fact that I was working as a journalist for 3-4 years. I used to write about women and children's issues and was much involved in the polio campaign in 2004. Now, the community has realized and acknowledged my leadership in some ways. These days, Muslim women too are looking for positions in state bodies. The state should have special programmes targeting the marginalized communities such as Muslims, *dalits*, *janajati* etc.

Q. Do you have any suggestions for the women's movement in Nepal?

A. In Nepal, violence against women is the most difficult problem it should be totally and fully stopped. It should be addressed by the laws and by every individual at home. Also, our participation and representation must be ensured; otherwise we cannot advocate or make law and policy for women's equality. Our equal citizenship rights - our identity - need to be guaranteed too, otherwise no one accepts your existence.

Mohna Ansari, a well-known rights activist, and Nepal's only female attorney from the Muslim community, worked as the Senior Advisor of IDEA International after the successful completion of her four year term in the National Women Commission (NWC) in June 2014. She was appointed as one of the commissioners for the National Human Right Commission (NHRC) in October 2014[2].

The Second Constitutional Assembly

Elections for the Second Constituent Assembly

Haque suggests that 'Muslim communities are and were used just as a vote bank by the political parties of Nepal'. He argues that the parties claimed they understood and raised the problems of the Muslim communities during the time of elections but then, after having encouraged their members to vote, reneged on any commitments or promises after the elections. 'Not a single party has raised the issue of Muslim representation either in the assembly or in cabinet, and thus Muslims remain the victims of discrimination and marginalization and are deprived of the opportunity of serving the nation politically and in the administration'. He notes that 'the election commission has not identified a quota of fixed seats for the Muslim candidates'.

Eventually, elections were held for a Second Constituent Assembly, on 19 November 2013, but the basis for these was less progressive and inclusive than before. The interim constitution required the representation of women, ethnic minorities, historically disadvantaged groups, and other groups in the Constituent Assembly. Specifically, women, *dalits*, oppressed communities, indigenous people, people from underdeveloped regions, *madhesis* and 'other classes' had to be proportionally represented in the lists of candidates nominated by the political parties for the PR system within the overall electoral procedure. Based on Articles 13 and 33 of the Interim Constitution, electoral law also expanded the definition of the special categories to include people with disabilities, poor farmers and labourers. No reference was made anywhere to Muslims.

The National Constituent Assembly Election Monitoring on Gender, Nepal (NMG) a loose network set up under the auspices of the National Women's Commission to monitor gender aspects of the election process was, however, specifically concerned to assess the involvement and/or lack of involvement of marginalised and/or excluded sections of the population in the election, notably women. The quota for women overall was 50 per cent and the NMG document referred specifically to indigenous ethnic groups, *madhesis* and Muslim women as disadvantaged groups.

Special voter education efforts targeting minority groups were made, to some effect, according to the report produced by the Carter Centre in its report on the elections to the Constituent Assembly. These were commanded by the Carter Centre and resulted, in its view, in a relatively high proportion of women voting. But the campaign suffered from the short time frame within which it was undertaken.

> 'On the issue of federalism, which was the sticking point the last time round, the Maoists have stuck to their ethnicity based provinces and an executive president directly elected by the people. The Nepali Congress wants a parliamentary system. Meanwhile the Communist Party of Nepal (UML) has given a party ticket to Najma Khatun, the widow of Mohammed Alam who died of gunshot wounds earlier this month. Alam had been shot by men on a motorcycle with Indian number plates in southern Nepal. The pro-monarchy Rastriya Prajatantra Party fought the election on a nationalistic platform, calling for a referendum on the status of the monarchy with the hope that Nepal might become a Hindu state once again'.

External Support to Muslim Candidates

It seems that for the most recent elections to the Constituent Assembly (2013), Pakistan launched a secret operation to increase the presence of Muslim members. Intelligence sources and reports from Kathmandu said that Pakistan was financing Muslim candidates across party lines through its embassy in Kathmandu. The plan was apparently to take the number of Muslim representatives in the Constituent Assembly from 25 to 40. Sources pointed out that Zafar Iftikhar, a Pakistani diplomat, was in contact with influential Muslim leaders in Nepal, like Dr. Moazzam and Nazrul Hasan Falahi (both from the *Islamic Sangh, Nepal*) and Taj Mohammad Miyan (who heads the *Nepal Muslim Maha Sangh*), and it was conjectured that funds would have been channelled through such local Nepalese Muslim associations.

The Muslim candidates for the 2013 elections to the Constituent Assembly did not stand on a single platform, but belonged to different political parties; nor were they able to count on Proportional Representation, where most of the 'minority group' candidates were successful in getting elected, as they were not identified by the electoral commission as a distinct group for this purpose, and so contested the Constituent Assembly elections under the First-past-the-post System only.

Reports named at least 12 candidates who had been externally funded from Pakistan. These were: Razi Haider Khan, Javed Khan, Haider Ali, Abdul Hasan Nuri Maqsul Ali, all of the UCPN (Maoist); Dr. Qamrul Hoda, Tajammul Mansuri and Afsaq Sheikh (all of the Rashtriya Madhes Samajwadi Party); Dr. Abdul Kalam Azad (of the CPN-UML), Mirza Arshad Beg (of the Sadbhavana Party); and Dr. Abdul Hussain Ansari (of the *terai*-based Madhesi Loktantrik party). In addition, Pakistan also funded independent candidates with what was considered to be 'winning potential'. Athar Kamal, who contested in Kapilvastu-5, was one such candidate. Nazma Khatun, the Muslim woman who entered the fray after the killing of her husband Mahmud (Mohamed) Alam, a CPN-UML candidate, also reportedly received financial help from the Pakistani Embassy.

Sources suggested that Pakistan provided Rs 4.5 to Rs 5 lakh in Nepalese currency to these Muslim candidates. In the first instalment, 11 out of the 12 candidates have been given Nepalese Rs 1.5 lakh. Afsaq Sheikh alone has received Rs 3 lakh. In the second instalment, Nepalese Rs 3 lakh was to be provided to each of the Muslim candidates in the fray. Sources said that apart from the candidates, the Pakistan embassy also provided funds to local Muslim youths and small-time leaders to mobilise support for these candidates.

Results of the CA Elections

Initial results showed the Nepali Congress winning a plurality of the first-past-the-post seats with 105 of the 240 seats available under this system; the CPM-UML was close behind with 91; and the CPN (Maoist) far behind, winning just 26. Smaller parties and two independent candidates won the remaining 18 seats. 335 seats were allotted by proportional representation using a modified Sainte-Laguë method of allocation.

A total of thirty political parties and two independents were represented in the Second Constituent Assembly. The Nepali Congress emerged as the largest party in the 2nd Constituent Assembly, winning a total of 196 of the 575 elected seats; the CPN (UML) was the next largest party in the Assembly with 175 and the CPN (Maoist) third with 80 seats. Nearly half (48 per cent) or 162 of the 335 seats allotted by PR were women; but only 4 per cent (4 out of 240) of those elected by the first past the post system giving women a total of only 172 seats (in comparison with the 403 men).

Out of the 59 recognised 'indigenous groups' (*janajati*) only 20 were represented with a total of 183 CA members from such groups, as compared with 218 in the First CA, although numerous *janajati* and *madhesi*-based political parties participated in the elections in addition to the handful of larger national parties, most of which put forward a number of *janajati* candidates. Only one *dalit,* however, was elected under the first past the post system, compared with seven in 2008. Eventually a total of 19 Muslims was elected (3.35 per cent of the total population) the best result yet.

A comprehensive report on the 2013 CA elections, undertaken by the Asian Network for Free Elections (ANFREL) did not mention Muslims as voters or candidates at all, although it referred specifically to women, *janajatis, madhesis, dalits* and disabled people. Equally a detailed assessment of the 2013 CA elections by Professor Bishnu Pathak *'Voice of the Voiceless People of Nepal'* (Transcend Media Service, 28 October 2013) which refers also to women, *janajati, dalits* and *madhesis,* fails to refer once to Muslims. The report produced in 2014 by the Carter Centre, 'Observing Nepal's 2013 Constituent Assembly Election, Final Report, which talks a good deal about the issue of representation for marginal and excluded groups, also fails to consider the situation of the Muslims.

The Composition of the Second Constituent Assembly

The Carter Center Report notes that 30 per cent of the elected CA members were women (172 out of 575), compared with the 191 female members elected to the First Constituent Assembly. It also notes that 41 per cent of those elected were from the 'Khas Aryan and other groups', 34 per cent were *janajatis,* 18 per *madhesis*, and 7 per cent *dalits*. No reference is made to the number of Muslims (19), some of whom were elected but as members of political parties and sometimes as *madhesis*.

This time, in fact, the number of Muslims elected amounted to 19 (3.35 per cent of the total), marginally more than in the first CA, but still not equivalent to the percentage of Muslims in the total population (around per cent). In the second CA election, five candidates from Muslim community were elected directly, four men and one woman. They were: Mohamed Mustaq Alam from Rautahat-2 (MJF-Democratic), Formullah Mansoor from Bara-3 (Nepali Congress), Najma Khatoon (Khatun) from Bara-4 (CPN UML), the widow of Mohammed Alam who died of gunshot wounds earlier in October, Abdul Razak Gaddi from Rupandehi-1 (NC) and Atahar Kamaal Musalman from Kapilbastu-2 (Independent).

In the elections to the first CA, the MJF had the most Muslim members by means of FPTP, but in the second CA election their FPTP representation decreased significantly. This may have been because the party had fragmented many times. There was now only one direct representative from the Madhesi Janadhikar Forum-Democratic, a party led by Bijay Kumar Gachhadar, two from the Nepali Congress, one from the CPN UML and an Independent member. Again, as in the first, in the second CA election results also, all the directly elected ('first past the post') Muslim candidates came from *terai* districts.

Table 39: Representation of Muslims in Second CA Elections

SN	Constituency	Elected candidate	Votes	Party
1	Rautahat-2	Md. Mustaq Alam	13,450	MJFN(Democratic)
2	Bara-3	Formullah Mansoor	10,456	NC
3	Bara-4	Najma Khatoon	12,361	CPN-UML
4	Rupandehi- 1	Abdul Razak Gaddi	14,400	NC
5	Kapilbastu -2	Atahar Kamaal Musalman	4,674	Independent

Out of eighteen Muslim CA members, 13 were proportionally represented by various political parties. Among the thirteen PR members, five were females and eight were male members. Three each of the Muslim PR members were from Nepali Congress and CPN UML, two each from UCPN-Maoist and Forum Nepal, and one each from RPP, FSPN and TMLP.

A focus group discussion held in Ek-laini Bazaar in Nepalgunj in the summer of 2015, as part of this project stated that there were 21 Muslim candidates for the CA fourteen (14) male members and seven (7) female members. They remarked that although there was a nominal 33 per cent reservation made in politics for minority groups, Muslims received only 5 per cent of places. Only 21 candidates for 601 assembly members was inadequate; given the Muslim population there should be at least 180 Muslim political leaders standing. From Banke, they said, there were two from the Nepali Congress Party (one male and one female) and one from the Madhesi Party (one female).

Muslim Initiatives in the Second Constituent Assembly

Attendance and participation by Muslim members of the CA during 2014 were said to be relatively high, second only (at 77 per cent) to hill *dalits* and *janajatis* (79 per cent). We have little inside information (as yet) on the role of the Muslim members of the Constituent Assembly or on what they have been able to achieve during their period in office. All we know is that it is not an easy task, with various often conflicting pressures on members to represent 'their community' and also to represent other constituencies of which they are a part. This assembly continued to operate during the first part of 2015, having missed its own self-defined deadline in January 2015, but there appears still (towards the end of August 2015) to be no agreement on a number of basic issues, and the progress achieved as far as the Muslim community is concerned remains limited. The sudden rise in the political profile of the Muslims in recent years has not only boosted the morale of the community from centuries long disadvantage, but has also provided them an opportunity to raise an assertive voice for sharing political and administrative power. Accordingly they have raised their demands to include a 10 per cent reservation in the Constituent Assembly, reserved seats in Parliament and government holidays on Muslim festivals. More recently, they have produced a Position Paper, in which they set out their demands for incorporation into the new Constitution (see Appendix 2).

The outcome of this initiative remains unclear as the final version of the new Constitution has not yet been agreed, despite the official promulgation of the new Constitution in September 2015 which proved highly controversial and to which further amendments are expected (for further discussion see below under 'Other Issues').

In March 2016, thirteen new members were elected onto the Central Committee of the Nepali Congress Party and many older faces disappeared; a major restructuring took place, and Aftab Alam failed to get re-elected under Muslim reservation quota but his position was taken by Farmullah Mansur, once again.

11

Citizenship in Historical Perspective

Citizenship

As Gaige remarked in 1975, 'citizenship bestows the right to participate in the governing process. It grants access to power. It is a symbol of legitimacy for people living within their national boundaries. Citizenship is a bond between the individuals and the government of a nation and, therefore, important in the process of national integration'. He also comments with remarkable pertinence for the situation exactly 40 years later that, in the case of Nepal, 'changing citizenship regulations reflect changes in the attitudes of Kathmandu's decision-makers towards plains people of the *terai*' (1975: 87).

From the late 18th century onwards, the attitude of the hill rulers of Nepal has been ambivalent towards the status of the people of the *terai*. For, although the land itself was regarded, following 'unification' under the successors to Prithivi Narayan Shah, as a resource to be exploited for their benefit and that of first the Gorkhali and then the new Nepali state, the people were considered at least 'quasi-foreigners' (Gaige 1975: 88). No administrative procedure was established to determine the status of individual *terai*-dwellers as Nepalese or Indian, and except during the Shiva Ratri festival, when 'Indians' were allowed to make pilgrimages to the Pashupatinath Temple in Kathmandu, *terai* residents as well as Indians were required to stop at the border town of Birgunj to obtain a passport before proceeding to Kathmandu. Passports were then checked at Chisapani Garhi on the way to Kathmandu.

This procedure was not modified until the early 1950s and not entirely abandoned until 1958. In 1951, the Public Representation Act affirmed the right to vote for any inhabitant who had resided in any constituency for at least 60 days. This Act, with its liberal and 'permissive' approach, set the tone for the Citizenship Act of 1952. Like most citizenship laws, it declared a citizen anyone who was born in Nepal, anyone permanently settled in Nepal who had at least one parent born in Nepal, or any woman married to a citizen. It also stated that anyone who had lived in Nepal for at least five years could acquire citizenship by 'naturalisation'. Gaige remarks, tellingly, that 'if discrimination against minority groups occurs in citizenship legislation, it is usually found in the naturalization requirements'. He comments that 'the five years residency requirement for naturalization is part of the citizenship laws in the neighbouring countries of India and Pakistan, and indeed most other nations' (1975: 89)[1].

Even then, extreme nationalist organisations, such as the Citizenship Amendment Committee and the Nepal Prajatrantrik Mahasabha, demanded that in the 1959 elections, only those who had lived in Nepal for at least 18 years should have the right to vote and this view was supported by the daily newspaper *Halkhabar.* Their views were not, at this time, the views of the mainstream of Nepali politics, but they were influential, particularly among those long-resident in Nepal with established land rights in the *terai* and documents to prove them ie the larger landowners and among the officials who were obliged to make decisions regarding the granting of citizenship and land rights.

Citizenship legislation in the 1960s followed the royal coup. In the 1962 Constitution, articles 7 and 8 focused on citizenship. Article 7 repeated Article 2 of the 1952 Citizenship Act, but Article 8, on naturalisation, required foreigners to be able to speak and write Nepali, to reside in Nepal, to renounce any other citizenship and to have resided in Nepal for at least two years in the case of a person of Nepali origin and not less than 12 years in the case of persons of other origin. The last of these was the most restrictive, extending by seven years the residence requirement for those of non-Nepali origin but shortening it for those of Nepali origin terms that, importantly, were not defined and left to the Nepalis. One of the clear intentions was to discourage immigration from India at a time when the definition of Nepal identity was becoming an integral part of the new national development strategy of the royal government and when the *terai* was beginning to open up as a result of the virtual eradication there of malaria.

Crucially, Nepali citizenship was required for the acquisition of land under the Lands Act of 1964. Neither the Lands Act nor the 1964 Land Rules stated specifically that tenants had to produce citizenship certificates before purchasing land, but the latter required considerable detailed information about citizenship status so that, in reality, tenants were required to prove their citizenship. This created considerable tension as many tenants were in no position to prove their citizenship, and riots in Nawal Parasi in 1966 and in two other mid-western *terai* districts in 1969 (referred to without being named in Gaige 1975: 98) occurred in part at least because of alienation caused by the government's citizenship and land reform policies.

In 1972, the government announced that it was formulating legislation to prevent foreigners from working as agricultural labourers in Nepal and to make the appointment of all new tenant farmers the responsibility of government officials, which tended to raise questions of citizenship. This created even further potential for discrimination against those without the required documentation for citizenship; and, as Gaige explained, the application procedures to gain citizenship were extremely demanding in terms of the 'proofs' needed (1975: 99-100).

This was also a period when large numbers of labourers from the poor Indian states of Uttar Pradesh and, especially, Bihar were flocking to the *terai* in search of employment. The opening up of the *terai*, initiated during the 1960s, was now in the 1970s attracting immigrants both from the hills of Nepal and from the Indian states the other side of the border, both as labourers and as farmers, and squatter (*sukumbasi*) settlements were beginning to acquire significance both demographically and politically. The pace of immigration into the *terai* from both hills and adjacent Indian states was to accelerate during the 1980s and into the 1990s, but by the mid-1990s, immigration from outside was being rapidly replaced by emigration abroad, mainly to the Gulf.

The Government of Nepal (GoN) set up the Dhanpati Commission in 1994, which documented the fact that around 3.4 million Nepali were without citizenship certificates and made recommendations to address this. In April 1997, a Monitoring and Evaluation Committee was established to provide citizenship certificates according to these recommendations. To make issuance of citizenship certificates easier, an amendment bill to the Citizenship Act of 1963 was submitted to Parliament in 1999 and passed unanimously by the House of Representative. However, the National

Assembly rejected the bill. It was finally passed on in July 2000, and sent to the king for promulgation. In February 2001, after eight months, the King sent the bill to the Supreme Court, which ruled that the bill was unconstitutional, alleging that it contradicted the citizenship provision already enshrined in the constitution.

After the signing of the CPA, the GoN finally enacted the Nepal Citizenship Act of 2006 which divided citizenship into three categories: Citizenship by Descent, Citizenship by Birth and Citizenship by Naturalization. The possibility of obtaining citizenship by birth was limited those born before 1990 and remained valid for only two years. The campaigned that followed in 2007 led to around 2.6 million citizenship certificates being distributed. Since the citizenship certificate distribution campaign on the basis of birth is over, however, children of those undocumented are bound to remain so. But other groups are also at risk. Even for those who benefited from the citizenship certificate distribution campaign, the citizenships by birth which they obtained do not necessarily entitle their children to citizenship certificates because of a narrow interpretation of the Citizenship Act which does not allow citizens by birth to transfer their citizenship to their children.

Lack of information, lack of money, lack of family support, lack of access to officials, lack of official and legal support are all reasons why some individuals still do not have citizenship certificates. Naturalisation also remains a problem. One CDO from the central *terai* is reported as saying "I wish the Rule [the 2006 Citizenship Act, Article 4] would be amended so that it would explicitly mention what is possible and what is not, as it does with regard to the children of naturalized Nepali citizens [Article 5.5]. Accordingly, the district administration has not provided citizenship certificates to such people. Many children are put in a similar situation to that which their parents found themselves in before the citizenship certificate distribution campaign". The problem of people without documents is far from solved; rather it has increased on par with population growth.

During a study undertaken in selected districts of the hills and *terai* in 2009 (Rana 2009), however, some key Muslim informants complained that they were still discriminated against in the process of distributing citizen certificate by the authorities because of their 'origin'. They were suspected of being 'foreigners' because of their possible Indian origin and said that they had to provide a good deal of evidence in order to receive their certificates. In fact, however, although a number of Muslims complained that they faced many problems to get a citizenship certificate from the authorities, most members of Muslim families had in fact received the citizenship certificate. In this study (Rana 2009), only 3 out of 240 families (1.25 per cent) had family members who did not have such a certificate; one out of 79 households in the hill areas and 2 out of 158 in the *terai*.

The certificate is issued only those citizens who are of the age of 16 years or above; and most cases of ineligibility related to persons who were under age. In the sample, 79 per cent of Muslims above 16 years age had a citizenship certificate, but it is noticeable that a higher proportion of men than women had their citizenship papers. It is also striking and counter-intuitive that a higher proportion of hill Muslims, both men and women, were without citizenship certificates, than of those in the *terai*. It is not clear why this should be so.

Table 40: Muslims with (and without) Citizenship Certificates (2009)

	Hill		Terai		Grand Total	Grand Total Received
	Total	Received	Total	Received		
Male	180	131 (72.77%)	342	303 (88.59%)	522	434 (83.14%)
Female	151	106 (70.19%)	324	248 (76.54%)	475	354 (74.52%)
Total	331	237 (71.60%)	666	551 (82.73%)	997	788 (79.03%)

In 2011, the UNHRC Office in Nepal produced a bulletin, based on a combination of fieldwork and secondary sources, concerned with 'people without citizenship certificates in the central *terai*' (*UN* RCHC 2011). It does not specifically identify Muslims in its discussion, but it comments that 'the number of people unable to prove their citizenship in the *terai* is high, most of whom are poor and uneducated' (p1).

Those interviewed for the bulletin told a tale of daily obstacles due to lack of citizenship certificates, of missed opportunities when trying to obtain such certificates, insufficient public information and officials facing ambiguous legislation... interviews with people living in the *terai* without citizenship certificates highlight the many difficulties faced in owning land, getting married, registering and educating children, or holding public office. Other civil rights are also forgone: participation in user groups, education stipends for disadvantaged children, social security allowances for senior citizens, and other forms of social protection. Not having citizenship certificates bar the vulnerable from social safety nets and make them particularly destitute' (p 1).

Since the citizenship certificate distribution campaign on the basis of birth of 2007 is now over, the children of those who remained undocumented are bound to remain so. But other groups are also at risk. Even for those who benefited from the campaign, the citizenship by birth which they obtained does not entitle their children to citizenship certificates, because of a narrow interpretation of the 2006 Citizenship Act, which does not allow citizens by birth to transfer their citizenship to their children. One CDO said he wished the Rule (2006 Act, Article 4) would be amended to mention explicitly what is possible and what is not, as it does with regard to the children of naturalised Nepali citizens (Article 5.5) (p. 5).

Introduced in Nepal in 1976, birth certificates are equally important as they are in practice even if not by law one of the documents requested to obtain citizenship by descent. While birth certificates are by law available as other personal events registrations to persons residing in Nepal, according to the Birth, Death and Other Personal Events (Registration) Act, 2033 (1976), in practice there are many hurdles to cross in order to obtain them, including the presentation of the father's citizenship and marriage certificates. For the children of those without citizenship certificates, the birth cannot be recorded and they are unable to establish any kind of legal identity. There are even cases where birth registration has not been granted to children of those given citizenship certificates on the basis of birth. Lack of birth certificate may deprive children of an education if there is not the support of the local community and the school to register them.

The New Constitution of Nepal (2015)

There was much debate during the period of the second Constituency Assembly regarding the drafting of a new Constitution over issues of citizenship, with many rumours circulating as to how access to Nepali citizenship would be defined. Eventually an official version was promulgated on 17 September 2015, but it provided extremely controversial in several respects, including with regard to the issue of access to citizenship, where it was stated that while the offspring of a Nepali man and a foreign spouse would have a right to Nepali citizenship, the same would not be the case for the offspring of a Nepali woman and a foreign spouse, unless that spouse already had surrendered rights to the citizenship of another country and had already become a Nepali citizen. A foreign spouse could acquire Nepali citizenship only after a lengthy period of residence. The offspring of a Muslim man with Nepali citizenship and a woman of Indian origin would be Nepali citizens; but the same would not be the case for the offspring of a Muslim woman with Nepali citizenship and an Indian husband.

The provisions for citizenship in the new Constitution are outlined below (*Copied from Section 11, Part 2, Constitution of Nepal, 2015) (final)*

(1) Those persons who have acquired citizenship of Nepal at the commencement of this Constitution and those persons who are eligible to acquire citizenship of Nepal under this Part shall be deemed to be the citizens of Nepal.

(2) The following persons who have their permanent domicile in Nepal shall be deemed to be citizens of Nepal by descent:-

 (a) A person who has acquired the citizenship of Nepal by descent before the commencement of this constitution.

 (b) Any person whose father or mother was a citizen of Nepal at the birth of such a person.

(3) A child of a citizen who has acquired citizenship of Nepal by birth before the commencement of this Constitution shall, if his/her father and mother both are the citizens of Nepal, shall be entitled to Nepali citizenship by descent upon his/her attaining the age of majority.

(4) Every child found in Nepal whereabouts of whose paternity and maternity is not known shall, until the mother or father is traced, be deemed a citizen of Nepal by descent.

(5) A person born to a Nepali citizen mother and having his/her domicile in Nepal but whose father is not traced, shall be conferred the Nepali citizenship by descent.

 Provided that in case his/her father is found to be a foreigner, the citizenship of such a person shall be converted to naturalized citizenship according to the Federal law.

(6) If a foreign woman married to a Nepali citizen so wishes, she

may acquire naturalized citizenship of Nepal as provided for in a Federal law.

(7) Notwithstanding anything contained elsewhere in this Article, in case of a person born to Nepali woman citizen married to a foreign citizen, he/she may acquire naturalized citizenship of Nepal as provided for by a Federal law if he/she is having the permanent domicile in Nepal and he/she has not acquired citizenship of the foreign country.

Provided that if his/her father and mother both are the citizen of Nepal at the time of acquisition of the citizenship, he/she, if born in Nepal, may acquire citizenship by descent.

(8) Except provided for in this Article, Government of Nepal may confer naturalized citizenship of Nepal according to Federal law.

(9) Government of Nepal may confer honorary citizenship according to Federal law.

(10) In case any area is annexed into Nepal by merger, the persons having domicile in such area shall be citizens of Nepal subject to a Federal

It follows from this that a person can only be a Nepali citizen by descent if both parents are Nepali citizens. The requirement that a child born to a Nepali woman and a foreign man must have been born in Nepal to become a naturalised citizen is no longer maintained. But a child whose father is of foreign origin or nationality cannot be a Nepali citizen unless that father becomes a naturalised Nepali citizen. This is normally a lengthy procedure and requires that the man be resident in Nepal.

The Right to Vote

As Gaige remarked back in the 1970s (see above) and the more recent UN RCHC Office report (UN RCHC 2011) emphasised, the right to vote is directly linked to citizenship. According to the Constitution, every Nepali citizen above 18 years has a right of vote; in order to vote, however, individuals must be registered on the electoral roll as citizens. As we have seen, in 1951, the Public Representation Act affirmed the right to vote for any inhabitant who had resided in any constituency for at least 60 days. This Act, with its liberal and 'permissive' approach, set the tone for the Citizenship Act of 1952. Like most citizenship laws, it declared a citizen anyone who was born in Nepal, anyone permanently settled in Nepal who had at least one parent born in Nepal, or any woman married to a citizen. It also stated that anyone who had lived in Nepal for at least five years could acquire citizenship by 'naturalisation'.

This legislation was 'hardened up' during the 1960s and thereafter, to make it more difficult for non-Nepali nationals to acquire Nepali citizenship. At the same time, in practice, an increasing number of people mainly but not only immigrants found it hard to register their citizenship and have their names put officially on the electoral roll, to enable them to vote in local and national elections. The 2009 study (Rana et al 2009) found that, although the names of members of 215 out of 240 families (90 per cent) were on the electoral roll, in 23 cases (10 per cent) they were not. The main reason for not being included in the electoral roll was lack of citizenship. The problem was most acute in the district headquarters (urban areas) in the *terai.*

Table 41: Muslim Households with Members Having Voting Rights (2009)

Responses	Hill			Terai			Grand Total
	District headquarter	Rural	Total	District headquarter	Rural	Total	
Yes	40	40	80	56	79	135	215
No	0	0	0	22	1	23	23
Don't know	0	0	0	2	0	2	2
Total	40	40	80	80	80	160	240

Political Representation

On the other hand, political involvement and even more so political representation of the Muslim communities also remained limited at the local level as well as at the national level, despite some interest among the various parties in gaining their vote. The UML was one of the first parties to directly appeal to Muslims, founding the Nepal Muslim Ettehad Association in the mid-90s; and the Maoists gained some popularity among Muslims by calling for secularism during the civil war. Peter Gill notes that 'many Nepalgunj Muslims became sympathetic to the party for its opposition to the Shiv Sena (Maoist cadres assassinated a Shiv Sena member in Nepalgunj in 2004)'. The Maoists also formed a Muslim wing, the Muslim Mukti Morcha (Gill 2017). But, as Gill reported from Nepalgunj in his article in *The Record* (February 2017) 'perhaps more than any one party, Madhesi activism over the past decade has had an impact on Muslim politics in Nepalgunj and on how Muslims see their own identity. One evening at Rahul's tea shop in the bazaar, Bijaya's friend Chaand dai introduced me to a local Muslim Maoist leader, Ather Husain Farooqui. He was in his 40s, a member of the central Maoist committee, and a former principal of one of the best Muslim private schools in town. Several months later, he was named chair of the Muslim Mukti Morcha.

Ather Husain told me that many Muslims in Nepalgunj supported the Madhesi movement in 2006–7, as well as the more recent blockade in the 2015–16, recognizing that they share with Hindu Madhesis a common legacy of exclusion by high-caste hill groups. He said that his party appealed to Muslims and Madhesis more generally, though he admitted there had been tensions. (Maoists killed a teenage Madhesi protester in Lahan in 2007, further inflaming the Madhesi movement, and many Madhesis continue to see them as fair-weather friends.)

I asked him whether he considered himself a Madhesi. "Look at me," he said. "When you see me, what do you think I am?" He was wearing a windbreaker jacket with sunglasses propped on his head, and he was clean shaven and had dark skin. Before I had time to answer, he said, "You think I am a Madhesi. Then I tell you my name, Ather Husain. Then what do you think I am? Muslim. Then I show you my citizenship card? And then you know my identity is Madhesi, Muslim Nepali. In that order." Almost as an afterthought, he added that, ultimately, economic class is the most important identity. We sipped our tea and watched cows pass by the tea shop.

Not all Muslims I met in Nepalgunj shared Ather Hussein's view that Muslims are Madhesis. I met a friend of Ather Husain's, a Muslim radio journalist, in his studio near Eklaini one evening. He was a plump man with an immaculately groomed mustache, and wore a look of perpetual disapproval on his face, though he kindly obliged my questions." Look, I'm a Muslim," he told me. "Around the world, Muslims have their own identity. Our community is international."

When I asked if he considered himself a Madhesi, he offered a non-ethnic reading of the term. "I'm a Madhesi because I live in the Madhes, below the hills. So are the Pahadis who live here, so are Muslims, so are Hindus." Unlike Ather Husain, he was a supporter of the UML. He said that although many Muslims were attracted to the Maoists and Upendra Yadav's Madhesi Janadhikar Forum (MJF) in 2008, helping them clinch two seats each from Banke, they later became disappointed with those parties after they failed to promulgate a new constitution on time. In the 2013 elections, the tables turned dramatically, and the UML won one seat and Congress three seats in the district. He said, "In my experience, security is most important [for Muslims] in politics. Muslims who vote for UML are voting for them because they believe the party will stand by them and keep them safe. It's not always safe here, for various reasons."

Muslims do not only show an interest in politics, some are also themselves actively involved. Involvement is, however, significantly less in the *terai* than in the hills. In a study of Muslim communities undertaken by Rana and others in 2009 in selected hill and *terai* districts (Rana et al 2009), it was found that 50 out of 240 families (21 per cent) had a family member who was also a member of a political party. In hills, the percentage was nearly 40 per cent but in the *terai* only about 12 per cent per cent). The largest percentage was, not surprisingly, in the hill district headquarters, where over half of the households (52.5 per cent) had at least one family member who was a member of a political party. This is, I suggest, a striking result, even if it fails to identify the party concerned.

Table 42: Membership of a Political Party (2009)

Responses	Hill			Terai			Grand Total
	District headquarter	Rural	Total	District headquarter	Rural	Total	
Yes	21	10	31	6	13	19	50
No	19	30	49	74	67	141	190
Total	40	40	80	80	80	160	240

It was also found that a small minority of Muslim households had family members who might be said to have achieved a 'leadership' role in local politics. Overall, just short of 8 per cent of all Muslim households had someone in such a position: 12.5 per cent of households in the hill areas and 5.6 per cent in the *terai*. In the hills, some 20 per cent of households had both party activists and people in leadership roles. Again, one might find this level of involvement quite surprising. Interestingly, and tantalisingly, Upadhyay commented, rather generally, on the basis of fieldwork in one Muslim hill village in Tanahun District, that 'some Muslims are quite active in local politics' (2014: 111). But he does not elaborate on this.

Table 43: Political 'Leadership' and Activism (2009)

Levels of Political Organizations	Number of Person
District level	2
Constituency level	3
Local Level	4
Member of fraternal organization of political parties	10

However, only two Muslims in the 2009 sample had reached district level in a political party, as members of a district committee; three were appointed up to constituency level and four appointed to bodies at the local level; more than half were members of 'fraternal organizations' of political parties.

As regards political representation, only 13 households out of 240 (5.4 per cent) had family members who had been elected to any political body, from local to national level, in the previous five years although it should be remembered that no local government elections have been held officially since 2002. In the hills, just over 10 per cent (11.25 per cent) of households had a family member who had been elected to a local body, but in the *terai* the figure was only 2.5 per cent; furthermore, this political representation was limited to the local level as ward or VDC representatives. Also, it was found that Muslims tended to be politically active almost exclusively in areas where the Muslim population was in the majority.

Table 44: Post in any Political Body from Local to National Level (2009)

Responses	Hill families			Terai families			Grand Total
	District headquarter	Rural	Total	District headquarter	Rural	Total	
Yes	5	4	9	1	3	4	13
No	35	36	71	79	77	156	227
Total	40	40	80	80	80	160	240

A small scale study in three wards in a single VDC in Bardiya District undertaken in 2010 (Khan 2011), gives a further indication of the constraints felt by Muslims as regards political participation. Most of the specific constraints expressed had to do with the status and capacities (or lack of them) of the Muslims themselves, or to do with barriers from outside, preventing them from greater involvement. Thus, in a sample of 100 interviewees, illiteracy and poor education was given as a reason by 17 per cent of those asked, poverty by 8 per cent; 12 per cent referred to discrimination and 9 per cent to 'lack of accessibility'. Just over half (51 per cent) referred to a combination of factors, including those mentioned by the others as primary causes for their lack of involvement in politics. Only three per cent expressed no particular opinion or 'did not know'.

Participation in 'External' Social Activities

Participation in 'external' social activities is a very important aspect of general social integration and ability to influence outcomes in the wider society. The 2009 Rana study attempted to analyze the participation of Muslim males and females residing in the district headquarters and rural areas of hill and *terai* regions in relation to social activities and household decision-making process. The level of their participation in social activities was based on the frequency of certain activities generally practised by Muslim males and females eg participation in madrasa meetings, mosque meetings, meetings of school management committee, political meetings, meetings of social organizations/club/NGHOs, labour contribution to community activities, donations to charities, or mosques, or other organisations within the past year.

It was found that meetings in the local mosque were the most frequent of all the 'external' social activities of the Muslims in the study area, which frequency was 3.65 times for a family per year. The second social activity in which most of the Muslims participated was *madrasa* meetings, third most common was some form of labour contribution within the community and fourth was 'political meetings' with an average frequency of 1.5 times per year. They also participated but less frequently - in other social activities (donations, meetings of social organizations, school management committees and local political bodies 1.06, 1.03, 0.54 and 0.53 times per family per year.

The participation of Muslim females in 'external' social activities was very low in comparison to that of males. In some areas, it was only nominal. For example, as regards participation in mosque meetings, which was the main area related to all Muslims' participation in 'external' social activities, the females' share was only 0.02 times per year per family. Their main areas of participation were related to labour contributions and to donations in which their participation was 0.58 and 0.23 times per family per year.

There was a considerable difference in relation to participation in social activities as between hill and *terai. In* the hills, Muslims participated in mosque meetings and madrasa meetings 7.40 and 6.34 times per year respectively; but the participation of *terai* Muslims in these activities was only 1.78 and 1.43 times a year respectively. In areas like labour contributions, participation in political meetings, donations and participation in meeting of social organizations, hill Muslim families participated 2.16, 2.19, 1.33, 2.00 times a year respectively; by contrast, Muslim families in the *terai* participated in these activities 1.44, 1.15, 0.93 and 0.55 times a year respectively.

It was found that only 13 out of 240 (5.41 per cent) families had held some 'leadership' position in any social, cultural, or professional organization in last five years. In the hills, this percentage was 8.75% and in the *terai,* it was 3.75 per cent. Muslims in the hills were leading those in the *terai* in relation to their leadership position in any social, cultural, or professional organization. Only one family member of all the households in the study area was a member of the central committee of a Muslim organization. Most who were members of any organisation were members of organizations involving Muslims only. Only 3 out of 13 family members were member of an organization other than a Muslim cultural organization: these were members of a School Management Committee and the Red Cross.

Table 45: 'Leadership' in any Social, Cultural, or Professional Organization (2009)

Responses	Hill families			Terai families			Grand Total
	District headquarter	Rural	Total	District headquarter	Rural	Total	
Yes	4	3	7	4	2	6	13
No	36	37	73	76	78	154	227
Total	40	40	80	80	80	160	240

Representation at the Local Level Today

While there is a good deal of information available regarding the position of women and their representation at the local level in Nepal, there is virtually nothing about the political representation of Muslims women. For example, the report produced by VSO, Women In Power: beyond access to influence in a post-2015 world, it is noted that 'the 2007 Interim Constitution mandated a 33 per cent quota for women across all boards including VDCs. Additionally, 10 per cent of the VDC budget is meant to be allocated to women and girls. However, both policies are being flouted. Women's participation and representation in the three local bodies (in the Women's Empowerment Action Forum project) is extremely low. Out of 3,915 VDC secretary posts, only 81 are occupied by women... In the VDCs where WEAF is working, the 10 per cent budget is being directed towards developing roads' (VSO 2015: 20).

We do not have very much detailed data on the political representation of Muslims at the local level at the present time. The last official local elections for DDC and VDC were in 1997 and it is only now in May 2017 that local elections are being held, for the first time in 20 years. In the interim, various local 'arrangements' have been reached as to how to represent local interests. It is likely, although this remains to be confirmed by future research, that these arrangements rarely involve Muslim representation, even where Muslims constitute a significant proportion of the local VDC community; and still less at the level of the DDC.

The fieldwork in the *terai* during June-July 2015 revealed the limited extent to which Muslims are represented. In the Madhesi Janaadhikar Forum (Democratic) district committee in Dhanusha District, for example, out of 31 members, only two were Muslims. The district committee was dominated by Yadavs (13 out of 31) and had very few representatives from other marginal or disadvantaged groups and, as far as I can see, no women. Nine, however, of the key informant interviews in Dhanusha district and Janakpur were with political activists, so it is not as though there was no political involvement at the local level by Muslims but it remains clearly limited.

An issue that has been relatively well covered in this report is that of the political marginalisation of Muslims and the lack of involvement in politics on the part of or by Muslims at local and at national level. Marginalisation is a function of the way in which Muslims are treated politically by the rest of Nepali society; lack of involvement in politics is both a function of marginalisation (ie external barriers to involvement) and of lack of interest (ie internal barriers to involvement). A key informant from Janakpur, Tahar Nadaf, commented during fieldwork in 2015 for this project, that

> 'Participation from the Muslims community in Nepalese politics is very limited. The people of the Muslim community are marginalized as regards political participation. Some people get a chance to participate, but they are not allowed to utter their own voice; they are forced to utter their parties' voice. Muslims are not in positions of decision making. So the voice of Muslim community is not raised in the House. The people from the upper classes in the political parties have oppressed the Muslims and the Madhesis. This is also a fact that most of the people from the Muslim communities are not interested in politics. They prefer to be involved in their own business and works; they are not interested in interfere in any other things etc.'

Another key informant from the Janakpur area, Vijay Kumar Dutta, remarked that

> 'In general, the Muslim community has no strong place in politics or indeed in other sectors either. Muslims are treated as second class citizens as regards rights and facilities given by the government and their agencies. As far as politics is concerned, Muslims are treated as foot-soldiers in politics; as a vote bank by the political parties. The reservation system has played a vital role in improving the condition and status of the Muslim community; but it is not sufficient and appropriate as it is not implemented properly.

Access to Information

One of the consequences of poor literacy rates and access to education is a relatively low level of access to information through the print media. In a recent survey (NEMAF 2016) of five districts in the Mithila 'belt' of the *terai,* 48 per cent of respondents had never read a newspaper and less than 4 per cent were regular newspaper readers and 13 per cent were occasional newspaper readers; also 34 per cent did not listen to the radio and 39 per cent did not watch TV. As a result, very low proportions of people in this region were aware of what happening at the village, district or national level.

Awareness of ward and VDC level planning was particularly low among madhesi *janajati, Muslims* and *madhesi dalits* (6, 6 and 7 per cent respectively); and their representation among those aware of what was happening at the local level was also low (8, 12 and 17 per cent respectively). Only 5 per cent of *madhesi dalits* and 7 per cent of Muslims were aware of Social Audit events in their VDC; only 4 per cent of Muslims and 5 per cent of *madhesi dalits* were aware of Public Audits in their VDC; and only 5 per cent of *madhesi dalits* and 6 per cent of Muslims were aware of public hearings in the previous year. Women were generally less aware than men.

A significant proportion of Muslims are also not aware of social security payments for senior citizens, disabled people, conflict victims and single women); they are in fact the least aware of all the social groups identified, with 40 per cent unaware and only 60 per cent aware, compared with *janajati and* high castes (36 per cent and 63 per cent for both); *madhesi dalits* were more aware (23 per cent unaware and 77 per cent aware).

New Demands from the Muslim Community

All the constitutions of Nepal developed and modified up to now have failed to provide full recognition of the rights of Muslim communities. This is a major component of their overall political, social, cultural and legal marginalisation and effective exclusion. Specific issues have been identified, however, and demands as regards incorporation into the draft Constitution made, in a document described by IDEA as a 'Position Paper of the Muslim Community', presented to the Constituent Assembly and relevant committees (see Appendix 2). This was produced prior to the promulgation of the Constitution.

The final version of the Constitution had not at this time been agreed or made public, although drafts had been circulated (during the final approval process in June-August 2015), including a version (translated by the UNDP) in English. The demands presented for incorporation in the new Constitution make clear the elements of the kind of 'special status' Muslims are seeking at the present time. It remains to be seen how many of those demands are in fact incorporated in the agreed Constitution when it is finally promulgated. In early July 2015, Muslim and Christian leaders pronounced the draft 'a sham', pointing out that it failed to honour pledges made by previous governments to protect and enhance their rights. The new Constitution was eventually approved in September 2015. It remained and indeed remains highly controversial and may well be subject to various amendments. Whether any of those address the concerns of the Muslim communities remains to be seen.

12

Other Key Issues

Education

The issue of education, which has been relatively well covered in previous sections, and identified as a key issue by most of those interviewed as part of the fieldwork for this project during the summer of 2015 that of the relatively poor educational status of Muslims, particularly of girls and women remains a key issue for consideration and action. This is, however a long term problem.

Non-formal education and functional literacy classes especially for girls and women might help increase confidence and enable females to engage more directly with the wider world; campaigns to alert parents to the benefits of education, particularly for females, and to the disadvantages of lack of education, sponsored and supported by respected Muslim men and women would be helpful; radio and TV programmes encouraging literacy and education for all, particularly for females could be considered.

Government support for Muslim education and for the effective integration of the *madrasa* system into the overall education system would be helpful in encouraging local communities to build, maintain and make use of local *madrasas* and see them as part of an integrated structure of educational institutions. Local resource centres and libraries would also help with literacy and education. Muslim organisations, like *Millat-e Islamiya* (MIN), which has a library in Kathmandu with more than 10,000 books in Urdu, English, Hindi, Nepali and Arabic, and whose vision is to develop it into a research centre with addition of books in different languages as also collection of audio-visual materials on different Islamic concepts and subjects, could do more to promote the development of libraries outside the Kathmandu Valley, particularly in the *terai.*

Recognising the poor state of education among the Muslim communities of Nepal, the MIN has started Qur'anic classes in Kathmandu where by a teacher appointed by the organization goes to the home of willing children to teach them Qur'an. At present, according to its website, such classes are running in three different locations in the city and 30 students are benefiting from it. This is of course extremely limited, but MIN is planning to expand the programme in future. MIN is also cooperating with *Islami Sangh Nepal*, Al-Hira Educational Society and Students' Education Foundation by providing them space for their offices in its own building. In cooperation with the Graduates' Association of the Islamic Development Bank, Jeddah, scholars in Nepal (GAIN), the MIN is running a clinic for poor people in its premises in Kathmandu. GAIN is providing the manpower and the MIN the space and the funds for the clinic. It works six days a week and is open for all, Muslims as well as non-Muslims. Service to humanity as well as *da'wah (call)* is the objective of these efforts.

NGOs and the 'Development' of Muslim Communities

This example raises the question of the role of specifically Muslim NGOs, and more widely that of NGOs in general, in providing support to local communities. As we have seen throughout this report, there are several national organisations that have a more or less 'developmental' orientation and undertake a range of activities to support the 'development' of Muslim communities across Nepal. National Muslim Forum Nepal describes itself as 'an Umbrella Organization of Muslim-led development organizations/ NGOs in Nepal'. It was established in September 2004 as an Islamic Federation by uniting local NGOs of Muslim from different districts. *Islami Sangh Nepal* also came forward and took initiative to assemble Muslim scholars, intellectuals, leaders and social workers at one platform to discuss review and analyzed the need to form an organization for advocacy for Muslims in Nepal.

There are also local NGOs, some of which were encountered during the fieldwork undertaken during the summer of 2015. All of these have limited resources, but they have the advantage of being rooted in local communities and of having very specific programmes and projects designed to benefit the Muslim community as a whole. Dastider traces the rise of NGOs as such to the early 1990s, and remarks that 'the shift in the nature and character of Muslim bodies in post-1990 Nepal is discernible as they attempt to focus on the socioeconomic and socio-political aspects of the problems faced by Muslims in democratic Nepal. Muslim organisations that functioned in the pre-democratic era existed solely for religious and cultural purposes, as permitted by the monarchy-led panchayat regime, and were therefore not actually working for the upliftment of poor Muslims. Many of the organisations in the *terai* even existed only on paper with the prime motive of receiving donations (*zakat)* from the Gulf. These organisations never antagonised the Hindu rulers with their demands and conformed to the low profile and non-assertive image of the community'.

There is a reference in Dastider (2000: 767) to Siddiqa (1993: 275-79) which apparently listed the Muslim welfare organisations operative at the time. A full listing of Muslim NGOs and of NGOs that include Muslim communities within their scope of work is not possible here, but this could be a valuable exercise for the future, and provide the basis for a greater awareness of the needs still unfulfilled as well as of the areas and regions already covered. A partial list of NGOs, political parties or groupings and other organisations is provided in Appendix 1.

While most of the efforts of Muslim associations and groups are devoted to the specific promotion of the Muslim community, there have also been some initiatives by Muslim associations to reach out beyond their own community to help others.

In August 2015, for example, the Lutheran World Federation (LWF) and Islamic Relief Worldwide (IRW) signed an agreement to cooperate in humanitarian relief efforts, a first collaboration of its kind in Nepal. Since then the two organisations have supported quake survivors in five VDCs of Rasuwa district. 'Faith based organisations working together to reach out to the most vulnerable show the way forward towards solidarity and social harmony in a divided world', said LWF Nepal Country Director, Prabin Manadhar.

> 'As the weather worsened, they distributed construction materials to build shelter and toilets to the people of Yarsa, a remote village of Rasuwa. The construction materials were a welcome gift for many in this Dalit village who have been braving the winter in animal sheds and under tarpaulin shelter. In the first phase of the collaboration between LWF reported that as the weather worsened Nepal and IRW, with the help of local partner

> Manikor Society, construction materials were provided to over 2,000 families. 'I feel so relieved today', said Sita BK, 42, according to the *Nepali Times, 'having* a toilet of our own will make a big difference'. The mother of three will however have to manage the construction of her new shelter and toilet by herself as her husband is away working in Malaysia. Like BK, many of those who walked several hours to reach Kalikasthan, where the supplies were being distributed, were mothers with young children. Their husbands are migrant workers in Qatar and Malaysia'.
>
> 'Forty-year old Subha BK who walks with the help of an artificial leg said: 'Life became difficult after I became disabled and my wife left me. But I am supported by my friends. With their help and thanks to these materials I can build myself a better shelter'. However, there were others like Dhan Bahadur BK, 60, who worried about rebuilding his home in the same location. 'No place is safe in our village. Unless the government provides us with land in a safer area we will continue to feel vulnerable'. In a world marked by religious strife the unique interfaith partnership stands as an inspiring example. As IRW's Regional Humanitarian Manager Umair Hasan remarked: 'Community integration and religious tolerance does not make for good headlines. But through this partnership we want to send a strong message to the world. It's a message of religious harmony and humanitarianism'.

A focus group held in Eklaini Bazaar, Nepalgunj in the summer of 2015, as part of the NEMAF/IDEA project, considered that although the poor status of Muslims generally was in part the result of discrimination and neglect by the government and the wider society, it was also in part a result of a lack of awareness or consciousness of Muslims themselves. This group suggested that 'Muslims are not aware about social issues which exist in the society. They are too busy collecting their two times meals. They do not know how to make proper communication with others. If an awareness programme could be organized in the Muslim communities from time to time, this would give them information about education, life style etc.'

There are other key issues, however, besides education and awareness, which demand immediate responses from the Muslim community and from the government, from those directly involved in drafting and finally approving the Constitution, and also from Muslim organizations and associations. One of these is the continuing minority status of Muslims in Nepal and whether this status is a help or a hindrance to the economic, social, cultural, and political development of Muslim communities in Nepal.

Social Exclusion

In the first chapter we identified the Muslim community as a disadvantaged community. In part this is, Muslims feel, the result of social discrimination against Muslims by others in Nepali society, and social exclusion from the mainstream by government and non-government agencies alike; in part, they recognise it is the result of their own practices and prejudices.

While it is generally felt among Muslims that they are the subject of social discrimination, there is very little specific evidence from surveys or studies to show what form such social discrimination takes. A small study in three wards of a single VDC in Bardiya District undertaken in 2010 (Khan 2011), however, gives us some idea of what ordinary Muslims in the *terai* experience. When asking about social discrimination against Muslims, 61 per cent of respondents (out of a sample of 100) said that they were treated badly in the public places, 16 per cent said that behaviour towards them was 'satisfactory', but only 7 per cent said other non-Muslims behaved well towards them in public places. Sixteen per cent said they had no opinion or 'did not know'. As regards treatment by officials, 47 per cent felt discrimination, 48 per cent did not respond and 5 per cent did not know. But 66 per cent felt they were treated badly in health centres by health professionals; while 31 per cent felt they were treated well.

In the economic sphere, many felt discriminated against in business and in employment contexts. Two thirds (63 per cent) of business men were concerned that they had been unable to obtain loans and 8 per cent said they were not allowed to open a business wherever they wanted to; 20 per cent cited a variety of reasons they felt discriminated against in 'doing service and business'; just under 10 per cent said they 'did not know'.

Mohamed Alimeem Rai, a key informant from the Nepalgunj area, interviewed during the summer of 2015 as part of this project, suggested that there were two major reasons why Muslims were disadvantaged, internal reasons and external reasons:

> 'Lack of education, lack of awareness and themselves. These are the main factors behind their poverty and backwardness. Due to lack of education Muslims could not improve their living standard, without getting education we can't think of how a person can survive, how he will communicate, how he will interact in the society. Everything depends on education. If a person is educated, he can earn more or his style of doing business is different and progressive. Lack of awareness is also a barrier improvement in economic condition. The second included: Government policy, political leadership, lack of facilities, lack of reservation and lack of suitable environment.
>
> 'The biggest factor in poverty and disadvantage is poor education. The government does not allow or recognize *madrasa* education where we can study modern education and religious education. Schools and its environment are also not as per Islamic law. The uniform is also not permitted as per Muslim demands'. By and large, all these factors are seen as crucial by Muslims, but their demands are not met, even if they would not harm anyone else'.

On the other hand, a recent study by NEMAF (2016) in five districts of the central eastern *terai* suggested that Muslims did not face difficulties in gaining access to educational services (only 15 per cent reported such difficulties, compared with other social groups between 20 and 27 per cent). But they did express some concern regarding their level of satisfaction with the services provided, with only 11 per cent fully satisfied and 36 per cent satisfied; 30 per cent were unsatisfied or uncertain. As regards access to health services, Muslims expressed the greatest concern about access to services (38 per cent) and at the lack of availability of medication (50 per cent) apart from Madhesi *dalits* (57.5 per cent) - but greatest satisfaction of all groups with the services provided (84 per cent).

Muslims still have not been able to achieve full recognition of their 'special status' as many argue is required, although there has been what might be term 'partial' recognition. The formation of a special Muslim Commission endorsed yet again in the Constitution eventually approved in September 2015 is significant, although its actions and activities appear to be limited; it has a website and does undertake certain initiatives. Certain 'concessions' have been achieved, as regards cultural, religious and social recognition. The new Constitution, approved in September 2015 by the Constituent Assembly, does also include specific reference in various sections to 'Muslims' as a particular social minority group, requiring special protection.

The Constituent Assembly has, for example, formally (on 16 September 2015) 'approved provisions to form seven federal commissions in the constitution to address the grievances of marginalised communities, including Tharus, Madhesis, Muslims, women and *janajatis* after the promulgation of constitution. The commissions will have the mandate to protect the rights of minorities. As well as formulating policies and programmes to promote the welfare of the respective communities, they will also offer recommendation to the government for its implementation. The commissions are also entitled to review whether the government has implemented its commitments for the welfare of the respective communities'. This, in effect, simply renews the mandate of the preexisting Muslim Commission.

The whole notion of 'social inclusion' on the basis of special identities for minority groups remains contentious, however, with many (some Muslims included) arguing for a more open and less discriminatory approach adopting universal human rights for voting (one adult, one vote with no 'special status') and enforcing all of the constitutional safeguards to protect and enhance the status of those who have in the past and still are socially discriminated against, not by adopting 'quotas' but by adopting a broad programme of positive discrimination. Others appear to prefer a notion of 'social inclusion' that privileges certain social groups for inclusion as 'disadvantaged minorities' but fails to mention or actively excludes others. Muslims have to decide how much weight to put on achieving 'special status' and how much on achieving basic human, civil and political rights in reality as well as in law.

In the context of Kymlicka's (1995) three types of rights, the Nepali state seemingly is acquiescing to the Muslims' special rights of representation; but some would argue that what is also required is 'a distinctive identity' to enable Muslims to exercise those in whatever circumstances are appropriate, in so far as they may constitute 5 per cent of the population but are not sufficiently concentrated geographically as to be able to bid for an autonomous region or state and self-government within a federal system. A combination of poly-ethnic and special representation rights would increase the participation of Muslims in the hitherto Hindu-dominated state institutions, and also, through financial support and legal protection, aid the Muslims in expressing their cultural practices and rituals and other aspects of their identity, without being eclipsed by the dominant Hindu majority.

These rights are important for both their intrinsic as well as instrumental value. As Young (1990, p. 92) has pointed out, they have *instrumental* value because the "participatory processes are the best way for citizens to ensure that their own needs and interests will be voiced and will not be dominated by other interests." But ensuring democratic participation of social groups also has an intrinsic value "over and above the protection of interests, in providing important means for the development and exercise of capacities." All in all, measures to increase public integration of Muslims is valuable not only because of its intrinsic value it gives a legitimate voice to Muslims in the political arena, but also because of its instrumental value in that it helps them influence decisions that might overcome or decrease their marginalization and exclusion from socioeconomic benefits accorded by the State.

Muslim groups have generally now established a clear link between inclusiveness and constitutional recognition; and almost all have come to believe that Muslims should be given constitutional recognition. Although there was always a debate as to the modes and strategies by which this objective could be achieved, it was also always strongly claimed that Muslims must have a well-defined legal-constitutional status per se in any future Constitution of Nepal.

Muslim groups generally identify two major ways in which this objective could be achieved by proportional representation and by affirmative action. Proportional representation has become a more generally accepted and legitimate mechanism for the inclusion of hitherto marginalized and excluded social groups in the political system although there have been signs in recent years of a certain backsliding in this regard. The combination of the two is further explained in Art. 63(4), which says: The principle of inclusiveness shall be taken into consideration by political parties while selecting candidates... the political parties shall ensure the proportional representation of women, *dalits*, oppressed communities/ indigenous groups, backward regions, *madhesis* and other groups, in accordance with the law."

Thus, proportional representation was clearly accepted in principle as a viable political tool to ensure the inclusion of marginalized groups. Muslims, who have been historically recognized as a social group in Nepal, also find the idea of proportional representation politically appropriate and acceptable to articulate their political claims. The problem is that they are not recognised as a distinct 'minority' group as far as proportional representation goes. They are lumped in with the *madhesis* for some purposes, and although the right to practise their own religion is accepted, as Haque remarks, 'the Muslims of Nepal are not given the right to practice Islamic personal law, because there are no such laws in the country, though Islam was introduced here in the fifth century of the Hijri calendar, according to existing historical records. It was Arab and Muslim traders who introduced Islam to Nepal. And they have to follow the non-Islamic rules regarding marriage, divorce, sacrifice of animals in the way of God during the month of Eid ul Azhah and others. Moreover it has been found that the local authorities tend to create problems during the registration and issuance of civil status certificates'.

The Issue of Religion

Outside this set of specific Constitutional demands for Muslims, the Muslim demand for proportional representation also underlines a crucial gap in the existing legal constitutional framework. The Interim Constitution does not explicitly recognize the multi-religious character of Nepalese society. The Fundamental Rights given in the Constitution do not directly address the question of religion and faith. Although there is an overarching right to religion (Art. 23), which says "every person shall have a right to profess, practice and preserve his or her own religion as handed down to him or her from ancient times paying due regard to social and cultural traditions", there is no provision for the specific protection of minority religions. The other set of rights, particularly the right to social justice, also do not look at the question of religious minorities. For example, Art. 13 (3) of the Fundamental Rights says: The state shall not discriminate among citizens on grounds of religion, race, caste, tribe, gender, origin, language or ideological conviction or any of these'.

But it does not specifically identify religious groups for specific treatment, although in other respects its identification of potentially or actually vulnerable groups is exemplary: 'Provided that nothing shall be deemed to prevent the making of especial provision by law for the protection, empowerment or advancement of women, *dalits,* indigenous ethnic groups (*adivasi, janajati), madhesis* or farmers, labourers or those who belong to a class, which is economically, socially or culturally backward, or children, the aged, disabled or those who are physically or mentally incapacitated'.

It is very clear that although the state does not formally permit discrimination on the basis of religion, it does not make any special provision for the inclusion of religious minorities. The state is prepared to identify 'special groups' in pretty much every way caste, class, ethnicity, gender, region, even age and physical capacity except by religion. In this sense, religion is not considered to be a legitimate category of social justice. Therefore, the Muslim demands for constitutional recognition is a twofold demand: (a) it claims that religious minorities be recognized as stakeholders in the wider constitutional agenda of inclusiveness. (b) Muslims specifically, being a distinctive religious ethnic social group, need to be identified as a legal-constitutional category.

Intra-Muslim Relations

We have seen, but not explored to any real degree, that the Muslim community in Nepal is divided in many ways economic, social, cultural, political and religious. Several of those interviewed during the fieldwork in the *terai* in summer 2015 were insistent that the sectarian differences between Barelwis, Deobandis, Wahabis, Tablighi Jama'at and Jama'at i Islami were not of major significance, although many of the quotations provided by Sijapati suggest otherwise (eg the statement by the President of the National Muslim Forum at 2011: 85). This issue remains to be examined more closely in future research.

As an indication of the kind of issue that triggers conflict between the various Muslim communities is provided by Zadfakir, who remarks (2001: 31) that, on 3 July 1998, *The Kathmandu Post* reported that 'a mosque at Jayaspur 5 (Nepalgunj) was partitioned today owing to simmering differences between the Deobandi and Barelwi sects of Muslims over the proper way of saying *namaj* (prayer). Senior members of the Muslim community say that the Charmari mosque could be the first in the world to be partitioned for a minor difference on the way to conclude the *namaj*. The Barelwis insist that the proper way to conclude the *namaj* is by reading a *salaam*, while the Deobandis do not consider the reading of the *namaj* as a must. Amidst heightened emotions, a Muslim volunteer, however, told the *Kathmandu Post* that 'the actual reason behind the partition is not the fight over the proper way to end the *namaj but* a big aid money that is due from the United Arab Emirates'.

The issue of foreign funding for the construction of mosques and *madrasas* is a very real one in Nepal today, both as regards the concern expressed by some non-Muslims, particularly those pursuing the Hindutva, that money from the Gulf states is leading to a growing Muslim or Islamic revivalism or fundamentalism, and as regards tensions between different Muslim communities. The case referred to by Zadfakir relates to divisions between the Deobadis and the Barelwis in Nepalgunj, in the western *terai*; but it is in the eastern *terai* that foreign migration to the Gulf, the flow of remittances, and links with the Gulf more generally are greatest, and where one might expect more in the way of influence (and funding) from Saudi Arabia, the UAE and other Gulf states. This again is a key area for further research.

Another religious or rather theological distinction that does seem to be important, however, is that between the various Nepali sects (*fikr*) and that of the Ahmadis (or Qadiani) who are regarded as heretics by most Nepali Muslims. The Ahmadis who present themselves and proselytise as the only true Muslims originate in the Punjab and believe that their founder, Mirza Ghulam Ahmad (d. 1908) was a Prophet. This for most Muslims is heretical. In 1974, Pakistan passed a constitutional amendment declaring the Ahmadis to be a non-Muslim minority, which made them extremely vulnerable. They have since then migrated to many different parts of the world and began to establish a presence in Nepal over a decade ago.

The discourses of the National Muslim Forum describe the Ahmadis as a 'growing threat' because of the disturbance (*fitna*) they are said to be creating among Nepali Muslims. Sijapati states that 'the Forum's General Secretary explains that the Ahmadis arrived in Nepal twelve years ago and since then have 'captured' several villages' (2011: 92). He sees the presence of the Ahmadis as a 'grave problem, which regardless of the differences of religion or sect, is a problem for us all'. Falling victim to the lure of money, it is suggested, some Nepali Muslims are being 'persuaded' to convert. This language is very similar to that used by Hindu revivalists concerning the threat of conversion to Christianity: that ordinary Hindus are being 'bought' by missionary money. Sijapati describes how already at the time she was undertaking her research 'the fight has already begun, for various *'ulama* have stood up to eradicate this *fitna* and have founded the Assembly to Protect the End of the Prophets[1] (*Majlis Tehafuz Khatm Nabuat*)' (2011: 92).

Hindu-Muslim Relations in Historical Perspective

In the last few years, what might be called the politics of religion has, for various reasons, become more acute. We shall therefore, briefly, consider the dynamics of Hindu-Muslim relations, which have become, arguably, more a matter of concern recently than they have been previously, in part as a result of the differing responses to the introduction of the term 'secularism' into the Constitution and into the politico-religious discourse within and between groups in Nepal (Seddon 2016, Niraula & Seddon 2017).

The issue of relations between Hindus and Muslims in Nepal might be said to fall into two parts: cooperation, on the one hand, and conflict on the other. The first of these is difficult to examine without further research, but there are competing views on the relationship between the two. It could be argued, on the one hand, that, particularly at a time when there is evidence of a resurgence of Hinduism and demands for a Hindu state to be reinstated (as we shall see below), an exclusive emphasis on 'Muslim identity' risks increasing social divisions between Muslims and non-Muslims (especially Hindus), thereby reducing the possibility of oecumenical united action across sectarian and community lines to transform and improve Nepali society. This becomes an increasing concern, if it is feared that Muslims are a risk to others, because they are thought to be becoming more radicalised both politically (terrorists) and religiously (fundamentalists).

On the other hand, it could be argued that a self-confident Muslim community, assured of its basic rights within Nepali society, would be in a better position and more likely to collaborate and cooperate with other groups to promote more general commitment on the part of government and civil society to improvements in social welfare for the disadvantaged.

As regards conflict, this may be regarded as the other side of the coin. In so far as Muslims remain distinctive and keep themselves to themselves, they may be able to advance a coherent and distinctive set of interests eg as a marginalised and disadvantaged community, a minority; but they may also increase the divisions that exist between Muslim and non-Muslim, just as an emphasis on caste and ethnic differences and divisions may exacerbate social tensions and real division, leading to a greater chance of conflict.

The Muslim presence in northern India had significant impact on the hill kingdoms of what is now Nepal; but, according to the *Vamshavalis*, the first Muslims actually to settle in Nepal arrived in Kathmandu from Kashmir only in the late 15th and early 16th century, during the reign of King Rama Malla (1484-1520 AD). Many of these 'Kashmiri' Muslims entered into the Kingdom as traders of woollen goods, who were permitted to settle in the Valley as a mid-point for their journeys between Kashmir and Lhasa; some married and settled in Nepal others settled in Lhasa (Dastidar, 2008). Sijapati suggests that 'as descendants of traders, the Kashmiri Muslims of Kathmandu have traditionally had strong ties with Nepal's monarchy, and have served in various positions in the court'.

Sijapati suggests that 'letters of Christian missionaries from the seventeenth century onwards attest to the presence of Muslims in Kathmandu' (2011: 20) and comments that 'prior to the unification of Nepal in 1768, Kashmiri Muslims enjoyed a relationship of mutual respect with the King through, in Gaborieau's words, 'their intermediary '*sufi-fakir*' leaders' (Sijapati 2011: 21). Oral histories recount how, in the 16th century, a Kashmiri fakir by the name of Shah Miskeen Baba employed his spiritual powers to persuade the Hindu Malla king at the time to give him land to establish a mosque in the Valley the Kashmiri Takia Jame Masjid - on the king's way (Raj Path) only a few hundred metres to the south of the king's palace.

This small Muslim community continued to live in the Kathmandu Valley even after the overthrow of the Mallas and the gradual 'unification' of what is now Nepal under the rule of the kings of Gorkha. They are referred to by early English residents in Kathmandu, such as Francis Hamilton and by Daniel Wright, who, in the introduction to his *History of Nepal,* refers to 'a few Musalmans, consisting of Kashmiri and Iraki merchants live in Kathmandu. The former have been established there for generations. Altogether they do not number more than about one thousand' (Wright, 1877). Conversion from Hinduism to Islam was already taking place; as early as 1803, Francis Hamilton remarked that 'while at Kathmandu, several Hindus of high caste among our followers chose to embrace the Musalman faith and thereby subjected themselves to severe restrictions and disgrace' (Hamilton 1971: 37-38). He added that 'Musalmans have become pretty numerous, and are increasing, as they are zealous in purchasing girls and in propagating their sect' (cited in Sijapati 2011: 146, footnote 25).

This may have been one of many factors leading the Ranas to codify the social status of different groups, including Muslims, in the Muluki-Ain of 1854. Other factors might have included concern about the influence of Christian missionaries (see below). In any case, it seems that reinforcement of the specifically 'Hindu' character of Nepal was felt to be required. In 1866, Jang Bahadur Rana emphasised that 'we have our own country, a Hindu kingdom, where the law prescribes that 'cows shall not be slaughtered', nor women nor Brahmans sentenced to capital punishment; a holy land where the Himalayas, the Basuhi Ksetre, the Arya Tirtha, and the refulgent Sri Pashupati Linga and Sri Guhyesvari Pitha are located. In this Kali age, this is the only country in which Hindus rule'.

'The Kali age' clearly was considered, by the Rana rulers at least, to bring with it new threats of subversion of the *asal Hindustan*, both from within and from outside. As we have seen, religious conversion was proscribed, but clearly did take place. Islam was, however, not seen as such a great threat to Hinduism until perhaps the second half of the 19th century, after the so-called Indian Mutiny, when significant numbers began to enter Nepal from India. Even the arrival of the Begum of Lucknow and her entourage does not seem to have created too much alarm in the capital, and it seems that such 'incursions' were simply absorbed and more or less integrated. The Muluki 'Ain provided a way of both including Muslims within the overall Hindu caste hierarchy while at the same time identifying them as distinct and different.

Even with the surge of Muslim immigration into Nepal in the aftermath of Indian independence in 1947 and the subsequent Partition, however, when undoubtedly there was a flow of Muslims into Nepal, there seems to have been relatively little concern expressed about either the growing population of Muslims or their tendencies towards proselytisation and conversion of Hindus, which have recently become an issue. Immigration into the *terai* from India began to be a political issue from the 1950s onwards, when it undoubtedly increased for reasons that are not entirely clear but may be related to growing sectarian and religious divisions and conflict in India following partition.

From the early 1950s onwards, after the overthrow of the Ranas, there was a growth in Nepali nationalism closely associated both with the construction of a renewed Hindu monarchy and also with the rise of new democratic forces. During the 1950s, there were occasional reports of large migrations of Muslims from Bengal into Jhapa district, but the 1961 census of Nepal indicates that little more than 3 per cent of the district's population was Muslim' (1975: 106).

The 'opening up' of the *terai* in the late 1950s and through the 1960s, in part as a result of malaria eradication and in part because of population pressure in the hills, led to mass immigration into the region from the north; at the same time, immigration into the *terai* from across the border was also increasing. Gaige notes that 'reports of large-scale migration from the Indian border states of Uttar Pradesh and Bihar, and West Bengal, periodically find their way into the Kathmandu press, most of them reports of Muslims escaping the wrath of their Hindu neighbours. Only the vaguest estimates of the numbers of migrants accompany these reports.

The late 1950s and early 1960s saw the formation of several Muslim associations, and in 1963, there was a nationwide conference of Nepali Muslims in Rautahat and an annulment of the previous requirement to obtain government permission to build a mosque within the kingdom. This marks the beginnings of efforts to develop a coherent and official 'minority' status for Muslims as a whole in Nepal. On the other hand, according to Gaborieau (1972), the change in self-identification from 'Hindustani' to 'Nepali' Muslims occurred in early 1960s because of the Panchayat Regime's policy of homogenizing the diverse groups of Nepalis into a single national identity and culture.

In the early 1960s, however, the fear of Nepali nationalists was largely that Naxalites and communists and the Terai Liberation Front all of whom were undoubtedly operating in the *terai* at that time were threatening the integrity of the nation; but these fears took on a 'communal' aspect as conflicts over land and land rights became entangled with claims of citizenship and nationality. These issues, which affected Muslim-Hindu relations, continued to be of some importance in maintaining a degree of suspicion and tension between the two 'communities'. There was real concern in some quarters that Muslims, who accounted for a mere 2.5 per cent of Nepali population in the early 1960s, were becoming rapidly more numerous and, in certain parts of the *terai,* threatened to 'overwhelm' the local population; although the validity of this charge is doubtful, it is evidence of the 'spectre of migration' fear (Gaige 1975: 177).

In the late 1960s, it was widely suggested by the Nepali press that immigration into the *terai* from India was increasing the economic, social and political problems of the regions, squatting on and effectively colonising the land, organising gangs of criminals (*dacoits*) and undermining law and order, exacerbating Hindu-Muslim relations (particularly in districts with high levels of Muslims, like Kapilvastu and Rupandehi) and creating problems around the definition of citizenship. The government-sponsored Peasants' Organisation certainly expressed the view that disturbances in Nawal Parasi in September 1966 were at least partly the result of citizenship problems arising from the abolition of the *ukhada* land tenure system, especially in Nawal Parasi and Rupandehi districts; while, in response to demonstrations of protest in Talihawa, the headquarters of Kapilvastu district, against the government compulsory savings scheme that took place in April 1969 when violence spread across Kapilvastu and Rupandehi districts, one ultra nationalist Kathmandu newspaper accused exiled Nepali Congress workers of facilitating the 'infiltration of a large number of Indian Muslims and other Indians into this region of Nepal to create disturbances' (cited in Gaige 1975: 177).

In 1972, Gaige adds, the press reported that large numbers of 'Bihari' Muslims were moving into Jhapa from Bangladesh because of persecution at the hands of Bengali Muslims following the establishment of an independent government there, and cites *Jana Jagriti Weekly*, 11 August 1972. He was doubtful, however, that significant migration of Muslims into Jhapa was taking place as a result of the creation of Bangladesh and inter-Muslim conflicts as a result of this political process. On the other hand, there is no doubt that there were significant distinctions in what became East Pakistan between the small minority elite of Urdu-speaking Muslims in Bengal and the majority of Bengali-speaking Muslims, who were predominantly poor and middle peasants and linguistic differences took on an increasingly class-based and political significance through the 1950s and 1960s, prior to the creation of Bangladesh as an independent country. At least one source refers to the 'large-scale exodus of Urdu-speaking Muslims during the liberation war meant that by 1974, Bengali (or Bangla as it was being referred to) was the mother tongue for almost 98 per cent of the Bangladeshi population' (G H Peiris, *Political Conflict in Bangladesh* 1998).

Despite the concerns expressed by Hindu nationalists and the largely Kathmandu-centred media, there is remarkably little evidence of systematic conflict, in fact, between local Hindus and Muslims in the *terai*, whether with respect to immigrants or established communities, throughout the whole period from the 1950s to the 1980s, despite a doubling of the Muslim population in this period, from around 200,000 to around 400,000. Indeed, even the All Nepal *Anjuman Islah*, established by the late King Mahendra to minimise and mitigate inter-communal problems, and ever wary of inter-communal tensions and conflict, was able to document only eight incidents of Hindu-Muslim conflict in Nepal between 1954 and 1981 (another source[2] suggests twelve between 1954 and 1977), almost all in the *terai.*

Most of these were associated with immigration and citizens' rights, and including disputes ranging from conflicts over access land to *taziya* processions, the construction of an *idgah* and a mosque, and the accusation of a Muslim slaughtering a cow. The latter was the largest scale incident of all, and took place in 1971 in the *terai* districts of Bara and Rautahat'. The Muslim accused of breaking the law by killing a cow was reportedly murdered by a Hindu from the same village, and riots lasting twelve days followed (Sijapati 2011: 55). This does not seem to suggest serious conflict.

Sijapati has argued that 'Muslims were no threat to the monarchy in the panchayat system' and it seems there was relatively little conflict at the local level; Sijapati actually suggests that this was a period of what some describe as 'assurance of royal protection'. Indeed, the *Muslim Sewa Sangh*, registered in 1974, apparently held a 'Quran competition' in the Police Club in Kathmandu, with the full cooperation of His Majesty's government, during which, however, 'all the statues of different Hindu gods and goddesses were covered with cloths' (Sijapati 2011: 28) presumably so as not to offend the sensibilities of the Muslims participating. This is not to say that there were no incidents at all; but they were limited in occurrence and generally quickly contained.

Hindu-Muslim Relations 1970s to 1990s

Numerous ethnic 'cultural' associations were formed during the 1970s and 1980s; Muslim associations were also emerging (as we have seen). One of these, the All Nepal *Anjuman Islah* (All Nepal Reform Council), was apparently 'active in quelling several outbreaks of violence between Hindus and Muslims in the late 1970s in the *terai*' (Sijapati 2011: 28). Sijapati does also refer to conflict between Muslims and Hindus in 1992 in Banke, which involved the Hindu desecration of a mosque and violent retaliation by Muslims, and clashes between Hindus and Muslims in 1994-95 in Nepalgunj over the building of a temple near a Muslim *musafir khane* (lodge) that involved three days of rioting and looting. She points out, however, that 'these were all localised conflicts that transpired near the southern border near India, and up until the 1990s, were ended swiftly with government intervention' (2011: 55).

Dastider comments that violent confrontations between Hindus and Muslims had occurred in the *terai* districts of Mahottari, Rautahat, Bara, Dang and Banke in the second half of the twentieth century, but also suggests that 'the few incidents of communal clashes between Hindus and Muslims, that have so far been reported (since 1990) from Tulsipur (Dang) in 1992, and Nepalgunj (Banke) in December 1994 and October 1995, confirm the belief that Muslims are safe in Nepal as long as they maintain their age-old submissive and non-assertive minority character. But as soon as they become a little assertive and aware about their democratic rights, they immediately attract the ire of the Hindu majority, and animosity and mutual distrust displace the harmonious relationship between the two communities' (2000: 769).

However, other sources appear to contradict this assessment of the situation in the 1990s. Lawoti, for example, reports that in Nepalgunj, five violent conflicts took place between Hindus and Muslims between 1992 and 1997 (Lawoti 1997). Also, Peter Gill, writing about Nepalgunj in *The Record* in February 2016, suggests that

> 'Tensions between Hindus and Muslims ran high in the 1990s. In 1992, Indian Hindu nationalists led an angry mob that destroyed the Babri Masjid in Ayodhya, Uttar Pradesh, claiming that the mosque had been built atop the site of an older temple to Lord Rama. Tensions spilled across the border. Fights began to break out between Muslims and Hindus in Nepalgunj, often over women or cricket matches between India and Pakistan. A chapter of the Shiv Sena, modeled on Bal Thackeray's Hindutva and Marathi nativist political organization in Bombay, opened an office. Tensions came to a head in the May 1997 municipal elections, in which the Shiv Sena supported candidates for Nepalgunj mayor and other positions. After Shiv Sena supporters reportedly blocked a Muslim from entering a polling place, a Shiv Sena member was shot and injured, and riots erupted in which many homes and businesses were destroyed. One Muslim from a nearby village was

killed and 27 people were injured; 90 percent of businesses damaged belonged to Muslims'.

Another example of Hindu-Muslim tensions in India spilling over into the *terai,* or Madhes, was when an Indian Airlines plane was hijacked from Kathmandu to Kandhahar in December 1999, and India seized the opportunity to claim that Nepal had become a hotbed of ISI activity against Delhi. When pressed by G M Banatwala, a Muslim member of the Indian Parliament, to pinpoint such institutions the Indian Home Minister, L K Advani, told him that such institutions existed on the Nepali side of the border! Prime Minister Atal Behari Vajpayee raised the issue with Nepal's Prime Minister G P Koirala during his state visit to India in December 2000; and when Prime Minister Sher Bahadur Deuba visited India in March 2001, the issue of ISI's activities against India from Nepalese soil was raised once again by Vajpayee.

Hindu-Muslim Relations in the 21st Century

Certainly, after 9/11, the Muslim *madrasas* and mosques were looked upon by the Nepali authorities with increasing suspicion; they were now suspected, by ordinary Nepalis as well as by the state, of harbouring and producing terrorists and of encouraging and promoting terrorism, despite vehement denial of this by Nepal's Muslim political and religious leadership. The courses of study they provided were scrutinized and they were pressurized to dilute their Islamic content and add more secular subjects. They began to feel threatened. The situation was particularly acute in the immediate aftermath of 9/11, but continued through the period of the US' 'war against terror'.

In May 2002, there were reports of two Nepali Muslims being killed by the army inside a mosque in Nawalparasi district, in the *terai.* The authorities acted on a tip-off that 'explosives' were hidden allegedly under a pile of sand inside mosque under construction. It was reported by the local authorities that 'during the army raid, explosives and bombs were found. The mosque was said to host a religious fair every summer and those killed had, allegedly, worked earlier in an ammunition factory in India. Eyewitnesses claimed that an *imam* of a mosque was arrested after the raid, whereas a Kathmandu-based daily reported three arrests.

This was a particularly significant episode in 2004 to which Sijapati devotes a whole chapter in her book on *Islamic Revival in Nepal* (Sijapati 2011), when, following the murder of 12 Nepali labourers by terrorists in Iraq, police in Kathmandu failed to prevent angry Hindu rioters from vandalizing mosques, beating up imams and threatening the lives of many Muslims. This anti-Muslim violence was the first such incident to occur in the Kathmandu Valley, and was particularly shocking to Muslims.

Kalo Buddhvar

There was, however, a particularly significant episode. The period of the Iraq war from 2003 onwards was of particular significance in Nepal because of the 'execution' at the end of August 2004 of 12 Nepali hostages by the Islamist group Ansar al-Sunna in Iraq. The Islamist group concerned actually identified the Nepalis as being employed by 'the West' and therefore as effectively supporting the intervention by foreign 'Christian' forces in Iraq and also (through ignorance) as Buddhists and Christians themselves. But in Nepal, this was seen as an attack by Iraqi Muslims on Nepali Hindus (non-Muslims). Protests and riots broke out in Kathmandu the next day, after newscasts had reported the incident. Local Nepali Muslims were the main targets, as well as their sacred buildings (mosques, *madrasas*, etc.), businesses and homes (Sijapati 2011: 49). This became known, to the Muslim communities in Nepal, as 'Black Wednesday' (*kalo buddhavar*). Megan Sijapati has provided a full account of this incident, in which rioters attacked the embassies of Middle Eastern governments, the offices of recruitment agencies (which send many Nepalis to the Gulf) and any office or building associated with Muslims or with Islam, including notably *madrasas* and mosques (Sijapati 2011: 48-70).

Thomas Bell also describes the events of that day in his book on Kathmandu (2014: 123-24). 'It was hard for me to reach the Kashmiri mosque because of police firing tear gas, but a couple of hundred rioters had the run of it before the police arrived. The ground was scattered with charred pages of Arabic; the prayer room was blackened; there were smashed plant pots and broken glass; a blackened tomb; water tanks knocked off the roof and split. The police were wandering around, spitting on the ground and poking things with their lathis. The Imam had been beaten up, then locked in a room for his safety... He was still locked in'. In the afternoon, the government declared a curfew, which was not lifted for four days. Helicopters flew low over the now empty streets, and no-one swept up the glass....'A Muslim leader detected complex planning, perhaps by Hindu fundamentalists: 'the way in which they opened the gate and entered the Mosque showed they used to visit', he reasoned. There were many other ideas circulating as to what 'lay behind' it all.

Years later, Bell met a leader of the Kashmiri community who had been the chairman of the mosque during the riot in 2004 and he was inside when it was attacked. 'We lost 4 crore 25 lakhs near about, and in our own property, in this office, I lost 2 lakhs near about', he said. All the labourers' passports they'd been holding were destroyed. 'You must have been terrified', 'Even today we are frightened', the old man said calmly.

In the newspaper *Republica,* Dev Kumar Sunuwar wrote at the time that 'Right after the gruesome killing of 12 Nepali hostages by militants in Iraq on September 1, 2004, Nepali Muslims didn't merely experience the violent attacks on their Jame Masjid (Mosque) in Kathmandu, but also the businesses they owned and the houses they lived in. But then, they have been living a fearful life, as they are always seen with scepticism and are portrayed as if they are terrorists'. Sunuwar generalises this very specific incident and suggests that Muslims have been categorised, increasingly, not just as a 'minority', but also as a 'threat'; Sijapati also, I believe, generalises from this very specific incident to develop a broader argument about the process of Islamic revivalism in Nepal and the growth of negative attitudes towards Muslims in Nepal, with a whole chapter in her book on *Islamic Revival in Nepal* devoted to 'religion, violence and Muslim Nepalis', entitled Kalo Buddhvar (Black Wednesday). How justified this may be, is a matter of debate, I suggest.

Deepening Tensions?

The National Muslim Forum was formed, following this incident in 2005 as a pan-Nepali Muslim organization, calling on Muslims across the country to unite as Muslims, whatever their differences, and to present themselves as a distinctive minority in Nepali society. Reports in 2007 indicated that a new alliance of Hindu groups, called the Nepal Armed Hindu Morcha, had formed with the objective of returning Nepal to its former status as a Hindu state through any means, including violence. At the same time, Muslim groups such as the Muslim Liberation Front, the Nepal Muslim Ettehad Organisation and the Islamic Federation of Nepal were cited in local media for their calls for greater representation of Muslims and recognition of religious rights in the central government.

This was a period of considerable tension and unrest in the *terai* as concerns regarding the effective marginalisation and even exclusion of Madhesis from political representation at the national level and the treatment of the Madhes as barely part of Nepal were expressed not only the political leaders of the various Madhesi parties and groupings but by ordinary people, including Muslims. In September 2007, there was a short period of sustained violence between Hindus and Muslims in Kapilvastu District, prompted by the murder of Abdullah Mohit Khan, a leader of the Madhesi Mukti Morcha party and formerly a member of an anti-Maoist resistance group. Hundreds fled the area, dozens were killed and hundreds more were harassed and victimised in retaliatory violence for Khan's murder, which one point took on the form of distinctly Hindu-Muslim reciprocal violence. The government failed to respond adequately during the weeks of tension and open conflict (Sijapati 2011: 136).

In recent years, Hindu extremists have tended to target not only Muslims but also, increasingly, Christians, as the number of those converting to Christianity has grown and Christians are seen as an 'existential threat' to Hinduism in Nepal. In August 2012, Release International, which calls itself 'the voice of persecuted Christians' reported (quoting AsiaNews and the BBC) that

> 'Hindu extremists in Nepal have threatened to attack Christians and Muslims unless they leave the country. Members of the Nepal Defence Army (NDA) made threatening phone calls to several senior church figures and issued leaflets threatening violence against both Christians and Muslims. In one call, extremists threatened to bomb a cathedral in Kathmandu – the target of a violent attack by the NDA in 2009. In another call, the group insisted that Nepal is a Hindu nation where Christians and Muslims are 'not welcome'. The threats have prompted a police investigation and forced churches to hire security guards. The NDA has claimed responsibility for several attacks on Christians, church organisations and mosques in recent years. It has taken advantage of political instability since the end of Nepal's civil war to pursue its armed struggle to create a Hindu state'.

But, even if the attention of Hindu extremists has tended to turn in recent years more towards Christians than towards Muslims, it is also the case that Hindutva the movement to sustain Hinduism has also been directed towards Muslims. One important factor has been the impact on Hindus in Nepal of the rise of the BJP and the success of Modi in India. It has been argued recently by the US Commission for International Religious Freedom (USCIRF) admittedly not an entirely disinterested organisation that although the Indian Constitution grants religious freedom to every citizen, religious tolerance and religious freedom 'continued to deteriorate in India in 2016'. It stated that

> Hindu nationalist groups and their sympathisers perpetrated numerous incidents of intimidation, harassment, and violence against religious minority communities and Dalits. The Indian government for the past several years, including that of the previous Manmohan Singh regime, have dismissed the findings of this annual report, which has always been critical of religious freedom in India. National and state laws that restrict religious conversion, cow slaughter, and the foreign funding of non-governmental organisations and a constitutional provision deeming Sikhs, Buddhists, and Jains to be Hindus helped create the conditions enabling these violations. While Prime Minister Narendra Modi spoke publicly about the importance of communal tolerance and religious freedom, members of the ruling party have ties to Hindu nationalist groups implicated in religious freedom.

These issues, combined with long-standing problems of police and judicial bias and inadequacies, have created a "pervasive climate of impunity" in which religious minorities feel increasingly insecure and have no recourse when religiously motivated crimes occur. Based on these concerns, in 2017 USCIRF again places India on its Tier 2, where it has been since 2009'..

Meanwhile, back in Nepal, Peter Gill reported from Nepalgunj in *The Record* (2017) that

> One December afternoon (in 2016) in Kathmandu, I got a call from Bijaya. The connection was bad, but I could make out that he was on his way to the capital because someone was in the ICU at Tribhuvan University Teaching Hospital. Ather Hussein, the Maoist leader, was there too, he said. He sounded worried. Ather Husain's number was busy, but I took a taxi to the hospital that evening and found him outside the ICU. He was talking intently with an elderly man and woman, whom I later learned

> were Muslim MPs from the Congress party. His eyes were red and he looked tired. When he saw me, he greeted me quickly and said that I could go in and see the patient myself. Still unsure of whom I had come to see, I followed another visitor into the room.
>
> Lying in one of the beds was Wajahul Khan, the maulana I had met the night of the teaching hosted by Chaand dai. He was unconscious, hooked up to a ventilator, his chest rising and falling to the rhythm of a machine. Tubes snaked into his nose and arm, and he had a large bandage on his head. It felt somehow invasive for me to be there, so I left quickly. Speaking with Ather Hussein and the other visitors, I learned Wajahul was in a coma. He had been attacked by an angry Hindu mob in Matehiya VDC, not far from where he lived, on Mawlid, the celebration of the Prophet's birthday. Religious tension had been brewing in the area for some time, at least since Muharram, whose lunar date coincided with Dasain celebrations this year. On Mawlid, tensions boiled over.
>
> According to a later independent investigation by Siraj Khan, a senior Nepalgunj *Gorkhapatra* journalist, a fight broke out between Hindu and Muslim young men in a Hindu village that the Mawlid procession was due to pass through. Several Hindus were injured, and the procession, led by Wajahul Khan and others, came to a halt outside the village and gradually began to disperse. At that point, a group of villagers seeking revenge for the earlier fight attacked the Muslim crowd using farm implements and homemade weapons. Wajahul was hit in the head with a heavy blunt object. One Muslim died immediately, and others were taken to hospital in Nepalgunj; five were evacuated to Kathmandu.
>
> None of this received significant coverage in the media. A few back-page articles were published in *Kantipur*, *The Kathmandu Post*, and *The Himalayan Times*, but the articles either omitted the religious aspect of the violence or buried the fact that people were killed'.

In fact, this was not the only such incident that took place in the region at around the same time. Christopher Sharma of *AsiaNews.it* reported that 'scores flee after Hindu-Muslim violence breaks out in southern Nepal'. It seems that the clashes took place in a predominantly Muslim village in Kapilvastu District, and followed the death of a Hindu man, punished by Muslims for refusing to join in the festivities for the birthday of the Prophet Mohammed (Mawlid), which fell on 12 December (2016).

> 'More than a hundred Hindu and Muslim men fled a village in southern Nepal… after the killing of a Hindu man in the village of Bidhya Nagar triggered a wave of sectarian violence between the two religious communities. The Hindus fled because the village has a Muslim majority, and feared more attacks. Muslims went into hiding to avoid police arrests for the sectarian violence… Several people were injured in the clashes, (and) six people were arrested after the police intervened, although investigations were stalled because many of those involved had fled the scene'.

This report also refers to clashes between Hindus and Muslims in the village of Matehiya in Banke District, where it was reported that two people had been killed and several injured, which triggered further violence and the damage and destruction of several homes and places of worship. As regards the incident at Matehiya, Gill reports that

> 'As terrible as the Matehiya violence was, things could have been worse had the violence spread from the village to the city. There were fears that something like the 1997 violence could recur in Nepalgunj, but mercifully, this did not happen. Ather Husain and others held meetings with the prime minister after it became clear that Wajahul was going to die, and emphasized the danger of bringing the body back through Nepalgunj, where some activists wanted to hold a public procession. The government transported the body back to his village, first by plane to Tulsipur, then by helicopter. Thousands of people came from the surrounding villages and Nepalgunj for the religious teacher's burial.
>
> I returned to Nepalgunj in January, interested to see how the public mood had changed. To my surprise, most people I spoke with said they felt little difference." It's impossible to know what people think, inside. But externally, people are not aggressive, either on religious or ethnic lines," a young man at a paan stall said. A reading glasses merchant said that in Nepalgunj, "If something happens, people know that you have to immediately sit down and discuss about it. Why? Because [violence] isn't destructive just for the individual, it is destructive for all of society, for Hindus and Muslims alike."

When I asked people why something like the 1997 violence had not recurred, both Hindus and Muslims highlighted the changes that had occurred over the past two decades. The city had experienced *bikas*, development, and people had become more educated. Some said that there was greater camaraderie between Hindus and Muslims after the Madhes Andolan of 2007, when Madhesis of both religions jointly clashed with Pahadis; the lines of division had become ethno-racial, not religious. When I pointed out that those accused of Wajahul's murder were Hindu Madhesis, people noted the different political context where the violence occurred. Until recently, there was no bridge across the Rapti River connecting Matehiya to the rest of Nepal, and mindsets were influenced more by Indian culture and politics. The Madhesi movement of 2007 had not had an impact there, they said

Others pointed to the leadership of Nepalgunj's civil society. NGOs like Fatima Foundation, Informal Sector Service Center (INSEC), and others have led periodic dialogue events over the last ten years, bringing together religious leaders, judges, and local politicians to promote social harmony. I learned of an organization called the Inter-Faith and Societal Goodwill Forum (*Antar Dharmik Tatha Samajik Sadbhav Manch*), founded in response to the 2006 riots by leaders from Hindu, Muslim, Sikh, and Christian faiths. The two primary leaders are a local *maulana* named Abdul Jabar Manjuri and the head priest of the Bagheswori temple, known as the Chandannath Yogi. They are an unlikely pair, sometimes seen riding around the city on a motorcycle the baba in front, wearing brass hoop earrings and handlebar moustache, and the maulana behind, with his hennaed beard, flowing kurta, and Nepali *topi*. They agreed to meet with me.

"When people do bad things, it's important to remember that it's individuals who do bad things, not religions," the priest told me. "Crimes are crimes. It's important not to make it about religion. For the people who want to blame a religion, as soon as the Hindu guru and the Muslim maulana sit down together, it's a good message. They don't get the opportunity. And we go ahead with legal procedures." The maulana told me that although he had never met the priest before the 2006 riots, he now considers him a good friend.

At the time of the riots, they were introduced by a local businessman and began walking the streets holding hands and admonishing restraint. In the subsequent years, they have worked with the local authorities and intervened in several religious disputes before they had the chance escalate, facilitating dialogue between the groups. They have received recognition from international donors and government officials. He explained that after the initial dispute during Muharram in Matehiya, he and the yogi had travelled to the VDC. At a meeting with villagers, he urged them to fight for justice, but not in the name of religion. "Fight for roads, fight for getting electricity. Why fight each other?" he recalls saying, lamenting that it seemed to do little good.

I asked them why the violence did not spread to Nepalgunj. The yogi praised the chief district officer, who held meetings with various community leaders to allay fears and anger. He added that he and the *maulana* had urged local journalists to cover the issue sensitively, and was happy that the national media had not given it heavy coverage, since sensational reporting could have made things worse. "The media shouldn't add to the fire." After our meeting, I walked with the maulana through the old bazaar. He told me he felt awful about what happened in Matehiya, but the main thing is to prevent this from happening again, for no more deaths to occur. He said this in an almost cheerful tone that could have been interpreted as a lack of sincerity, but I don't think that's what it actually was. He had a point. His and the yogi's efforts to keep the issue out of the public eye may have helped the situation from getting out of hand in the short run, but I wondered about the long-term implications of sweeping it under the rug'.

What Gill does not mention is the fact that there had been other incidents in the region during the Mawlid. The *Europe Balkan Latest (EBL) News* covered one such at Narainpur village, also in Banke District not far from Nepalgunj, on 13 December 2016, where it reported that

'A man was killed and 15 people were injured in a clash between Hindu and Muslim groups in south-western Nepal near the Indian border, local police said Tuesday. Violence erupted late Monday when thousands of Muslims participating in a rally to mark the birthday of the Prophet Mohammed entered a Hindu neighbourhood in the village of Narainapur in Banke district, police inspector Laxman Shahi said. "Before the rally, the Muslims had agreed with the Hindus to not enter the Hindu neighbourhood. But some left the main road and went to the area. That's when they clashed," he said. The police said the dead man was a 45-year-old local. "We fired seven rounds of tear-gas shells to control the crowd. The situation is still tense, but it's under our control," Shahi said adding that a few houses were also damaged during

> the clash. Around 200 police officers were assigned to the area. Hindus make up more than 80 per cent and Muslims 4.4 per cent of Nepal's 26 million people. Communal violence is rare in the country, but religious riots have occurred in the past in Nepalgunj, a town 36 kilometres west of the village.

It is not clear whether these incidents indicate a rise in the tensions between Hindus and Muslims in Nepal's *terai*, or were simply unfortunate examples of the ever-present potential for violence in multi-faith, multi-cultural settings and were triggered by the breaking of agreements about the limits to expressions of distinctiveness. The rise of Hindu fundamentalism in Nepal is undeniable, and some have argued that there is a process of revivalism, if not radicalisation, taking place among Muslims.

Muslim Radicalisation and Revivalism

There has been increasing concern expressed by some in Nepal and not only by Hindus it has to be said - in recent years, regarding the potential 'radicalisation' of Nepal's Muslims under influence from outside, for example from Saudi Arabia, from Pakistan and, most recently from a local Indian franchise of the Islamic State. With the rise of radical Islam in the Middle East and the formation of Al Qaeda in Afghanistan during the 1980s, and the rise of the Taliban in Afghanistan and Pakistan in the 1990s, and then, even more dramatically after 9/11, Islamists and indeed Muslims in general and their alleged 'breeding grounds' the *madrasas* have come to belooked upon with increasing suspicion.

Upadhyay remarks that the situation has changed particularly since 2005-2006, with the removal of the monarchy and declaration of 'secularism' when, as he puts it, over-dramatically I suggest, 'the various political changes... opened a floodgate for the various Islamist groups from across the border to increase their activities in Nepal. With financial support from the Muslim world, there was a speedy growth of *madrasas* and mosques on both sides of the 1,751 km Indo-Nepal border, particularly along the northern Indian states of UP and Bihar' (2014: 35). He goes on to argue that in the last ten years, 'some Muslim organisations that were operating as socio-religious organisations became aggressive in challenging their centuries-old subordinate status. This led to communal conflicts in some of the districts of the *terai* region where Muslims are in competitive strength' (2014: 37).

He refers in particular an incident in Kapilvastu where 'a violent communal riot erupted in 2005 that ended with the killing of numerous innocent Hindus and Buddhists. The communal riot ended with government interference, but the scars of communal violence are still fresh in the minds of the Hindu and Buddhist population'. He asserts that 'the rising strength of the Muslim population in Kapilvastu is attributed to cross-border migration of Muslims from UP and Bihar states of North India. The open border is fuelling the Islamic fundamentalists on both sides of the border' (2014: 37). This, I suggest, is an assertion with limited empirical justification, although the recent (2016) clashes in Banke and Kapilvastu Districts may indicate the development of new elements in local Hindu-Muslim relations.

As Sijapati describes in some detail, many Muslims in Nepal have undoubtedly participated in what she refers to as a 'religious revival', in which they are offered 'new affiliations and new meaning systems based on common belief and practice as opposed to the traditional categories of caste background' (Sijapati 2011: 8). This suggests an increasing assertion of Muslims sharing Islam as a distinctive religion, as opposed to being 'Muslims' within an overall predominantly Hindu caste system or just one more distinctive social group in the context of contemporary Nepali society. She observes, significantly that this religious revival has been 'intrinsically linked... to the influence of imported Salafi-oriented ideologies and funding from Gulf countries for the building of mosques, Islamic centres and education... The new reform movements are heavily informed by more rigid interpretations of Islam disseminated from the Persian Gulf, where Nepalis are travelling in increasing numbers, and Pakistan and India' (Sijapati 2011: 9).

Even in Nepal, which was relatively remote from the areas of 'Islamist terrorism', *madrasas* have often been and continue to be suspected, by ordinary Nepalese as well as by the state (and even outside observers), of harbouring and producing terrorists and encouraging and promoting terrorism, despite vehement denial of this by the concerned management bodies. The courses of study they provided have, accordingly, been scrutinized and the madrasas pressurized to dilute their Islamic content and add more secular subjects. The situation became particularly acute in the aftermath of 9/11, but continued through the period of the US' 'war against terror' in the years after 2001, and war in Iraq from 2003, and remains an area of concern to some.

An increasing awareness of conflict throughout the Middle East and, closer to home, in Afghanistan and Pakistan in particular, and in the Indian sub-continent, between Islamists and others, has pervaded the attitude of many Nepalese towards Muslims in their own country. But "Nepali Muslims neither have attacked anyone nor do they have any sort of armed groups, as there are several as such in the Tarai where over 90% of Nepal's Muslims reside," says Nazrul Hussain Falahi, General Secretary of the National Muslim Forum, Nepal (NMFN) an umbrella organization of Muslim-led development organizations in Nepal. "Then how come we Muslims are terrorists? We're a peace loving people and want peace and harmony in the country."

The links between the indigenous Muslim community in Nepal and Islamist terrorist groups in Pakistan and elsewhere have never been demonstrated, but it can be argued that fears, expressed in the aftermath of 9/11 and at various points during the next decade as the US administration under President George W Bush pursued the global 'war against terror', continued to be held by various elements of Nepalese society, and this exacerbated the already-existing social and political discrimination resulting from their perceived status in Nepalese society associated with the overall classification of the population on the basis of caste, class and ethnicity, both in official and in unofficial policies and practices . One source (www.harunyahya.com/en/|Articles/29455/al-muslims-have-a-responsibility) concerned about the state of Hindu-Muslim relations in Nepal suggests that

> 'In 2004, these racist (Hindu) groups set fire to houses, workplaces, associations and mosques belonging to Muslims' and also that 'in March 2008, they hurled four bombs at a mosque in Biratnagar in which more than 50 Muslims were praying, thus causing the martyrdom of three Muslims and dozens more to be injured. In the time that followed, many mosques in the towns of Biratnagar and Bukraha, which have substantial Muslim papulation, were attacked by radical, racist Hindu organizations'.

In September 2007, according to the Pluralism Project (at Harvard University) sectarian violence between Hindus and Muslims broke out again, this time in Kapilavastu District, west of Kathmandu. Reports indicated the riots were sparked by the assassination of an Islamic leader, leading to Muslim reprisals and Hindu counter reprisals that lasted for two days and claimed several lives.

There are few reports of any troubles between this incident and now. Worries about the threat of 'fundamentalist Islam' in Nepal continues, however, to thrive in certain quarters. In October 2014, for example, it was reported that 'amid reports of criminal activity and growing religious fundamentalism in border areas, Nepal's Armed Police Force (APF) and India's Sashastra Seema Blal (SSB) were enhancing intelligence-sharing activities along their 1,880 km border…'. The moves followed a visit by the Indian Home Minister, Rajnath Singh's visit to Kathmandu the previous month during which he expressed his concern regarding the growth of Islamist fundamentalism in the border areas. As part of the measures introduced to control the infiltration of Islamist fundamentalists into Nepal, *madrasas* were being required to report on any visitors, especially foreigners. Members of the Indian Mujahiddin (IM) were thought to have crossed the border to try to recruit fighters, and the IM leader Yasin Bhatkal was arrested in Nepal in 2014.

On 16 July 2016, the daily newspaper *Republica* which has a certain reputation for imflammatory reportage carried an editorial which spoke of the risk of terrorism in Nepal and linked this with the potential radicalisation of Nepali Muslims through unregulated *madrasas.* There was considerable anger and outrage at this, not least from Muslim organisations; and the newspaper published an apology two days later. It also reported the comments of some of the Muslim organisations which had protested at the editorial. "To try to relate Nepali Muslims with any violent activities taking place elsewhere is absolutely unjust for this community because Muslims in Nepal have never resorted to any violent activities let alone raising arms," said Samim Miya Ansari, president of National Muslim Struggle Alliance, during a discussion with a team of journalists at *Republica.*

Ansari led a delegation of representatives from various Muslim organizations to the head office of Nepal Republic Media at Bag Durbar, Kathmandu. MP Mohammad Zakir Hussain of CPN (Maoist Center), Dr. Shamim Ahmad, country director of the World Assembly of Muslim Youth, Nazrul Hasan Falahi, former president of *Islami Sangh Nepal*, and Mohammad Shahid Ali, spokesman of the struggle committee, were among those who expressed their concerns during the discussion. Hussain said that the government has remained apathetic toward the requirements of Madrasas despite their repeated attempts to draw the attention of both the government and Parliament toward the situation. Falahi said that international communities can learn from the exemplary inter-faith harmony in Nepal.

Hindu-Muslim Cooperation

On the whole, though, despite this history of tension and sometimes of conflict between Muslims and Hindus, relations between Nepali Muslims and other social groups in Nepal have been, I would suggest, for the most part, relatively unproblematic as far as open conflict is concerned. Whether it is possible to discern a trend involving a deterioration in inter-communal relations is hard to say. Also, we are not in a position to comment in any detail at this point on the extent to which there is effective cooperation between Muslims and non-Muslims across the religious-community divide a) in everyday life, b) in local community activities involving both government and non-government organisations and associations, and c) at a wider level in local and national forums and associations.

The study of a hill Muslim village in Tanahun District by Upadhyay, however, provides an indication of the nature of interaction between Muslims and other groups in this one case at least. In this Muslim village of 64 households (and 466 inhabitants) there is routine interaction with other groups in Kihun VDC, the majority of whom are Brahmins and Magars, and thus Hindus and Buddhists, albeit main in regard to festivals and what might be termed cultural interaction rather than in daily social and economic interaction. As Upadhyay puts it:

> 'Kihun VDC is a confluence of an assortment of caste/ethnic groups living together... People of Kihun join each other in the ceremonies of social fairs and festivals. There is good participation from the Islamic community in the sociocultural activities of the village, especially in the festivals of Hindus. In this regard, there is harmony between Muslims and Hindus. They have the practice of close friendly ties (called *miteri saino* in Nepali... Due to educational awareness and modernity, the rigid caste-based relationship and commensality that prevailed between the people in the village in the past is diminishing fast in the present. Collectively, the people share the common practices in their own way. The Hindus and the Muslims relationship and brotherhood are becoming more amicable despite religious differences' (2014: 64).

On the other hand, Upadhyay also refers to the persistence of social and economic discrimination against the Muslim community by the Hindu upper castes in particular. In fact, he states, baldly, that 'the higher Hindu caste groups of Kihun VDC treat the Muslims as untouchables' (2014: 82). This discrimination is most evident in the schools, where Muslim pupils are discriminated against both by the teachers and by some of their fellow students (2014: 122-24). Upadhyay even refers to the fact that 'Muslim students sit separately on back benches (as they are regarded as untouchables) and are also deprived of using educational materials and equipment in many cases... Muslim students feel discriminated (against), depressed, frustrated and (tend to) terminate school (2014: 140-141).

At the local level, it seems clear that Muslim communities also retain a degree of insulation from other local communities, as a result of distinctive cultural and social practices not only are Muslims different and are seen to be different, in some respects they relish that difference and to a significant extent promote it. They keep their women indoors and covered up, and their girls tend to be removed from school after only a few years. They tend not to be involved in local activities, and specifically not in politics, not just because of marginalisation and exclusion but to some extent at least because of a lack of interest or wish to be so involved. Their involvement with non-Muslims in local community activities is, it would seem from the fieldwork undertaken during the summer of 2015 in the *terai,* somewhat limited, although it certainly does exist and this is something that should be subject to further research.

There are numerous specifically Muslim associations and NGOs which operate locally, with a view to promoting the welfare of the Muslim communities and/or of specific sections of the local Muslim community. Some of these were identified during the fieldwork in the summer of 2015. At the national level also, there are numerous Muslim associations and organisations, some of which were contacted during this research and identified.

But again the level of collaboration and cooperation between Muslim and non-Muslim Nepalis appears, on the basis admittedly of incomplete information and this is a topic that demands further research to be limited. Michael Hutt describes how, at the time of the debates over the 1990 Constitution, 'those demanding a secular state included Buddhist, Muslim and Christian associations, ethnic organisations representing the predominantly non-Hindu Tibeto-Burman tribes, and leftists, liberal and republican elements' (Hutt 1993: 37), suggesting that the Muslims formed part of a broad 'front' aligned in favour of religious pluralism and against the idea of a Hindu state.

But there are few examples, that we have come across, that indicate a commitment on the part of Muslim associations and organisations to collaborate with other non-Muslim organisations, let alone multi-faith organisations, at local or at national level. The exception is the Inter-Religious Peace Committee representing the Hindu, Buddhist, Christian, Muslim and Jain communities which was formally established as the Inter Religious Peace Council in October 2006 (having been founded over two years before), with Muslim representation in the form of Najarul Hussein as joint secretary. In 2007, a student project on 'inter-faith dialogue and religious understanding of peace' at Dickinson College in Kathmandu commented that 'the only inter-faith organisation (in Nepal), the Inter Religious Council of Nepal (IRCN), has been active in bringing together civil society and religious leaders, and encouraging sand challenging other religious communities to be vocal and active to bring peace in the country'. But the project complain s that too little had been done among students, and proposed to remedy this.

Sijapati also refers to the IRCN and reports in her study on *Islamic Revival in Nepal*, how it met in January 2010 to discuss how best to ensure an oecumenical vision for a new Nepal. The visions of the different faith communities differed in many respects, but all agreed that a multi-faith perspective was essential to the realization of a coherent and unified yet diverse nation. They criticized the rejection of religion implied in an atheistic or irreligious perspective of a secular Nepal, and agreed that Nepal would survive only if the convictions of religious communities inform the shape of the new secular state (Sijapati 2011: 137).

An example of attempts by individuals to bridge the divide between different religious communities is provided by the gift made by former Minister and leader of Nepali Congress (NC), Mohamad Aftab Alam, who in March 2015 pledged Rs 551,000 for the construction of a Hindu temple and a religious guest house at Shivanagar in Garuda Municipality in Rautahat District. Alam, a Muslim, attended the Shreemad Bhagawat Saptaha Gyan Mahaygya, a Hindu religious function, organised by the Municipality and announced his donation at that time. Speaking at the programme, former minister Alam said it is every citizens' duty and responsibility to preserve the religious and cultural faiths of all religions and community'. The NC Rautahat District President, Krishna

Prasad Yadav, also promised, on the same occasion, to contribute Rs 500,000 for the construction of the temple.

In a few cases although it may well be that these are only the tip of the iceberg as regards more positive inter-communal relations individuals have maintained close personal relationships across the religious divide. On 11 April 2016, Gani Ansari reported for the *BBC Nepali Service* on his relationship with Ram Narayan Gupta:

> I am a Muslim. He is a Hindu. Nearly 25 years ago, when our society was more conservative than it is today, our grandmothers tied the knot of life-long friendship, referred to as *miteri saino* in Nepal, between us. At that time, neither I nor he knew the difference between Islam and Hinduism. It was not my choice to be a Muslim, nor was it his choice to be a Hindu. We grew up together, and we still celebrate our friendship free of any religious prejudices. But when I read or hear about sectarian violence, I wonder why people following separate religions cannot be friends like us…
>
> … I came to Kathmandu for higher education, but I still visit my friend in the village at least twice a year to celebrate Eid and Holi. Some Hindus do not drink water touched by their Muslim neighbours. Some Muslims do not drink water in Hindu households. But Ram Narayan and I eat together, without fearing religious consequences. My Eid is joyless without my Hindu friend. His Holi is joyless without me, a Muslim. He always cooks *halal* meat whenever I visit him.
>
> A few months ago, my friend invited me to his marriage ceremony. I took leave from my office to attend his wedding in Bisrampur of Parsa district. I reached home, dropped my bags, and went to my friend's house. He had bought me a sherwani, his relatives wanted to apply henna on my hand. I felt shy, but they insisted. And I had to comply. The next day, I accompanied my friend to bring home his bride. I sat next to him right through all the Hindu rituals. The priest chanted Hindu mantras for hours, which was different to my culture. In Muslim society, the *maulana* needs no more than a few minutes to complete the ritual of marriage.
>
> It is not just marriage that sets us apart from Hindus. We bury our dead, they cremate theirs. We need to take bath before

participating in last rites, they take bath only after taking part in funeral. Allah is the only god to us, the Hindus have countless gods. In spite of these differences, we have been friends over the last two decades. Our inter-religious friendship flourished because we always respected each other's faith. The *azan*'s call blaring out of the loud speaker of our mosque never disturbed him. The ringing bells at their temples never irritated me.

We have learnt to value our interfaith friendship and religious harmony from our parents. Even now, when the Hindus in our village organise a religious *yagya*, we Muslims always contribute. When we build a mosque, they are ready to help us. But I feel Nepali society's traditional harmony is now being divided by caste, ethnicity and religious groups. If we cannot nip it in the bud, we will regret losing our historical religious coexistence'.

Secularism and Hindutva

Back in the early 1990s, when the notion of secularism was first discussed in the context of a new Constitution, as Hutt remarked (1994: 37), 'the debate on 'religion' quickly became an impassioned argument between proponents of a secular state and proponents of a Hindu state'. Those demanding a secular state included Buddhist, Muslim and Christian associations, ethnic organisations representing the predominantly non-Hindu Tibeto-Burman tribes, and leftist, liberal and republican elements. An enormous demonstration organized by the Nepal Buddhist Association to demand a secular state brought some 10,000 marchers out onto the streets of the capital on 30 June (1990).

These demands were strongly opposed by traditionalist Hindu organisations, particularly by the *Sanatan Dharma Seva Samiti* and the Nepal Committee of the *Vishwa Hindu Parishad.* The Interim Government's minister of housing, Achyut Raj Regmi even threatened to go on hunger-strike if the constitution made Nepal a secular state. Concern was expressed that 'the declaration of Nepal as a secular state would open its borders to a flood of Christian missionaries, who might have political as well as religious patronage and motives' (Hutt 1994: 37). The Constitution of 1990, while reinstating the multiparty system, still barred people of different ethnic communities from forming political parties to promote the interests of their communities and religious groups from forming religious parties. Meanwhile, all "mainstream" political parties were dominated by high caste Hindus. The Supreme Court also declared it unconstitutional for *janajatis* to use their mother tongue in local administration

The Interim Constitution of 2007, however, provided explicitly for freedom to practice one's religion; it also specifically denied the right to convert another person[3]. No laws specifically affecting freedom of religion were changed. Nonetheless, many believed that the declaration made it easier to practice their religion freely. Government policy contributed to the generally free practice of religion and the government itself took positive preliminary steps with respect to religious freedom. Although there were no registration requirements for religious groups, there were legal registration requirements for NGOs. Organizations had been prohibited from registering if their names contained religious words.

However, this began to change in April 2007 when the Government allowed the registration of an organization with the word "Bible" in its title. Christian, Muslim, and Jewish religious organizations claimed that, unless registered, they would be restricted from owning land, an important step for establishing churches, mosques, synagogues, or burial sites. An organization that provided religious services and *kosher* foods to Jewish adherents (generally tourists) complained that the organization was not able to legally register as a religious organization and that its workers had to enter the country on business visas. Foreign workers in the Christian missionary hospitals and schools also entered the country with visas designating them as technical workers for local or international NGOs sponsoring the hospitals and schools; if they were found to proselytize, they were to be expelled from the country, but there were no expulsions during the reporting period.

For decades, dozens of Christian missionary hospitals, welfare organizations, and schools have operated in Nepal. These organizations claimed that they did not proselytize and tended to operate relatively freely. Missionary schools were among the most respected institutions of secondary education; and many members of the governing and business elite graduated from Jesuit high schools. Some foreign Christian organizations, however, had direct ties to local churches in Nepal and sponsored pastors for religious training abroad. Specific holy days, most of them Hindu, were recognized as national holidays. These were Mahashivaratri, Buddha Jayanti, Falgun Purnima, Krishna Asthami, Dasain, and Tihar. Although public schools did not teach religion, most had a statue of Saraswoti, the Hindu goddess of learning, on their grounds. Many began the day with a Hindu prayer to the goddess.

Other festivals and holy days, however, more closely linked with other religions, were also recognised and celebrated, including Easter and Christmas. Civil servants could take off religious holidays and celebrate them at home (on private property) without government interference. The Government had no formal policy on inter-faith understanding, but the Inter religious Council of Nepal, consisting of representatives of the Hindu, Buddhist, Muslim, Christian, and Baha'i faiths, was active in promoting peace in the country. The growing number of cultural and religious organisations was generally tolerated.

A year later, on 28 May 2008, at its first session, the recently elected Constituent Assembly of Nepal made a momentous decision: that Nepal would no longer be a Hindu monarchy but a secular republic overturning, in effect, more than two centuries of history. Already, a year or so earlier, in January 2007, the Interim Parliament constituted on the basis of the composition of the National Assembly ten years previously, in 1997, when the last elections had taken place had promulgated the Interim Constitution, which declared Nepal to be a secular state. Now, the 4th Amendment of the Interim Constitution brought in by the Constituent Assembly in May 2008 stated unambiguously that Nepal would be 'an independent, indivisible, sovereign, secular, inclusive and federal democratic republican state'. All the languages spoken as native tongues would be languages of the nation; Nepali would be the official language, but nothing shall be deemed to prevent the using of any language spoken as the mother tongue in a local body and office.

It stated that 'the Rights to Freedom include the right to live with dignity and no law shall be made that provides for the death penalty. Every citizen shall have the following freedoms: freedom of opinion and expression; freedom to assemble peaceably and without arms; freedom to form political parties; freedom to form unions and associations; freedom to move and reside in any part of Nepal; and freedom to practice any profession, carry on any occupation industry and trade. These, subject to laws to impose reasonable restrictions on any act which may undermine the sovereignty and integrity of Nepal or which may jeopardise the harmonious relations subsisting among the peoples of various castes, tribes, religions, or communities or on any act of defamation, contempt of court or incitement to commit an offence or on any act which may be contrary to public decency or morality.

Madrasas, but not mosques which receive no government funding, were now required to register with local district administration offices (part of the Home Ministry) and supply information about their funding sources to operate; some Muslim leaders criticized the move as discriminatory; but the registration requirement has not been enforced. Muslims were not restricted from participating in the Hajj, although the Government did not subsidize the pilgrimage.

The Rastriya Prajatantra Party of Nepal (RPP-N) a centre-right, culturally conservative and royalist political party and a splinter group of the Rastriya Prajatantra Party (RPP) strongly objected to the declaration of a secular state, and supported the maintenance of Nepal as a Hindu kingdom. It had registered with the Election Commission of Nepal ahead of the April 2008 Constituent Assembly election and sought to form a front of royalist parties. The RPP-N won only four seats in the April 2008 Constituent Assembly election; and at the first meeting of the CA on 28 May, the RPP-N was the only party to oppose the declaration of a republic.

Its leader, Kamal Thapa, subsequently said (on 20 June 2008) that the country faced an impending 'disaster', and that the party's policies and programmes would remain the same despite the political change. On 13 July 2008, he described the abolition of the monarchy as merely "an interim decision", and emphasized that the RPP-Nepal sought the restoration of the monarchy. The party boycotted the July 2008 presidential election, on the grounds that the major parties were treating the election as a partisan contest. In August 2008, some senior leaders left the party and joined the RPP.

On the other hand, in line with the Interim Constitution's position on religious tolerance and wishing to redress the balance in this domain, the Maoist Prime Minister Prachanda signed a six-point agreement in March 2009 with the United Muslim National Struggle Committee, pledging to form a Muslim Commission and provide a constitutional guarantee for 'Muslim identity' through the nationalization of Muslim holidays and the establishment of political quotas, a permanent Hajji committee, an Islamic Affairs Commission and an Islamic School Board, and through the introduction of Islamic personal law (based on the *shari'a*) for Muslims. In May 2009, however, Prachanda resigned, leaving Muslims unsure that the agreement would remain valid.

In January 2010, a meeting of Nepal's Inter-Religion Council representing the Hindu, Buddhist, Christian, Muslim and Jain communities met to discuss how best to ensure a vision for a new Nepal. Their visions differed in many respects, but all agreed that a multi-faith perspective was essential to the realization of a coherent and unified yet diverse nation. They criticized the rejection of religion implied in an atheistic or irreligious perspective of a secular Nepal, and agreed that Nepal would survive only if the convictions of religious communities inform the shape of the new secular state (Sijapati 2011: 137).

By contrast with this attempt to generate support for a secular state in which all religions were respected and in which there was a positive contribution to be made by the different faith communities to a new tolerant multi-faith society and state, the predominant mood among Hindus and particularly Hindu nationalists has been to reject the idea of a secular state and to return to a Hindu state.

Throughout the last eight years, since the formation of the first Constituent Assembly in 2008 and its declaration of Nepal as a secular republic, forces loyal to the notion of a Hindu monarchy as central to Nepal's identity, unity and stability have continued to argue for a return to the status quo ante as regards this basic feature of the state and have tended to oppose the very notion of 'secularism', often equating it with 'atheism' or even with anti-Hinduism. With the rise of Narendra Modi within the BJP during 2013 and his subsequent nomination as Prime Minister of India in 2014, there can be little doubt that politically active conservative and nationalist Hindus in Nepal saw a new opportunity to maintain or rather re-gain their previous largely unquestioned dominance. The significance of this cannot now be underestimated; it has coloured much of Nepal's political debate over the new Constitution and has encouraged the old Hindu establishment to see new hope for a reinforcement of the status quo, rather than a basis for a progressive and inclusive transformation of Nepal.

In October 2009, twelve Bahun organisations from all over Nepal met in Devghat and decided to merge to form one national organisation, the Brahman Samaj Nepal (BSN). It spread rapidly to establish branches in 68 out of Nepal's 75 districts, omitting only the Himalayan region. Between October 2009 and May 2012, the BSN organised many programmes ranging from peaceful demonstrations with religious hymn-singing to more politically aggressive 'torch' rallies (*masal julus*) and general strikes (*bandhs*). A torch and motorbike rally held in Pokhara on 5 February 2012 is claimed to be the largest demonstration the city has ever seen. The BSN estimates its membership to be over 200,000.

Several grassroots Chhetri organisations also merged to form larger organisations. Although relatively more organised and more numerous, the Chhetris have not managed to unite behind one single organisation. The largest, however, the *Kshatree Samaj Nepal* (KSN), claims to have some 500,000 members; this organisation is based in Pokhara. Others formed in Kathmandu, like the *Khas Chhetri National Federation* (KCNF). But more substantial and more united was the *Khas Kshetri Unity Society-Indigenous Nationalities* (KKUS-IN) based in Biratnagar, though it claims to have branches in 48 districts. Established in 2006, the latter this group was led by former UML leader Yuvaraj Karki. It argues that Chhetris are in reality *adivasi janajati* (or disadvantaged indigenous people), hence, like the KCNF, it invokes the Khas title, and is in favour of identity-based federalism and a separate Khasan state, on the basis that the Bahun ideology has ruined the country. The KSN disagrees, arguing that Chhetris are indigenous but not *janajati*.

An alliance called the Khas Chhetri National Front was formed in 2009 but it failed to unite the various groups. The KSN continued to grow and became dominant. On 22 May 2010, KSN agitation, in particular a relay hunger strike, culminated in negotiations with the government which reached agreement on two points: 1) there should be further study regarding the status of the Chhetris as an *adivasi* but not a *janajati* group, and 2) government reservation policy should be based on class, not ethnicity. A task force was formed and led by the KSN Chairman. On 11 February 2012 he submitted a 130-page report to the Minister of Local Development, documenting the 'indigenous character' of the Chhetris.

The conservative and royalist RPP-N contested the 2013 Constituent Assembly elections in November 2013 and this time won 24 seats out of 575 seats under the system of proportional representation, making it the fourth largest party in the House (it had only four seats in the previous Constituent Assembly). In an interview with the *Kathmandu Post* on 29 December 2013, Kamal Thapa of the RPP-N indicated that he might be able to compromise on the issue of the Hindu monarchy, suggesting that 'despite the fact that we have received six times more votes than last time, we still don't have enough. So it is not just our agenda that will be established. A compromise is necessary and the people recognise that the NC-UML is capable of finding this compromise'.

The next day, some 20 Central Committee (CC) members - including former minister Tanka Dhakal and former Kathmandu mayoral candidate

Rajaram Shrestha, registered a new party the 'Nepali Rastriya Prajatantra Party' (NRPP) with the Election Commission. The Election Commission turned down the breakaway group's claim to the PR seats won by the RPP-N and Tanka Dhakal and several others later announced their return to the RPP-N, stating that 'splitting the RPP-N at this moment is not in our interest. It will weaken democracy'.

But the RPP-N was not the only party to harbour concerns about the declaration of Nepal as a secular state and to favour the restoration of the monarchy and a Hindu state. The Nepali Congress Party (NCP), although historically (in the 1950s and 1960s) a republican, democratic socialist party, has grown increasingly conservative over the years, to the point where it was prepared certainly in the 1990s and even during the latter part of the Maoist insurgency to accept the strong hand of the monarchy (first Birendra and then Gyanendra) on the rudder of the state, only baulking when the latter launched his royal coup and opting for democracy over the monarchy. It was, even then, a very late 'convert' to the emerging republican trend at the time of the Jana Andolan II and would undoubtedly have preferred a 'conservative democracy' with a constitutional monarchy to anything more radical until it became clear that this would be unacceptable to the emerging pro-republican forces inside Nepal and indeed (at that point) to India.

There has always been a strong current on the right of the NCP as indeed has also been the case for the CP-UML supporting the monarchy and the Hindu state; it was this tendency in the NCP (and in the UML and RPP) that was courted by the key foreign powers India, the USA and the UK during the crucial period between the Jana Andolan II and the promulgation of the Interim Constitution, when it was hoped by those 'external forces' that there was still a chance to secure a 'conservative alliance' around the Palace, if the king had been willing to accept a constitutional role. This faction of the NCP had been relatively quiet for some time, firstly because the NCP was able to a large extent to dominate the political debate between 2006 and mid-2008 and then because it was preoccupied with its power struggle with UML and the CPN (M) over who ran the interim government and how. The NCP would also re-emerge at the end of 2013, after the elections for the second Constituency in a more powerful position than before, able to assert its numerical preponderance in the CA, together with the UML, to keep the Maoists on the back foot.

Some nine months later, however, the disquiet of many NCP members with respect to the notion of a secular state, and even with the notion of federalism, was becoming too great to be contained. The party began to show new signs of division on these issues. In September 2014, it was reported by *Telegraph Nepal.com* that

> 'If leader Khum Bahadur Khadka of Nepali Congress is to be trusted, then his party senior leaders including his party president and Prime Minister Sushil Koirala, vice president Ram Chandra Poudel and senior leader Sher Bahadur Deuba too, are not at all happy with the decision to undermine Nepal's Hindu identity. "They have not been able to express their words freely in public but internally they too are not pleased with the choice of declaring the country a secular one," said Khadka, while addressing an interaction program in Kathmandu, September 12, 2014.

Khadka suggested that "the majority of the Nepali Congress central committee members are in favour of reviving the country's Hindu identity," and continued: "In the party's next central committee meeting, I will forward the proposal to revive our Hindu identity and declare the constitution without federalism." "The decision to declare the country secular was conspiratorial by all means because the parties had no public mandate to do so," he said, adding that "we will be left with no option than to set the new constitution ablaze if it endorses the secular declaration." "I can clearly see that if secularism is continued, then in the next 10-12 years Nepal will plunge into religious conflict," he concluded.

A month later, in October 2014, it was reported widely in the press that several Nepali Congress leaders had openly launched a campaign to revive Nepal as a Hindu state. The campaign, which has adopted the slogan "Nation, Nationality and Sanatan Hindu State", is led by former minister and party leader, Khum Bahadur Khadka, and was launched at a public event in Kathmandu, at which several former ministers, lawmakers and party leaders expressed their support for the proposal to reassert the country's Hindu status. The programme was organised by the Civil Struggle Committee for a Sanatahan Hindu State Nepal, with BP Chintan Pratisthan as the coordinator.

This was the first time since 2008 that the pro-Hindu leaders in the party had publicly and collectively urged for the revival of a Hindu state. The NCP, which had agreed to make Nepal a secular state in 2007, did not make any official comment over the campaign; but former

Speaker Taranath Ranabhat said that the demand was 'logical since Hindus and Buddhists that fall under the Omkar clan together combine to account for 90 percent of the nation's population', and NCP leader Chirinjivi Wagle asserted that 'a huge sum of money has been poured into the nation in an attempt to convert Hindus'. This latter assertion was not documented, although it is certainly the case that some of the Muslim candidates for the second Constituency Assembly elections received support from outside, mainly from Pakistan, and there is undoubtedly considerable effort put into encouraging conversion to Christianity by Christian missionaries and development agencies, despite their protestations that they do not proselytise. In any case, 'secularism is the seed for (the) disintegration of the state,' Wagle declared.

The Hindutva movement does not, however, see Islam, or Muslims, as a particular threat; whereas the recent growth of active prosyletisation by Christian groups, particularly from the USA and from Korea, is undoubtedly regarded as such. Peter Gill, reporting from Nepalgunj in February 2017 in *The Record*, comments that when he spoke with Dhawal Shamshere Rana, the local RPP politician, he did not see Islam or Muslims as a threat to Hinduism or the country. 'The problem here and in the rest of the country is conversion into Christianity," he said. "This has been done in a very systemized and organized way which is leading to problems and tensions. We've realized there is a certain purpose to it, and we are trying to stop that."

The declaration of Nepal as a 'secular' state is seen by many, not just in the RPP but also in the NC, as a denial of Nepal's inherently Hindu 'nature'. Deep Kumar Upadhyay, central working committee member of the NC, also bemoaned the party's decision to accept a secular state: "NC should rectify its decision. If the party fails to act on it soon, it will come right back at us." Senior advocate Kumar Regmi presented his views on the relevance of a Hindu state in Nepal; and several of the pro-Hindu state NCP members present including Kul Bahadur Gurung, Pushpa Bhusal, Laxman Ghimire, Purna Kumar Sharma Limbu, Marshal Julum Shakya, Duryodhan Singh Chaudary, Parvati Chaudary, Swarna Jawrchan and Keshav Thapa - said they would press the House to declare Nepal a Sanatan Hindu State in the new constitution. Khum Bahadur Khadka said that his party had 'made a mistake' by adopting the idea of secularism, a mistake that the party should now correct. He warned that the country could face religious conflict if the new Constitution fails to declare Nepal Sanatan Hindu State, hinting at a new 'Hindu movement and possible 'uprising'..

Thus, although Nepal was actually declared a secular state for the first time some eight years ago, the last few months of 2014 perhaps not surprisingly in view of the lack of progress towards a consensus on state restructuring - saw heightened debate on the subject. Some began to call for the reinstatement of a Hindu state, often in the name of unity and integrity but sometimes as a response to alleged proselytization by Christians and Muslims. Others (including Muslims and Christians) were alarmed by this increasingly aggressive Hinduism. In the meanwhile, many were calling for political quotas and other forms of positive discrimination for some 'minorities' but not others, in the name of 'social inclusion'; while others were increasingly fearful (particularly from a 'gender perspective') about partiality and exclusiveness in determining the rights of citizenship, and other rights. By the end of the year, secularism had become increasingly controversial even embattled.

Foreign Interventions

The temperature was raised still further when, in December 2014, the British Ambassador expressed his view that any new Constitution would 'enshrine equality for all, without discrimination based on gender, sexual orientation, caste, ethnicity, religion or language, and with a particular focus on ensuring enjoyment of those rights by the most marginalised in society such as *dalits*', and would also ensure that 'the right to change religion is protected, and that the right to hold opinions and to express them freely will remain strong.' Although he was clearly endorsing a broad commitment to human rights without discrimination, his legitimate but perhaps ill-advised intervention as an official representative of a foreign power drew a critical response from certain media outlets and political commentators; but it was his apparent emphasis on 'the right to change religion' that aroused the greatest reaction, particularly among those sections of the press and political spectrum defensive of the special place of Hinduism in Nepal.

Less than a month later, in mid-November 2014, Kamal Thapa of the RPP-N addressed a meeting in Dangadhi and told the audience that if the new Constitution were to be pushed through by a two thirds majority vote in the Constituent Assembly, it would be against the agreed system and process: 'it would be better to organize a referendum to decide on federalism, democratic republic and secularism while drafting the new statute', he said. He asserted that the declaration of Nepal as a secular state was 'at the behest of *international power centres* (sic) 'although he failed to identify these foreign influences and warned that the political parties that played a key role in making Nepal a secular state would be 'wiped out' of the political spectrum sooner or later. He promised that 'millions of people' would gather on behalf of the RPP-N outside the Constituency Assembly building to put pressure on the major parties to ensure that the new Constitution reinstated Nepal as a Hindu state.

There are several reasons for the concern expressed by those advocating a return to the status quo of the Hindu state (and possibly to a monarchy) and a reluctance to follow the programme of 'social inclusion' and federalism being promoted by the Madhesi parties and the Maoists. One which receives the most rhetorical attention and insistence is the assertion that the institution of a secular state, and of federalism in particular, represents a threat first to Hinduism and then to the integrity of Nepal as a state. There is little evidence of the former. Statistics show that 80 per cent of the population still identifies itself as Hindu. There is also little evident appetite for separatism apart from a minority, exemplified by *madhesi* militants like Dr. C K Raut among those advocating federalism. Another, and closely related to this, is the argument that 'social inclusion' as currently advocated by its supporters risks the sharpening of ethnic and caste divisions and the spectre in particular of ethnic 'identity' based states. The combination of federalism and pursuit of a 'social inclusion' agenda, it is felt by some, risks promoting social and political conflict and disintegration.

The fear of undue influence from 'outside' Nepal, from 'international power centres', invoked by Kamal Thapa, deserves more detailed attention. We have already referred to the adverse responses to the verbal intervention by the British Ambassador in November 2014; more recently, in early February 2015, there have been strong objections to meetings between EU representatives and the *madhesi* activist, Dr. C K Raut. One English-language weekly, the *People's Review*, has been particularly exercised by Westerners' agendas and interference.

But the *People's Review* is also concerned about undue interference by what it terms 'the South', by which it means India in general and the Modi BJP government in particular. In its edition of January 29 February 4 2015, for example, it suggests that 'it is clear that the Indian embassy is backing the agenda of Madhes Pradesh. One other possible interpretation of the concern with 'external forces and power centres' is, therefore, that Nepalese Hindu nationalists feel threatened by the influence that India undoubtedly has had in the past on political developments including, during the key period from 2006 to 2008, the promotion in Nepal of republicanism, federalism, 'social inclusion' and secularism and is now having, through the nexus of Hindutva and right-wing Hindu fundamentalists, since the election of Modi as Prime Minister of India.

The Maoists, many of whom are of course Hindus despite their adherence to an essentially atheistic political ideology, have, in the past albeit much less in recent years have often expressed their concern about 'Indian expansionism' as a threat to national integrity, but they have also relied heavily on support from India over the years and this has rarely been linked to the idea of a threat to republicanism, federalism, 'social inclusion' and secularism all of which the Maoists appear to espouse.

Muslims in the Secularism Debate

Until fairly recently, as far as I can determine, the Muslim community as a whole has tended to support the 'secularist' agenda, on the basis that it implies not only tolerance of all religions but active recognition and endorsement of the pluralism of faiths in Nepal, which would benefit their claim to be a religious minority, generally marginalised and discriminated against. But in recent years, there has emerged a growing concern on the part of some at least of the Muslim leadership, in part about the growing political uncertainties and potential social division in the face of the very slow and uneven progress made towards the drafting of a Constitution agreed by all the key players, and in part about what is seen as the rise in proselytization by Christian groups and missionaries. Some Muslim leaders have come out in favour of the idea of a return to a Hindu state, within which, they feel, they had a clear and established place and which controlled Christian proselytization.

In fact, such activity is still proscribed, but there is a growing feeling, it seems, that formal proscription is not effective and that state 'secularism' has somehow given the green light to missionary activity. On 12 August 2015, one of the Kathmandu dailies carried the headline 'Muslims want Hindu state to stop Christian proselytization'. In fact, the concern was expressed by only a few Muslim local leaders, but they articulated what some are concerned is a new but growing orientation. An article by Devendra Basnet reported from the district of Dang, in the western *terai* that

> 'It may come as a surprise that a rigid follower of Islam has been actively supporting the ongoing agitation for a Hindu state. Amjad Ali, chairman of Rapti Muslim Samaj, is fully committed to Islam. However, he is not only seriously involved in such agitations but also speaks out openly to explain his reasoning to the masses. "It is to protect Islam," he clarifies. "With the growing influence of Christianity among followers of the Hindu faith", he said, "the presence of Christian missionaries has been hugely noticed in the Muslim communities also. Missionaries have managed to convert great numbers of Hindus. How can the Muslim community be spared the same fate if we leaders don't speak up? "I've opened my mouth demanding that Nepal to be declared as Hindu state in order to protect my own religion." Although he has received mixed reactions from his own community, he is adamant that only the proclamation of a Hindu state can protect his religion from the growing influence of Christianity.

CPN-UML CA member Anarkali Miya said she has personally experienced missionaries trying to influence the Muslim community to follow Christianity. "When I was studying in class eight, an unknown person used to send me a Bible in an envelope every month," she said, Christian missionaries have greatly intensified their activities these days. "Hence, the risks of our community being lured by them are very high," Miya further said. "For all these reasons, I believe the country should not adopt the concept of secularism. It will only create more problems in future."

Other Muslim leaders also said that missionaries have been trying to lure their community into following Christianity through offers of employment, development and various other benefits. Udbudhin Faru, chairman of *Muslim Mukti Morcha* which is affiliated to the UCPN (Maoist), also acknowledged the increasing influence of Christianity in the Muslim community. However, he said he is compelled to stick to the concept of secularism because of his party's policy. According to him, about a month ago missionaries reached settlements where his relatives lived and handed them bibles. "They requested my relatives to read it and decide for themselves. Although my relatives didn't care, the incident is a clear indication that the missionaries have intensified their campaigns," said Faru, adding that the distribution of bibles is going on extensively in Bhaluwang and surrounding villages.

"Every religion is equally important. But persuading people to convert to another religion should be condemned," said Barfi Khatun of Bhaluwang. "Let us visit the mosques to offer our prayers freely and without any hindrance. The government should at least safeguard our rights."

The article continues, however, to comment that 'according to Muslim leaders (in Dang), the attempted proselytising by missionaries has so far been unsuccessful. But although there is no evidence of Muslims converting to Christianity in Dang district, the same couldn't be said about other districts. Salim Shah, former district chairman of *Muslim Samaj* which is affiliated to the Nepali Congress, said, "I've seen a large number of Muslims in Rupandehi, Nawalparasi and other districts being converted to Christianity. We had no problem when Nepal was a Hindu state and our religion will be protected when the country is proclaimed a Hindu state once again," he said. On the same day, 12 August 2015, another newspaper also carried an article stating that 'Muslims in Nepal demand a Hindu state', in response to the statement by Amjad Ali. Here it was reported that

> 'Muslims in Nepal have backed the ongoing campaign for reinstating the country's erstwhile Hindu identity, saying they are more 'secure' under a Hindu state than under a secular Constitution. It is to protect Islam. "I have opened my mouth demanding that Nepal be declared a Hindu state in order to protect my own religion," said Amjad Ali, chairman of the Rapti Muslim Society, who is also involved in the protest programmes demanding a Hindu state in Nepal.

The main concern, it appears, is the alleged activities of Christian missionaries. CPN-UML CA member Anarkali Miya said she has personally experienced missionaries trying to influence people from other faiths to follow Christianity. "I believe Nepal should not adopt secularism. It will only create more problems in future," Miya said. Udbudhin Fru, chairman of Muslim Mukti Morcha affiliated to the UCPN (Maoist), also admitted the growing influence of Christianity in Nepal.

> 'Turning the country secular is nothing but a design to break the long-standing unity among Muslims and Hindus. So there is no alternative to reinstating the country's old Hindu State identity in order to allow fellow citizens to live with religious tolerance," Babu Khan Pathan, chairperson of the *Rastrabadi Muslim Manch* in Nepalgunj, was quoted as saying by *The Himalayan Times*.

> "We don't need a secular identity, but want to see the country called Hindu State as this ensures safety and security for all," Pathan added and claimed that around 80 per cent of Muslims in Banke are in favour of a Hindu State identity.
>
> 'In a campaign to "reconvert" the country as a Hindu state, Muslim leaders in Nepal are lashing back at the constituent assembly for attempting to declare the country "secular" in its draft constitution. The Muslim leaders feel that Nepal remaining as a "Hindu nation" helps them feel more secure and allows the citizens to live with religious tolerance. On July 6, the *Sanatan Hindu Rastra Maha Abhiyaan*, led by Nepali Congress leader Khum Bahadur Khadka, submitted a memorandum to Constituent Assembly Chairman Suhas Nembang opposing the inclusion of the term "secular" in the preamble of the draft Constitution'.
>
> 'Muslim leaders of the country are of the opinion that the present secular status had added to the insecurity of the peacefully living Muslim population in the country. Rastrabadi Muslim Manch Nepalgunj a pro-monarchy party, which, along with other pro-Hindu organisations, has been supporting the campaign as the country plans to adopt a new Constitution. The party's Chairman, Babu Khan Pathan, told *The Himalayan Times*, "Turning the country secular is nothing but a design to break the long-standing unity among Muslims and Hindus. So there is no alternative to reinstating the country's old Hindu State identity in order to allow fellow citizens to live with religious tolerance." Pathan added, "We are Nepali Muslims and proud of it, because we have our unique culture of being the Muslims of this land. 80 percent of the Muslims in Banke are against Nepal being a secular state."
>
> 'Amjad Ali, chairman of the Rapti Muslim Society, who is involved in the protest programmes demanding a Hindu state in Nepal said, "It is to protect Islam. I have opened my mouth demanding that Nepal be declared a Hindu state in order to protect my own religion."

This news item was reproduced in many outlets, including *The NewsMinute* online (on 13 August 2015,http://www.thenewsminute.com/article/muslims-nepal-ask-hindu-nation-say-no-secularism-33143#sthash.xe55xDs1.dpuf) with minor variations.

It is not yet clear whether the expression of concern among some Muslim leaders about Christian proselytisation and preference for a return to the status quo of a Hindu state, on the basis that it promoted tolerance between religious groups but banned conversion, will become more widespread, or not.

Perhaps it is significant that on 6 September 2015, a mixed crowd on Buddhists, Muslims, Bon and Christians gathered outside the Constituent Assembly to call for tolerance and secularism. I have argued that it will be 'up-hill work' to maintain secularism in Nepal against the rising tide of Hindutva (Seddon 2015), but we shall see. For, the very next day, it was reported that the Rastriya Prajatantra Party-Nepal (RPP-N) said it would fight to remove any reference to 'secularism' from the new Constitution and restore the Hindu state instead right up until the last moment of constitution drafting process. A central committee meeting of the party held on 7 September 2015 decided that the party would be active to establish its agenda in the constitution up until the last minute, according to party co-spokesperson, Mohan Shrestha.

In the event, the final version of Constitution retained its reference to Nepal as 'an independent, indivisible, sovereign, secular, inclusive, democratic, socialism-oriented federal democratic, republican state'. It also emphasized that Nepal embraced 'multi-caste, multilingual, multi-cultural and diverse geographical specificities' and proposed to 'end discrimination relating to class, caste, region, language, religion and gender discrimination, including all forms of racial untouchability'. It also states that 'reasonable restrictions' may be placed on any act which may jeopardise 'the harmonious relations subsisting among the people of various caste, ethnicity, religion, or community.'

It remains to be seen how not just the RPP-N but also those Muslim leaders who spoke out in favour of a Hindu state will proceed in the coming months and years. I have argued elsewhere (Seddon 2015) that maintaining secularism in Nepal in reality will remain 'an up-hill struggle'. On Friday 25 September 2015, however, Muslims in Nepal celebrated the first Eid after the country was declared 'secular' by the new constitution. Hundreds gathered to offer prayers at the Kashmiri Mosque, Bagbazaar. In June 2017, the government postponed the second round of the local elections to avoid clashing with the end of Ramadan. This is some form of recognition.

Notes

1. Probably better translated as 'Assembly to Protect the Finality of Prophethood' – meaning to protect the idea that Mohammed was the last of the Prophets.
2. Uphadhyay 2014: 34)
3. Article 23 of the Interim Constitution protects the rights of all religious groups by guaranteeing the individual the right "to profess and practice his/her own religion as handed down to him/her from ancient times having due regard to traditional practices." It also states "no person shall be entitled to convert another person from one religion to another and shall not take actions or behave in a way that would create disturbance in another's religion."

Conclusion & Acknowledgements

Many aspects of the social, cultural economic and political situation of the Muslim community and of the Muslim communities of Nepal remain unclear. All that has been possible in this book is to bring together a wide range of information relating to the past and present to provide an introduction and an overview.

Much remains to be done, both as regards research into the situation of the Muslim Communities of Nepal and as regards policy and practice by Muslims and non-Muslims alike to contribute to improving the everyday lives of Muslims throughout Nepal and their rights and their representation in politics and in other areas of economic and social life in Nepal.

The original project and the report to IDEA, and also this book that has arisen out of that report, are all intended as a contribution to this 'project', and to encourage and promote further discovery, discussion and debate.

I wish to thank Mohna Ansari in particular for encouraging me to explore the possibility of undertaking research on the Muslim Communities of Nepal, and for introducing me to IDEA. I wish to thank IDEA for providing financial and logistic support, and NEMAF for its active involvement and particularly to Tula Shah, the Director of NEMAF, for his leadership and his encouragement to me and the other members of the NEMAF team.

I hope that it will be possible to take this research into the Muslim Communities of Nepal further in the future, with a view to providing further information, analysis and insight into the situation of the Muslim communities, and also to clarifying further this time, to a greater extent than was possible in the original project, in collaboration with representatives of the different Muslim communities and the Muslim community as a whole the challenges and the opportunities that face them.

David Seddon
July 2017

Appendix 1

Muslim NGOs and other Groups/Associations

Al Hira Educational Society

Al Madat Foundation Nepal

All Nepal Anjuman Islah (ANAI)

Al Madat Foundation

Banke UNESCO Club

Fatima Foundation

Grammi Uttahan Abhiyan (Bara)

Health Services and Relief Association

Imam Ahmad bin Hambal Development Center, Taulihawa, Kapilvastu

International Islamic Federation of Student Organisations (Kuwait)

Islami Sangh Nepal

Islamic Center of Nepal

Islamic Federation of Nepal

Islamic Yuva Sangh (IYS)

Jama'at-i Islami

Jami'at Ahl-e Hadis

Jami'at Millat-e Islamiya

Madhesi Mukti Morcha

Madhesi Muslim Forum

Madrasa Islamiya Sangh

Markab Imam bin Hamwal

Millat-e Islamiya (formerly Jami'at Millat-e Islamiya)
Muslim Ekta Sangh (MES)
Muslim Ettehad Sanghathan (UML)
Muslim Forum Loktantrik
Muslim Liberation Front
Muslim Mukti Morcha (CPN-M)
Muslim Student Education Foundation
Muslim Women's Welfare Society
Narool Islam Jalpapur
National Muslim Forum
Nepal Buddhijivi Muslim Sangh
Nepal Federation of Nationalities (NEFIN)
Nepal Masjid Foundation
Nepal Muslim Ettehad Organisation
Nepal Muslim Awam Sahara
Nepal Rastriya Muslim Manch
Nepal Muslim Samaj
Nepal Muslim Sangh
Nepal Inter-Religious Council
Rastriya Muslim Manch (aka National Muslim Forum)
SISA (Dang)
United Muslim National Struggle Committee
World Assembly of Muslim Youth

Appendix 2

Some Special Issues Relating to Muslim Community to be Incorporated in the New Constitution

1. Preamble: Provision of 'declaring the nation free from discriminations based on class, caste, geography, language, religion, untouchability and gender and being a secular state, and with the determination of building an equitable society based on economic equality, prosperity and social justice on the basis of proportionally inclusive and participatory nation by eliminating all forms of discriminations like political, economic, social and cultural' should be stated.
2. Definition of the State: Nepal is an independent, indivisible, sovereign, secular, proportional, inclusive, federal democratic republican welfare state, free from caste based discrimination and untouchability and oriented toward socialism should be defined as definition of the state.
3. Fundamental Rights: No discrimination shall be made among the citizens in the application of law and on grounds of religious belief should be guaranteed.

Constitution should guarantee special provision through the law for the protection, empowerment, development or positive measures or compensation of minority Muslim Community.

Rights Relating to Muslim Community: Following issues relating to the rights of Muslim Community should be included under separate Article of the constitution under fundamental rights.

- Right to participate in the policy making level which affect themselves

- Rights relating to cultural heritage, traditional knowledge, skills and technology
- Right relating to language, script and culture
- Right to information and communication in mother tongue
- Right to social security
- Rights relating to special representation in all mechanism of the state

Rights relating to Women: Proportional representation of Madhesi and Hilly Muslim women should be ensured in all rights to be given to women by the constitution on the basis of their population.

Rights Relating to Religious Freedom: Every individual shall have the right to religious freedom, meant to follow or not to follow, practice and protect the religion as per their conscience. There should be full respect of the principle of secularism. Muslim community should have the rights to establish trust of their religion and operate it.

Rights Relating to Education and Culture: Muslim Community should have right to get education in mother tongue and they should have right to protect, promote and follow their culture.

Right to Social Justice: Socially backward minority Muslim community should have right to participate in all political mechanism, agency, area and public service on the basis of the principle of proportionality and inclusion with proportionate representation of their population.

4. **Directive Principles and Policies of the State:**

   Directive Principle of the State: The social objective of the state shall be to develop healthy social life based on justice and morality by eliminating all forms of economic and social disparities and maintaining harmony among different castes, tribes, religions, languages, areas, races and communities, and to manage special provisions including positive discriminations for the overall development of *Muslim* community.

   Policies of the State: State shall pursue the policy to ensure the proportional inclusive representation of the Muslim community in all level of bodies, agencies and areas for the state federal, provincial and local on the basis of their population.

Policies and Obligation of the state: State shall pursue the policies to uplift economically and socially backward Muslim community by managing special measures of positive discrimination in the area of education, health, shelter, food sovereignty and employment.

State shall pursue the policy of providing employment on proportional basis for Muslim community in all public and private industrial institutions and non-governmental sector.

State should pursue the policy of providing ownership over the land to the landless Muslim community and policy of guaranteeing economic and social rights to them.

5. Provision relating to the Executive:

Representation of Muslim community: The State, while constituting the council of ministers, shall ensure compulsory and proportional representation of the Muslim community in the posts of deputy prime ministers, ministers, state ministers and Assistant ministers.

Appointment of the provincial chief: President, while appointing chiefs of the provinces, shall appoint a person from Muslim Community to the chief of the one of the provinces out of total provinces.

Formation of Provincial Council of Ministers: State shall ensure compulsory and proportional representation of Muslims and backward communities while appointing council of ministers including the posts of deputy chief ministers, ministers, state ministers and assistant ministers.

Provision of Executive Chief and Deputy Chief of Local Bodies: There shall be compulsory and proportional representation of Muslims and backward communities while filing candidacy and electing for the post of executive chief and deputy chief of the local bodies by counting the seat number of the nation as total seat number to ensure their proportional representation on the basis population.

Formation of Executive Organ of Local Government: State, while constituting the executive organs of the local government, shall ensure the compulsory and proportional representation of the Muslim and other backward communities and manage the work division.

Formation of all level of government services and operation: Federal, provincial and local government shall constitute public service and necessary other services to conduct administration with compulsory and proportional representation Muslims and other backward communities.

6. Provision relating to Legislature:

Formation of House of Representatives: Proportional representation of Muslim community should be ensures on the basis of their population counting the total seat number while constituting house of representatives of the federal house of representatives. Muslim community should have representation in all committees of the federal legislature and at least one chief of the parliamentary community should be from Muslim community. Inclusive representation should be respected in the election to the post of Speaker and Deputy Speaker.

Formation of Federal National Assembly: Provision should be managed to ensure the proportional representation of the Muslim Community in the total number of the seats of the federal national assembly. The representation with compensation of the Muslim Community in the national assembly should be ensured if their representation could not be managed in the House of Representatives. Muslim community should have representation in all committees of the federal national assembly and at least one chief of such community should be from Muslim community. Inclusive representation should be respected in the election to the post of chairperson and vice chairperson.

Formation of Provincial Assembly: Provision should be managed to ensure the proportional representation of the Muslim Community in the total number of the seats of the provincial assembly. Muslim community should have representation in all committees of the provincial assembly and at least one chief of each committee of the provincial assembly should be from Muslim community. Inclusive representation should be respected in the election to the post of speaker and deputy speaker.

Formation of Local Legislature: Constitution should guarantee the proportional representation of Muslim community in the legislature of the local bodies in the each local body where the Muslim community is residing. Provision should be managed to ensure at least one member from Muslim community in the chief, deputy and chairperson of the committees.

7. Provision relating to Judiciary:

Appointment of judges of all levels: Proportional representation of Muslim and other backward community, on the basis of their population, should be ensured while appointing judges in the courts including Supreme Court, High Court and district courts.

Formation of separate court: Provision of separate court or separate bench in each district should be managed for the judicial solution of disputes to be erupted within the Muslim community based on their culture, religion or traditional law and custom, their family dispute and violence against women within the Muslim community.

Formation of the mechanism to appoint of judges in all level: At least one member representation from Muslim community should be ensured in the judicial council and such body to be formed to recommend the judges for Supreme Court, High Court and district courts and all courts.

Formation of Judiciary Service Commission in all level: At least one member representation from Muslim community should be ensured in the constitution in the commissions which have the power to appoint, transfer, promote and take disciplinary action of the employees in the judiciary service of federation, province and local level.

8. Provision relating to Commission:

Proportional Representation in All Commissions: Muslim Community should have proportional and inclusive representation in all constitutional bodies.

Muslim Commission as a separate constitutional body: There shall be one separate Muslim Commission as a separate constitutional body with following rights. The commission shall have one chairperson, four members including two women members having representation from Terai and Hilly Muslim community. Provincial offices of the commission should be opened in all provinces where the Muslim community resides.

1. To recommend the government of Nepal by conducting a study and investigation on the Muslim community.
2. To submit report with clear suggestions to the Government of Nepal on provisions to be managed concerning to the protection of the language and culture of the Muslim community, their uplift and development, and the situation of the class and community of Muslim.
3. To submit report to the Government of Nepal on national policies and programs concerning benefit of Muslims for implementation.
4. To submit suggestions to the government for the effective implementation of the laws if they are not implemented properly by monitoring the special provisions for the liberation and benefit

of the Muslim community and existing laws relating to benefit of the Muslim community.

5. To assess, monitor and evaluate policies and programs relating to mainstreaming Muslim community into the national development and proportional representation of them in all other state organs and recommend the Government of Nepal for the effective implementation of them.

9. Formation of Province and Protection of the special rights of Muslim Community:

Provinces should be built and names should be given by considering the identity of the Muslim community and continuing their residents.

Local Muslim should have special rights while using natural resources in the provinces where the Muslim community has majority.

There should be a provision of equitable distribution of the economic resources and revenue allocation.

10. Miscellaneous Provisions:

Formation of Constitutional Council: At least one Muslim member representation should be there in the constitutional council which recommends chief justice and office bearers of other constitutional bodies.

Appointment of Nepali Ambassadors and special representation: Representation of the Muslim Community should be ensured on the basis of inclusive principle while appointing Nepali ambassadors and special representative as per the constitutional provision.

National Security Council: Representation of Muslim community should be ensured on the basis of inclusive principle in the national Security Council which recommends for the appointment of the chief of the army staff, mobilization of Nepal Army, management of Nepal Army and recommends the government for preparing national security policy.

Formation of Army Service Commission: There should be representation of Muslim Community on the basis of inclusive principle in the Army Service Commission which recommends the government for the appointment in Nepal Army, transfer of the Nepal Army, promotion of them and taking disciplinary action to them.

Representation in other security bodies: Representation of Muslim community should be ensured on the basis of inclusive proportional principle and their population while appointing personnel and staff of the Nepal Police, Armed Police Force and National Investigation Division.

References & Bibliography

- *The Constitution of Kingdom of Nepal* (2015) www.sambidhan.org

- *The Constitution of Nepal,* (1962) www.ccd.org.np

- *Nepal Human Development Report*(2014)

Hamid Ansari (1981), 'Muslims in Nepal', *Institute of Muslim Minority Affairs Journal,* 1981, vol. 3, no. 1. pp. 138-58

Hamid Ansari (1981) *Muslims of Nepal,* CEDA Papers, Rural Development Group, TU, Kathmandu

Hamid Ansari (1980)'Muslims in Nepal', *Journal Institute of Minority Affairs,* Vol. 2, No. 2-3, 1980

Hamid Ansari (1980) *Indian Ethnic Groups in the Nepal Tarai,* Centre for Nepal and Asian Studies (CNAS), Kathmandu

Tahir Ali Ansari (1980) "*Muslim minority in Nepal*", Institute of Muslim Minority Affairs, K.A. University, Jaddah

Tahir Ali Ansari (1988)'The Muslim Minority in Nepal: A Socio-historical Perspective',*Journal of Muslim Minority Affairs,* Volume 9, Issue 1, 1988, pp. 159 – 166

Thomas Arnold (1896) *The Preaching of Islam: a history of the propagation of the Muslim faith,* A Constable & Co, Westminster

The Asia Foundation (2013) *Labour Migration Trends and Patterns: Bangladesh, India and Nepal, 2013,* The Asia Foundation

The Asia Foundation et al (2010) *Preliminary Mapping of Gender-Based Violence,* The Asia Foundation, DFID & Saathi, Kathmandu

Asian Development Bank (2012) *Country Poverty Analysis,* Nepal

Lynn Bennett(2006) '*Unequal Citizens, Gender, Caste and Ethnic Exclusion in Nepal*', DFID/World Bank, Kathmandu, Nepal

Lynn Bennett and D. R.Dahal (nd), '*Preliminary Exploration of Caste/ Ethnic and Regional Identity Dimensions of the Nepal 2006 Demographic and Health Survey*,' (Draft)

Lynn Bennett, Dilli Ram Dahal and Pav Govindasamy (2008), *Caste, Ethnic and Regional Identity in Nepal: Further Analysis of the 2006 Nepal Demographic and Health Survey*. Calverton, Maryland, USA: Macro International Inc.

Lynn Bennett and Dillip Parajuli (n.d.), *Nepal Inclusion Index: Methodology, First Round Findings and Implications for Action* (Draft)

Lynn Bennett & Dillip Parajuli (2013) *Nepal Inclusion Index: making smaller social groups visible and providing a baseline for tracking results on social inclusion*, Himal Books, Kathmandu

Lynn Bennett, Bandita Sijapati and Deepak Thapa, *Forging Equal Citizenship in a Multicultural Nepal,* World Bank/DFID, Himal Books, Kathmandu

Chandra Bhadra(2009),'State of Nepali Women'. In *South Asian Journal SAPANA Network*, South Asian Free Media Association, Lahore, Pakistan.

D. N.Bhatta &A.Haque (2014) 'Health problems, complex life, and consanguinity among ethnic minority Muslim women in Nepal',doi: 10.1080/13557858.2014.980779. Epub 2014 Nov 14.*Ethn. Health* Dec. 2015, vol.20,no 6: pp 633-49.

K. B. Bhattachan, Hemchuri,K. K., Gurung, Y. B. and B. K., C. M. (2001), *Existing Practices of Caste-Based Untouchability in Nepal and Strategy for a campaign for its Elimination*, Action Aid/Nepal, Kathmandu

Dor Bahadur Bista (1985), *Ethnicity, its Problems and prospects*, Kirtipur. Kathmandu: CNAS.

HMG NNEPC (1956) *Education in Nepal*, Nepal National Education Planning Commission, Kathmandu

Dor Bahadur Bista (1960), *People of Nepal*, Kathmandu, Ratna Pustak Bhandar.

Dor Bahadur Bista (1967), *People of Nepal*, Department of Publicity, Ministry of Information & Broadcasting HMG

Harvey Blustain (1977) *Power and Ideology in a Nepalese Village*, PhD Dissertation, Yale University, December, 1977 [Unpublished].

CBS (1993) *Population Census 1991*, HMG, Kathmandu

CBS (1995) *Population Monograph of Nepal,* CBS, Kathmandu

CBS(2003) *Population Census 2001* Kathmandu: His Majesty's Government of Nepal, National Planning Commission, Central Bureau of Statistics

CBS (2004), *National Living Standards Survey II,* HMG Central Bureau of Statistics, Kathmandu

CERID, (2002) *"Access to Education for Disadvantaged Group"* Kathmandu: Research Center for Educational Innovation and Development

CERID, (2003) *"Access of Muslim children to Education"* Kathmandu: Research Center for Educational Innovation and Development

CERID, (2004) *"Access of Muslim Children to Education: Phase II"* Kathmandu: Research Center for Educational Innovation and Development

CERID, (2006) *"Linking the Madrasas with Mainstream Education in Nepal"* Kathmandu: Research Center for Educational Innovation and Development

CERID, (2007) *"Institutional scope and need of Mainstream education in Madrasas and their autonomy"* Kathmandu: Research Center for Educational Innovation and Development

CERID, (2008) *"Formal Education in Madrasas of Nepal: A Study on Emerging Trends and Issues"* Kathmandu: Research Center for Educational Innovation and Development

Deepak Chaudhary (2015) *Tarai/Madhes of Nepal: anthropological study* (upgraded edition) Ratna Pustak Bhandar, Kathmandu

Circular of Department of Education, Nepal, Dated 30 Kartik 2063

J.R.I. Cole (1989,) *Religion and State in Awadh, 1722-1859: Roots of North Indian Shi'ism in Iran and Iraq,*University of California Press, Berkeley, Los Angeles, Oxford

Core Group (2009) *Creating Healthy Families in Nepal: sustaining family planning practices among marginalised groups,* Save the Children Fund, USAID & Core Group, March 2009

Dilli Ram Dahal (1978), *Indian Ethnic Groups in Nepal Tarai: A Study of Immigration Patterns and Socio-Economic Behavior,* Kathmandu: Centre for Nepal and Asian Studies, Tribhuwan University, 1978.

Mollica Dastider(1995),*Religious Minorities in Nepal: An analysis of the state of the Buddhists and Muslims in the Himalayan Kingdom*, Nirmala Publications, 35, New Delhi

Mollica Dastider (2000) 'Muslims of Nepal's Terai', *Economic and Political Weekly*, vol.35, no. 10, March 4-10, 2000)

Mollica Dastider (2000) 'Muslims Mobilisation and the State in Nepal, 1951-95', *European Bulletin of Himalayan Research,* vol.18, pp. 20-35

Mollica Dastider(2007),*Understanding Nepal: Muslims in a Plural Society*, New Delhi: Har-Anand Publications

Nurran Davids (2016) 'Religion, culture and exclusion of Muslim women: on finding a re-imagined form of inclusive-belonging', in *Knowledge and Culture*, Addleton Academic Publishers, pp. 46-59

DFID (2013) *Regional Dimensions of Poverty and Vulnerability in Nepal: Background Reports*, DFID/UKAID, Kathmandu

Alfiani Fadzakir (2001), *The Muslims of Kathmandu: a study of religious identity in a Hindu kingdom,* Unpubl. PhD thesis, Department of Human Sciences, University of Brunel

Fatima Foundation (2006) 'Islam Ma Mahila Adhikar', 'Mahila Ra Netritwa', 'Samaya Anusar Ko Islamic Sonch', 'Islam Ko Najar Ma Purush Ra Mahila Bich Ko Samanta',Nepalgunj, Banke

Marc Gaborieau (1972), 'Muslims in the Hindu Kingdom of Nepal', *Contributions to Indian Sociology*, vol 6, pp. 84-105

Marc Gaborieau (1978) 'Aspects of the lineage among the Muslim bangle-makers of Nepal', *Contributions to Indian Sociology*, vol.12, no.2, pp. 155-71

Marc Gaborieau (1981), 'Peasants, urban traders and rural artisans: Muslim minorities in the Kingdom of Nepal', *Institute of Muslim Minority Affairs Journal*, vol.3,no. 2, pp. 196-205

Marc Gaborieau (1981) 'Muslims in the Hindu Kingdom of Nepal', in (ed) T.N. Madan, *Muslim communities of South Asia: culture, society, and power*

Marc Gaborieau (1981) 'Peasants, urban traders and rural artisans: Muslim minorities in the Kingdom of Nepal',*Journal Institute of Minority Affairs,* Volume 3, No. 2, 1981.

Marc Gaborieau(1993) 'Varying Identities of Nepalese Muslims', *Comparative Studies of South Asia, Africa and the Middle East,* Volume 16, No. 2, 1993, pp. 39-46.

Frederick H Gaige(1975),*Regionalism and national unity in Nepal.* New Delhi: Vikas Publishing House

Ernest Gellner (1969) *Saints of the Atlas*, Weidenfeld & Nicolson, London

Ernest Gellner (1981) *Muslim Society*, Cambridge University Press, Cambridge

Om Gurung (2009) *Social Inclusion: policies and practices in Nepal,* Occasional Paper no. 11, Central Department of Sociology & Anthropology, Tribuvan University, Kathmandu

GSEA (2005) *Citizens With (out) Rights: Nepal, Gender and Social Exclusion Asssessment, Summary Report,* Gender & Social Exclusion Assessment (GSEA) Team & Advisory Group, DfID and World Bank, June 2005

Mohamed Hafiz and Zahid Parvez (2006) *Linking Madarsas with Mainstream Education in Nepal*, CERID, Tribhuvan University, Kathmandu

Mohamed Hafiz & Zahid Parvez (2008) *Formal Education in Madarsas in Nepal*, CERID, Tribhuvan University, Kathmandu

Mohamed Hafiz & Zahid Parvez (2009) *Quality Education in Registered Madarsas*,CERID, Tribhuvan University, Kathmandu

Mohamed MozammilHaque, 'Islam in Nepal', *Wordpress*,

Krishna Hachhetu (2009) 'Social Exclusion and Nepali Muslims: a case study of Bank District', *Contributions to Nepalese Studies*, vol.36, special issue, pp. 83-130

Clare Hennig(2014) 'A minority within a minority', *Nepali Times Buzz,* 11-17 July 2014

HMG (1958) 'Notice', *Nepal Gazette*, vol. vii, no. 43, 10 February 1958

HMG NEC (1961) *Report of the National Education Commission*, Kathmandu

HMG (1962) 'Education Act, *Nepal Gazette*, vol. xii, Extraordinary Issue, no. 12, 25 July 1962

HMG (1990) *Constitution of the Kingdom of Nepal, 2047* (1990) www.sambidhan.org

HMG *(2003) Population Census 2001* HMG NPC Secretariat, Central Bureau of Statistics, Kathmandu

(2063 bs) Interim Constitution of Nepal (2063 BS), www.unmin.org

Andreas Höfer (2004), *The Caste Hierarchy and the State in Nepal: A Study of the Mulki Ain of 1854.* Lalitpur: Himal Books, 2004.

Ahmad Imtiazi (1973) *Caste and Social Stratification among the Muslims.* Daryaganj, Delhi: Manohar Book Service.

Hari Bansh Jha (1993) *The Terai Community and National Integration in Nepal*, Centre for Economic and Technical Studies (CETS) in cooperation with the Friedrich Ebert-Stiftung (FES), Kathmandu

Humayun Kabir (2011) "Reflections on the Muslim Minority's Demands in New Nepal", unpublished paper (March 31, 2011), Postdoctoral Research Fellow HiPeC, Hiroshima University

Abdul Salam Khan (n.d.)*A Study on Citizenry Rights of Muslim Community in Western Nepal*, AResearch Apprenticeship (Code No SIRF/MM RA/09),Submitted to the Social Inclusion Research Fund Secretariat (SIRF), SNV Nepal

Abdul Salam Khan (2007) *A Study of the Muslim Minority in Kapilvastu and Gorkha Districts in Nepal*, a report submitted to SNV

Abdul Salam Khan (2071 vs) *Nepal ra Nepali Musulman*, Sopan Press, Dilli Bazaar, Kathmandu

Sakheena Khan(2011), *Enhancing Participation of Muslim Women in Politics, Final Report* (Mentor, Prof. Dr. Indira Sharma), Social Inclusion Research Fund (SIRF), SNV, Nepal (Code No SIRF/MMRA/2011)

SeemaLuitel(1999) *Gender Disparity and Girls Education in Nepal.* Kathmandu: Centre for Educational Innovation and development (CERID). 36

Monika Mandal (2013) *Social Inclusion of Ethnic Communities in Contemporary Nepal*, KW Publications

MOES (2005) *EFA theme wise strategies and action plan*, Kehar Mahal, Kathmandu: Government of Nepal, Ministry of Education and Sports

MOES (2064 BS) *School Sector Reform Core Document*, Government of Nepal, Ministry of Education and Sports, Kehar Mahal, Kathmandu

Muluki Ain 1854 as cited by Yadav Niraula, http://ezinearticles.com

Ahmad Mumtaz, *Madrasa Education in Pakistan and Bangladesh.* http://www.apess.org

Abul Hasan AliNadvi (1999) "*Islam Main Aurat Ka Darja Aur Uske Huquku -wa-Farayez*" (in Urdu), Jamiaut-ul-Moomenaat Islamiya: Lucknow.

NEC (2002) *Literacy Situation in Nepal* His Majesty's Government, Ministry of education and Sports, Nonformal Education Centre, Sanothimi, Bhaktapur

NEMAF (2016) *Local Governance and Access to Basic Services*, analysis of public perception across 20 VDCs of 5 districts of Mithila Belt in Madhes/Terai, Report December 2016

Badri Prasad Niraula (1995) 'Internal Migration', in: *Population Monograph.* Kathmandu: Central Bureau of Statistics.

Bhanu Niraula (1997) 'Does Caste/Ethnicity Matter in Fertility Transition? An Analysis of

Nepalese Data', in *Nepal, Population Journal*, Vol. 6, No. 5, PAN, July 1997.

Yadav Niraula, *Caste System in Nepal*, http://ezinearticles.com

J P Pandey et al (2013) *Maternal and Child Health in Nepal: the effects of caste, ethnicity and regional identity – further analysis of the 2011 Nepal Demographic and Health Survey,*Ministry of Health & Population and various *donors*, Kathmandu,March 2013

Nazima Parveen (nd) 'Politics of 'Inclusiveness': a study of contemporary Nepalese Muslim political discourse', www.asianscholarship.org/asf/ejourn/articles/Parveen.pdf

Nazima Parveen (2010) 'Politics of 'Inclusiveness': a study of contemporary Muslim political discourse', *Contributions to Nepalese Studies*, Vol. 39, No. 1

H.M. Zahid Parwez(1998) *Enhancing Educational Awareness in the Rural Muslims*, CERID TU, Kathmandu

H. M. Zahid Parvez (2003) *Access of Muslim Children to Education*, CERID TU, Kathmandu

H. M. Zahid Parvez (2004),*Access of Muslim Children to Education, (Phase II)* CERID, TU Kathmandu.

H. M. Zahid Parvez (2005) *Linking the Madrasas with Mainstream Education in Nepal*, CERID TU Kathmandu

Joanna Pfaff-Czarnecka (1997) Vestiges and visions: Cultural change in the process of nation building in Nepal in D Gellner, J Pfaff-Czarnecka and J. Whelpton (Editors), *Nationalism and Ethnicity in Hindu Kingdom : The Politics of Culture in Contemporary Nepal.* pp 419-470. Amsterdam: Hardwood Academic Publishers

Tariq Rahman (2004), The Madrassa and the State of Pakistan, *Himal South Asian* (February, 2004) http://www.himalmag.com

Swayam Prakash J. B. Rana, Abdul Quaiyum, Pasang Sherpa & H Mohamed Zaheed Parwez (2009) *Exclusion issues of Muslims of Nepal and role of education in their social inclusion* (Draft Report) Submitted to the Social Inclusion Research Fund, SNV Nepal (Research Fellowship (Code Number: SIRF/RF/07), Kathmandu

Tunga Rai (2009) 'Social Exclusion and Inclusion in Nepal" some examples from dalits, Muslim and indigenous communities', *Contributions to Nepalese Studies*, vol.36 special issue, pp. 221-243

Abdul Rauf (ed) (2000), *Nepal Mein Urdu Sha'ari*, Urdu Pakistan Studies Chair Research Centre, Tribhuvan University, distrib. by Discovery Publishing Nepal & Everest Bookstores, Kathmandu, September 2000 (Urdu)

H. G. Rawlinson (2001), *Ancient and Medieval History of India*, Bharatiya Kala Prakashan,

Edward Sachau (1910), *Alberuni's India*. Kegan Paul, Trench, Trubner & Co Ltd.

Abdul Salam, *A study of problems of Muslim Minority in Kapilbastu and Gorkha Districts*, June 2007, p. 42

Vikash Raj Satyal (2003), in *Sambal*, the IIDS Newsletter, nos. 25 and 26, December 2003

David Seddon (1998) 'Missing Girls', *Quarterly Development Review*, vol. xv, no. 19, June-August 1998

David Seddon (2015) *Muslim Communities in Nepal: an Overview*, unpublished draft report for IDEA, August 2015

David Seddon (2015) 'Muslim Communities in Nepal', *Quarterly Development Review*, vol. xxix, no. 33, November 2014-January 2015, Kathmandu

David Seddon (2015) *Nepal: maintaining secularism – an uphill struggle*, Society for Humanism (SOCH) Nepal, Kathmandu

David Seddon (2017) '50 Years of Change in the West (Central) Terai', forthcoming

David Seddon, Jagannath Adhikari & Uttam Niraula (2017) 'Secularism, Christianity, Hinduism and the Issue of Conversion in Nepal', forthcoming

Cholraj Sharma (nd) '*Nepalgunj Bazaar ka Musulman laru ko samajik Tathat Arthik Jeevan*', unpublished paper, Tribhuvan University, Kathmandu (cited in Dastider 2000)

Pitamber Sharma (2008) *Unravelling the Mosaic: spatial aspects of ethnicity in Nepal*, Himal Books, Kathmandu

Suhindra Sharma(1994) 'How the Crescent Fares in Nepal', *Himal,* November/December, 1994

Suhindra Sharma (1995) 'How fares the crescent in Nepal?' *Himal*, May 1995, http://www.himalmag. com/ component/ content/ article/ 3033-How-the-cresent-fares-in-Nepal.html

Pasang Sherpa (2012) 'Socio-economic Condition of Nepalese and Indian Muslims: a comparative study', *Indian Streams Research Journal,* Vol. II, Issue. X, DOI : 10.9780/22307850, http://isrj.org/UploadedData/1568.pdf

Muhammad Siddique (2001), 'Muslim population in the kingdom of Nepal: some outstanding features', *Journal of Muslim Minority Affairs,* 21. 2. 2001

Shamina Siddika(1993) *Muslims of Nepal*, Gazala Siddika, Ratna Book Distributors Pvt., Sociology and Anthropology, vol.1, Kathmandu

Megan AdamsonSijapati (2007)*Shaping Muslim Identities: Alterity, Conflict and Islamic Revival in Nepal*, PhD Dissertation, University of California—Santa Barbara, December 2007 (unpublished).

Megan Adamson Sijapati(2011) "Muslims in Nepal: The Local and Global Dimensions of a Changing Religious Minority', *Religion Compass*

Megan Adamson Sijapati(2011) *Islamic Revival in Nepal*, London and New York: Routledge

Megan Adamson Sijapati (2012), 'Mawdudi's Islamic Revivalist Ideology and the Islami Sangh Nepal', *Studies in Nepali History and Society,*

Megan Adamson Sijapati(2012), 'The National Muslim Forum Nepal: Experiences of Conflict, Formations of Identity" in (eds) Mahendra Lawoti and Susan Hangen, *Ethnic Conflict and Nationalism in*

Nepal: Identities and Mobilization after 1990 (London and New York: Routledge, 2012), pp. 102-120

Megan Adamson Sijapati (2013) *The National Muslim Forum, Nepal: experiences of conflict, formations of identity*, The Cupola, GettysburgCollege

Bandita Sijapati,'Debates on Muslims in Nepal" (background study for Bennett, Lynn, Bandita Sijapati and Deepak Thapa. *Forging Equal Citizenship in a Multicultural Nepal.* World Bank/DFID (Forthcoming).

Bandita Sijapati (2010) *Public Discourse and Action to Address Muslim Exclusion*, Unpublished Report

Yginder Sikand (2001), *Himal South Asian* (November 2001), http://www.himalmag

Mukta S. Tamang & Manju Thapa Tuladhar (eds) (2014) *Social Inclusion Research: a source book,* Mandala Book Point, Kathmandu

Meeta Thapa (2009) *Country Profile of Excluded Groups in Nepal*, Kathmandu, May 2009

Shanker Thapa, 'Caste Hierarchy and Interethnic Stratification in the Muslim Society of Nepal' *Tribhuvan University Journal Volume* XVIII, June edited by T.N. Madan 1995

Gerard Toffin (2013) *From Monarchy to Republic: essays on changing Nepal*, Vajra Books, Kathmandu

Anjar Ujma (2003). *Islamic Education: A Brief History of Madrassa, with comments on Curricula and Current Pedagogical Practices*; http://www. wordbank.org

Sayyid Jalauddin Umari (1986) *The Rights of Muslim Women: an appraisal*, Markazi Maktaba Islami Publishers. Delhi.

UNDP (1998), *Nepal Human Development Report 1998.* United Nations Development Programme, Kathmandu

UNDP (2004), *Nepal Human Development Report 2004: Empowerment and Poverty Reduction.* United Nations Development Programme, Kathmandu

UNDP (2009) *Nepal Human Development Report 2009*, United Nation Development Programme, Kathmandu

UNDP & NPC (2014) *Nepal Human Development Report: beyond geography – unlocking human potential,* United Nations Development Programme & Government of Nepal National Planning Commission, Kathmandu

Chandra Upadhyay (2017) 'Society and Culture of Muslims in Nepal's Terai: a study of Ghuski Village in Sunsari District', *Dundubhi, a Journal of Multi-Disciplinary Research,* vol.3, no. 3 September 2017?

Chandra Updahyay (2016) 'Exclusion within the Excluded: Status of Muslim women in Nepal (a Study in Bhutaha Village of Sunsari District), *Research Highlights,* vol. iii no 4, Future Fact Society, Varanasi (UP) India, pp. 67-70

Prakash Upadhaya (2014) *Social Ethnography of The Hill Muslims of Nepal,* Adroit Publishers, New Delhi

R. Upadhay (2007), 'Muslims in Nepal: Becoming an Assertive Minority', 4 October 2007. Downloaded from *Madhesi.wordpress.com.*

VSO (2015) *Women in Power: beyond access to influence in a post-2015 world,* Voluntary Service Overseas

Waliuddin Muhammad '*Mishkatul Masabih*' (Hadith)

Index

D

E

F

N

O

T

U

V

W